WHEN SCHOOLS COMPETE

WHEN SCHOOLS COMPETE

A CAUTIONARY TALE

EDWARD B. FISKE

and

HELEN F. LADD

BROOKINGS INSTITUTION PRESS
Washington, D.C.

Copyright © 2000
THE BROOKINGS INSTITUTION PRESS
1775 Massachusetts Avenue, N.W., Washington, D.C. 20036
www.brookings.edu

Library of Congress Cataloging-in-Publication data

Fiske, Edward B.
    When schools compete : a cautionary tale / Edward B. Fiske and Helen F. Ladd.
        p.   cm.
    Includes bibliographical references and index.
    ISBN 0-8157-2836-0 (cloth : alk. paper) — ISBN 0-8157-2835-2 (pbk. : alk. paper)
        1. School improvement programs—New Zealand—Case studies. 2. Education—Social aspects—New Zealand—Case studies. 3. Education and state—New Zealand—Case studies. I. Ladd, Helen F. II. Title.
    LB2822.84.N45 F58 2000
    379.93—dc21   99-050858
                                                                        CIP

9 8 7 6 5 4 3 2 1

The paper used in this publication meets minimum requirements of the American National Standard for Information Sciences—Permanence of Paper for Printed Library Materials: ANSI Z39.48-1984.

Typeset in Minion

Composition by Cynthia Stock
Silver Spring, Maryland

Printed by R. R. Donnelley and Sons
Harrisonburg, Virginia

To Julie, Ethan, Suzanna, and Haven

Contents

Tables

Preface

SELF-GOVERNING SCHOOLS, parental choice, market competition—these ideas are being proposed in countries around the world as ways of organizing and managing state education systems. Significant experimentation with such ideas has taken place in many countries, including England, Australia, New Zealand, and Chile, and they have attracted growing attention in the United States. For more than a decade American school districts have sought to decentralize the running of schools through policies such as school-site management. A sizable movement has developed around the concept of charter schools, and several cities and one state are currently experimenting with publicly and privately funded school voucher programs for low-income students.

Whether such reforms, or various packages of them, are desirable for the United States or other countries is vigorously contested. Judgments about the potential benefits of these ideas, as well as the general relevance of economic models to educational systems, tap into deeply held values, and discussion in the United States has been hampered by the lack of extended and widespread practical experience with them. To move the debate about such matters forward it would be useful to have a large-scale experiment in which self-governing schools operated in a competitive environment with extensive parental choice over a long period of time.

This book is about such an experiment. In 1989, the island country of

New Zealand, with its 3.8 million people, adopted a school reform that overnight transferred operating responsibility from the Department of Education to each school's newly elected governing board of trustees. Two years later, in 1991, with a new government in power, New Zealand enacted further reforms that introduced full parental choice of schools and encouraged the development of a competitive culture in the state education system. Its cultural similarity to the United States and other English-speaking countries, the presence of significant minority groups within its student population, and the fact that it implemented the reforms boldly make New Zealand as reasonable and useful a laboratory to observe these ideas in practice as one could hope to find.

Regardless of whether one favors or opposes the move to inject more competition into education, this book should provide valuable new insights. For some, the key lessons will emerge from New Zealand's failure to implement some ideas in their pure form. For others, they will emerge from the effects of New Zealand's decisions about thorny issues related to rationing places in oversubscribed schools or intervening in the activities of low-performing schools. Still others will be most interested in the new evidence on how the reforms increased polarization and exacerbated the problems of the unsuccessful schools or in what New Zealand's experience implies about charter schools and voucher programs.

Research Strategy

Numerous articles have been written in educational and other journals both in New Zealand and abroad about particular aspects of the Tomorrow's Schools reforms, and the Ministry of Education has engaged in monitoring activities for its own purposes. This book, however, represents the first attempt by outside researchers to undertake a comprehensive analysis of the impact of these reforms and to draw lessons for other countries. In addition to a review of existing scholarly literature on the Tomorrow's Schools reforms, our research took the following three forms.

Analysis of Data

Most of the tables in the book are based on our original analysis of data provided by the Ministry of Education and other sources. The ministry data included information on variables such as annual school enrollments, funding for schools, the socioeconomic characteristics of students by school, and test results by school on school-leaving exams. We also relied on information from the 1991 and 1996 New Zealand censuses of population and housing that was available by small geographic area through the SuperMap system. Our analysis focused on the three urban areas of Auckland, Christchurch, and Wellington because the challenges facing schools in these areas are most comparable to those of other developed countries.

We supplemented our empirical analysis with two major empirical studies by other researchers: survey research done by Cathy Wylie for the New Zealand Council for Educational Research during the period 1989–96 and the Smithfield project, a multiphased study of how competition played out in a few urban areas during the early 1990s.[1] Brief descriptions of the sample sizes and designs of these two studies can be found in appendix B.

Visits to Schools

To understand the impact of Tomorrow's Schools at the grass-roots level, we visited forty-six state primary and secondary schools, mostly in the three major urban areas. We observed classes, attended board of trustee meetings and open houses for prospective students, and talked with principals, teachers, parents, board members, and others regarding the reforms and how they were personally affected. In addition to providing evidence on the practical effects of the reforms, the school visits contributed to our data gathering and analysis in two important ways. First, they afforded an opportunity to gain insights from a variety of stakeholders into how to understand and interpret particular data, such as information about the funding of schools. Second, discussions with principals and others frequently raised important questions that lent themselves to quantitative analysis, such as which schools were obliged to accept students suspended

1. The survey research is found in Wylie (1997). The Smithfield project emerged in the form of a series of reports to the Ministry of Education during the 1990s and then in revised form in Lauder and Hughes (1999). Wherever possible we refer to the material in the 1999 book. We cite the original reports only for material that was not included in the book.

from other schools. As with our analysis of the school data, we concentrated our observations in the country's three major urban areas. (See appendix A for a list of the people we interviewed and the schools we visited.)

Interviews with Policymakers

On the basis of initial impressions from the school visits and data analysis, we held a series of discussions with senior officials of the Ministry of Education, legislators, and leaders of unions and other professional educational associations. These unstructured interviews were designed to broaden and test our understanding of the nature of the reform and of the reform process. We also benefited from the work of two applied historians, Graham and Susan Butterworth, who were completing an administrative history of the education reforms based on their extensive interviews with many of the relevant players within the government.[2]

Acknowledgments

As a husband-wife team who had the opportunity to spend five months in New Zealand in early 1998, we are extremely grateful to the institutions and people who made that opportunity available and productive. First, and most important, we thank the Fulbright program, which provided a lecturing and research grant for Helen Ladd to work in the public policy department at the Victoria University of Wellington. Second we are grateful to Victoria University, including the Institute for Policy Studies, for providing office space, research support, and collegiality for us both. Third we thank the Smith-Richardson Foundation for supplemental research support for travel and research assistance.

2. Butterworth and Butterworth (1998). In 1994–95, the Butterworths conducted a series of twenty interviews with the main architects of the reforms, which they supplemented in 1996 and 1997 with ten additional interviews and a few group interviews. Commissioned by the Ministry of Education, the study was intended to provide a historical record of the changes associated with the demise of the Department of Education and the establishment of the Ministry of Education. Earlier, Susan Butterworth had been commissioned to write a short administrative history of the department for training purposes.

The main contributors to this study are the many New Zealanders who shared their insights, their experiences, and their data with us (see list in appendix A). They include people in policymaking positions in the Ministry of Education, the Treasury Department, and elsewhere in the government; principals, trustees, teachers, parents, and students in the forty-six schools we visited; our colleagues and students at Victoria University; others involved with education policymaking and research; and the participants in our numerous public presentations in June 1998.

Among these people, some should be singled out. At the Ministry of Education, we are particularly grateful to Howard Fancy, the secretary of education, who spent many hours with us, and to Nicholas Pole, who provided us with much of the original data. At Victoria University, our heartfelt thanks go to Claudia Scott, Bob Stephens, Jonathan Boston, John Martin, and Arthur Grimes. At the school level, a number of principals in the Wellington area deserve special thanks for the extensive amount of time they spent with us.

Both for advice and ideas along the way and for their contributions to the final manuscript, we particularly thank Susan and Graham Butterworth, Cathy Wylie, and Martin Connolly. The Butterworths shared with us their manuscript in progress on the history of the reforms and commented closely on the first three chapters of this book. Cathy Wylie of the New Zealand Council for Educational Research shared with us her extensive research and knowledge and provided comments on the entire manuscript. Martin Connolly, formerly of the Education Review Office in Dunedin and now employed at the Ministry of Education, served as our primary contact for follow-up information once we returned to the United States and devoted a huge amount of time to ensuring the accuracy of our statements and the plausibility of our interpretations. To all of these people we are extremely grateful.

We are also grateful to our research assistants at various stages of this project. Rebecca Gau from Duke University helped us prepare for our visit to New Zealand, Samuel Buckle, Linyan Liu, and Pauline Ngan assisted us during our five months at Victoria University, and Susan Timberlake from Duke University helped prepare the final tables and figures. Finally, we thank all the people who shepherded this book through to publication. These include our Brookings editors, Christopher Kelaher and Janet Walker, and our copy editor, Diane Hammond. We could not have asked for a more congenial and helpful group of assistants and editors.

New Zealand's Bold Experiment

I

1 | *Introduction*

IN 1989 New Zealand embarked on what is arguably the most thorough and dramatic transformation of a state system of compulsory education ever undertaken by an industrialized country. Under a plan known as Tomorrow's Schools this island nation of 3.8 million people abolished its national Department of Education, which had overseen state schools for decades, and turned control of its nearly 2,700 primary and secondary schools over to locally elected boards of trustees.[1] Virtually overnight, legal responsibility for governing and managing New Zealand's state schools shifted from professional bureaucrats to boards dominated by lay volunteers, and one of the world's most tightly controlled public educational systems became one of the most decentralized. The Labour Party government in power at the time also installed new systems for financing state schools and holding them accountable, and it replaced the Department of Education with a much smaller Ministry of

---

1. Throughout this book we use the term Tomorrow's Schools to refer to the set of reforms that were enacted between 1989 and 1991, including the 1991 changes made by the government controlled by the National Party that introduced full parental choice. We use *Tomorrow's Schools* to refer to the policy paper, whose full title is *Tomorrow's Schools: The Reforming of Education Administration in New Zealand*, that outlined the Labour government's 1988 reform package.

Education charged with making policy recommendations rather than running schools.

Two years later New Zealand ratcheted the stakes of school reform up another notch. A newly elected National Party government committed to New Right social principles abolished neighborhood enrollment zones and gave parents the right to choose which school their child would attend. Primary and secondary schools found themselves competing for students against other schools in an educational marketplace. Public relations and marketing skills became as integral to the job description of principals as knowledge of curriculum and the ability to manage a faculty.

The story of how the Tomorrow's Schools reforms played out in New Zealand is an engrossing drama of educational reform on a grand scale. A succession of leaders from both major parties embraced radically new approaches to public education, implemented their respective visions over the opposition of unions and other professional educational organizations, and then, having achieved most of their stated objectives, were forced to recognize that, like the system it replaced, the new order of public education contains some important flaws. New Zealand's experience with school reform is a tale of bold thinking, aggressive political leadership, resolute commitment to large-scale social engineering, and unforeseen consequences.

The real importance of New Zealand's ambitious educational reforms, though, lies not so much in this boldness and scope as in the ideas and theories they embraced. For this reason the relevance of the New Zealand experience extends far beyond the shores of this island nation. The reform agenda was driven by ideas that are part of a global marketplace of ideas about school reform and are the object of experimentation, debate, and controversy in the United States and most other developed countries. What makes the Tomorrow's Schools reforms so significant is that New Zealand has been working with these ideas longer—and has taken them further—than virtually any other nation.

The ideas for which New Zealand is a global laboratory include the following:

—Decentralized management: Countries around the world have tried to decentralize their public school systems under plans that carry names such as *school-site management* or *school-based management*. New Zealand took the additional steps of shifting the control of schools from professional educators to parents and of selecting trustees through popular elections.

—Parental choice: Popular support is developing around the world for the notion that parents should have the right to select the school their child will attend. New Zealand has given families this right at both the primary and secondary levels.

—Competition among schools: Closely related to parental choice is the idea that forcing schools to compete for students in an educational marketplace will increase the quality of education. Whereas this notion is still in the experimental stage in the United States and other industrialized countries, New Zealand has made it a fundamental building block of its state educational system.

—Charter schools: The Tomorrow's Schools reforms established a state educational system that embraces many of the central features of what are known in the United States as charter schools. That is, it combined central funding and accountability with provisions for local schools to manage their own affairs. Although there are some important differences between the New Zealand system and American charter schools, the parallels invite close examination by those interested in the charter school movement, proponents and critics alike.

Theories of how to improve the quality of schooling are often debated in the abstract and on the basis of first principles. If they are to be implemented, however, they must be done so in specific social, political, cultural, and economic contexts that not only provide a reality check on their validity but also inevitably have the effect of shaping the ideas themselves. New Zealand offers such a context for this cluster of ideas. It offers a lens by which other nations can see into their own future if they decide to put the same ideas into practice. New Zealand is a living example of what can happen, for better and for worse, when schools are given managerial autonomy, when an entire school system opts for parental choice, and when ideas of market competition are applied to the delivery of a social service.

The purpose of this book is to describe the evolution of the Tomorrow's Schools reforms with an eye to identifying the lessons that New Zealand's experience with self-governing schools operating in a competitive environment holds for the United States and other countries, both developed and developing. We hasten to add that our purpose is not to cast judgment on whether the course New Zealanders followed was the right one for their own country. They must answer that question for themselves. Nor is the goal of this book to make abstract categorical judgments about controversial school reform strategies such as self-governing schools, competitive models of education, or parental choice. Rather, our objective is to look at how New Zealand implemented these ideas and to draw relevant lessons from its experience.

Three Strands of Tomorrow's Schools

The school system that emerged once the dust of the Tomorrow's Schools reforms had settled has three defining strands, each of which constitutes a sharp departure from past practices in New Zealand and other countries.

The first strand is the concept of self-governing schools. With the implementation of the Tomorrow's Schools reforms in October 1989, New Zealand moved abruptly from a tightly controlled system of governance and management to one that offers local schools a high degree of autonomy and flexibility in managing their own affairs. By turning control over to locally elected boards of trustees, reformers sought to make schools more responsive to local constituents. They also sought to increase the quality of teaching and learning by locating hiring, pedagogical, and other decisions as closely as possible to the point of implementation.

The second strand is the notion of schools as agents of the state. Central to the thinking of Tomorrow's Schools is the understanding that local schools, while enjoying operational autonomy, nevertheless act on behalf of the state. The government uses schools to achieve the national purposes that justify the establishment of a system of compulsory education, notably the creation of educated workers and citizens. In line with its stake in compulsory education, the national government provides most of the financial support for schools, sets curriculum guidelines, and oversees the system of accountability. There are tensions built into any system that seeks to combine school-level autonomy with national purposes.

The third strand is a competitive environment. The new educational order in New Zealand relies on competitive market pressures, including parental choice, to increase academic quality and to foster accountability both in individual schools and the system as a whole. The assumption is that the overall public good will be served by motivating schools to pursue their own interests in a competitive environment.

Running through these three strands is a crosscutting theme that is attracting growing attention in most industrialized countries. This is the concept of the local school as the fundamental building block of a public educational system. Such an approach contrasts with systems built around districts, regional bodies, or national ministries of education.

Impact of the Reforms

The reader should know at the outset that we are not able to make definitive judgments about whether the implementation of these three strands in the Tomorrow's Schools reforms has improved the overall level of student achievement in New Zealand. The country does not have a national system for assessing student performance in core academic subjects, and the architects of the reforms did not attempt to create a comprehensive picture of the old system to act as a benchmark for evaluating the new one. The only direct information available on student achievement consists of scores on school-leaving exams and other examinations that are taken by some, but by no means all, secondary students. Moreover, while the professional judgments of principals and teachers shed some light on how the reforms affected student learning, the picture is clouded by the fact that curriculum reforms were being implemented at the same time as the changes in governance and enrollment policy.

Effects of Each Strand

Despite the absence of longitudinal data on student achievement, ample evidence from a wide variety of sources allows us to identify both strengths and weaknesses in each of the major strands of the Tomorrow's Schools reforms. These can be summarized as follows.

SELF-GOVERNING SCHOOLS. There is universal agreement that overall the new decentralized administrative structure is superior to the bureaucratic system that it replaced. The Tomorrow's Schools reforms succeeded in breaking up an educational bureaucracy that many people believed had become overly bureaucratic, inefficient, and out of touch with the needs of local communities.

Virtually all schools have established parent-controlled boards of trustees, and in this sense the reforms achieved the goal of shifting the governance of local schools from professionals to the 15,000 amateurs who agreed to serve as school trustees along with some educational professionals. At the primary level, board members, principals, teachers, and parents alike have welcomed the new financial, managerial, and educational authority the boards enjoy. At the secondary level, where schools have a long tradition of boards of governors, the new boards of trustees have willingly embraced the enhanced control of their budgets and hiring policies brought by the reforms. At both the primary and secondary levels parents feel more welcome in schools, and teachers and principals say they are more responsive to parents' wishes.

The ability of boards of trustees and schools to shoulder new administrative responsibilities has varied widely. Some schools in distressed urban areas and in the countryside have had difficulty assembling boards, and a minority of schools are overwhelmed by the management tasks thrust upon them. The Ministry of Education has conceded that the new system does not work for 10–20 percent of schools, including some entire regions, both urban and rural.

SCHOOLS AS AGENTS OF THE STATE.   The model of schools as agents of the state has worked reasonably well in the sense that the Ministry of Education is clear about its curricular goals for the system, and the Education Review Office, which operates independently of the ministry, has put in place a viable accountability system based largely on governance and management criteria. At the same time, the government has developed few outcome measures on which to focus its accountability efforts. Inadequacy of funding has been a continuing concern, as has been the level of trust between the government and the schools, which is quite low. Perhaps most important, reformers underestimated the extent to which self-governing schools, especially those serving the most disadvantaged students, require continued support from the state they serve as agents.

A COMPETITIVE ENVIRONMENT.   The introduction of a culture of competition into the delivery of public education has produced, at best, mixed results. On the consumer side, parental choice has become an integral part of compulsory education in New Zealand and is now widely accepted as appropriate. Parents, especially well-educated ones and upwardly mobile parents, including Maori and Pacific Islanders, have not hesitated to make use of their extended right to choose among schools, and the choices they have made have had a large impact on enrollment patterns, especially in urban areas. With some exceptions, even vocal critics of the way choice has been implemented understand both that parental choice is desirable and that putting the genie back in the bottle no longer seems to be a political option.

Genies aside, the particular model of parental choice adopted by Tomorrow's Schools fell far short of the ostensible goal of offering choice for all students. Many parents, especially those with low incomes, are not in a position to exercise choice either because no alternative options exist where they live or because they cannot afford the transportation, fees, and other costs of enrolling in a desirable school. In addition, since oversubscribed schools have the right to designate which students they will accept, the system quickly flip-flopped in some fast-growing urban areas from one in which parents and children choose schools to one in which schools choose students. Parental choice, in short, gave way to school choice.

On the supply side of New Zealand's new educational marketplace, the introduction of competition for students has kept principals on their toes and made them more alert to the needs of their students. It has also generated some undesirable side effects, including a decline in professional collegiality. Principals and even teachers have become less willing to share pedagogical and other ideas with their counterparts at schools with which their school is competing for students. Some principals say they are under pressure to engage in recruiting practices that make them ethically uncomfortable.

Broad Consequences and Concerns

Although the New Zealand reform experience has resulted in clear benefits to many schools and students, it also highlights the systemic problems that can emerge from the interaction of the three strands. While such problems need not necessarily emerge in other countries that embrace the concept of self-governing schools operating in a competitive environment, they are likely to occur unless countries are vigilant about building safeguards into the system that were lacking in New Zealand.

POLARIZATION. The most obvious negative consequence of the Tomorrow's Schools reforms is that enrollment patterns in New Zealand, which once prided itself on being a relatively egalitarian society, became increasingly stratified. Our data show that in the five years following the introduction of parental choice in 1991 New Zealand students sorted themselves out by ethnic group and to a lesser extent by socioeconomic status to a degree that cannot be explained by changes in ethnic and demographic residential patterns. Data also show that much choice is motivated by considerations related to a school's mix of students and that the system has produced both white and brown flight from unpopular schools. While general social and economic polarization is a fact of life in most industrialized countries, including New Zealand, the Tomorrow's Schools reforms appear to have exacerbated this phenomenon.

WINNERS AND LOSERS.   The concept of an educational marketplace presumes that some competitors will succeed and others will fail. Moreover, in a free market economic system, it is inevitable—even desirable—that some competitors will go out of business. New Zealand's application of the principle of competition to the delivery of compulsory education created a situation in which the most popular schools position themselves to serve primarily academically motivated students from families with high socioeconomic status. They attract the best teachers and can concentrate on teaching a relatively narrow range of academic subjects well. By contrast, a significant number of schools at the other end of the popularity spectrum must deal with increasing concentrations of difficult-to-teach students: those with learning or behavioral problems, those for whom English is a second language, or those living in poverty or in dysfunctional families.

What does a state educational system do when a school becomes noncompetitive—that is, bankrupt—in the sense that it is unable to attract a critical mass of students? Closing such schools down posed political problems, largely because of concerns about where the students would go. The Ministry of Education was slow to acknowledge the seriousness of the problems faced by schools with high concentrations of difficult-to-teach students, and it has struggled to find a basis for intervening to assist them that is consistent with the principles of self-governance.

New Zealand's experience with Tomorrow's Schools thus raises the question of whether it is appropriate, practically as well as morally, to organize public education in such a way that, when the system is operating the way it is designed to function, there will be failures as well as successes among both institutions and individuals. One might justify the deliberate creation of relative failures if competition served to enhance the overall quality of all schools, in effect raising the tide for all boats. Or such a policy might be defended if some sort of safety net were in place to catch the expected losers early on and to take the steps necessary to make them into viable schools. Neither condition appears to have been present in New Zealand, although the ministry has belatedly started to assist schools battered by the cumulative effects of the reforms.

BALANCING COMPETING INTERESTS.   The Tomorrow's Schools reforms failed to provide adequate mechanisms for balancing the interests of the various stakeholders in the state educational system. For example, the reform package defined the community that local schools serve rather narrowly as current parents in a particular school, and some boards of trustees of primary schools took advantage of their new autonomy to add two more years to their programs. In many cases such unilateral actions created serious enrollment problems for nearby intermediate schools. While such decisions might be desirable in particular cases, the New Zealand educational reforms did not include formal mechanisms for the balancing of the narrow interests of a particular group of parents against the legitimate needs of broader communities, including those of parents in nearby schools and the state school system as a whole. The issue of how to balance the legitimate interests of various stakeholders also arose in relation to the question of how to ration spaces in oversubscribed schools.

New Zealand's experience has the potential to inform the debate over school reform efforts in other countries in several other important respects. Among the questions we address are

—What challenges arise in a system of parental choice when many schools become oversubscribed?

—To what extent can the problems of failing schools be addressed through managerial reforms?

—What lessons emerge about the potentials and pitfalls of self-governing schools?

—What is the proper role for central government in a decentralized system, especially in the areas of finance and accountability?

—What lessons does the New Zealand experience hold for charter schools or educational voucher programs?

Relevance of New Zealand's Experience to Other Countries

Readers are entitled to ask what possible relevance the experiences of a country with a population of 3.8 million persons and where sheep outnumber humans by a ratio of more than twelve to one might have for the United States and other major industrial nations. This is a fair question and should be addressed at the outset.

New Zealand is, to be sure, not heavily populated. But its population is roughly equivalent to that of the median American state. Since public education in the United States is constitutionally a responsibility of the fifty states and the territories, the Ministry of Education in Wellington is the functional equivalent a state department of education. Similar comparisons can be made with Australia, where public education is run by the seven states and territories, five of which are smaller than New Zealand.

New Zealand has a long-standing and impressive reputation among developed countries for social innovation. It created the first welfare state, was the first democracy to give women the vote, and its educators are known for their pioneering work in the field of literacy. New Zealand was the birthplace of Reading Recovery, an approach to reading instruction that has been widely emulated in the United States and other countries. As a country of immigrants and a member of the British Commonwealth, New Zealand has close social, economic, and cultural ties to European countries, and the problems with which it is grappling, including difficult issues related to education in inner cities and to the Maori and Pacific Islander minority groups, are similar to those of all nations associated with the Organization for Economic Cooperation and Development. In the preface to his book *Making Peoples: A History of New Zealanders*, the historian James Belich describes New Zealand as "an historian's paradise: a laboratory whose isolation, size, and recency is an advantage, in which grand themes of world history are often played out more rapidly, more separately, and therefore more discernibly, than elsewhere."[2]

Because New Zealand began overhauling its educational system in 1989, it has had more experience with ideas such as self-governing schools and parental choice than virtually any other developed country. It thus offers a splendid place to observe the long-term effects of such ideas. Perhaps most important, the reforms were carried out in bold relief, which makes it easy for outsiders to observe the effects, positive and negative, of the central ideas of Tomorrow's Schools. The country's leaders did not experiment with halting and incremental reforms of a state educational system in need of far-reaching reforms. Rather, they threw out the old system in toto, put in a new one, and left fine-tuning until later. The high relief of the New Zealand school reforms reflects the national character. New Zealanders as a people are not prone to halfway measures. They tend to act decisively, carry ideas to their logical conclusion, and only then, if need be, pick up the pieces. "We tend to run with things and improvise as we go along," observed Jill Stanley, the principal of Porirua School near Wellington.

2. Belich (1996: 7).

New Zealand's parliamentary system also lends itself to decisive actions. A relatively small number of persons with a commitment to certain policies can gain control of the cabinet and thus be assured that these policies will hold sway in Parliament as a whole. Indeed, leaders of both the Labour government that launched the reforms and the National government that expanded on them embraced rapid change as a matter of political strategy. At one point David Lange, who was Labour prime minister from 1984 to 1989, suggested that he and his fellow political leaders might relax and take a "tea break" from the social upheaval they were leading. Roger Douglas, the minister of finance and a primary architect of the changes, promptly dismissed any relaxation of the pressure. Significant social reform requires "quantum leaps," he said. "Moving step by step lets vested interest mobilize. Big packages neutralize them. Speed is essential.... Once you start the momentum rolling, never let it stop."[3]

3. Address to Australian Education Council conference, Adelaide, Dec. 1990, quoted in Lauder (1993).

2 | *Background and Context*

Bruce Murray is a former cricket player who played for New Zealand in international test matches and is still remembered as one of the country's best opening batsmen ever. A tall man with a gentle but determined manner and a wry, sometimes acerbic sense of humor, Murray is the principal of Tawa College, a thriving high school near Wellington where he keeps a Bruce Murray autograph cricket bat in his office.

Murray is a product of the school system that he has served as a principal for eighteen years. His mother was a seamstress who never went to high school, and his father tried a variety of jobs, including farming on a plot of land that, Murray quipped, "was so steep you could farm both sides of the acre." With the decline of wool prices during the Depression, his father was barely able to support the family. They lived in state housing, and the four children attended state schools. They all went on to successful careers in education and other areas of social service, much of it in developing countries. Murray is proud of the fact that, despite their poor beginnings, he and his siblings never became charges of the state and that they were "able to make a contribution to the world community." He attributed this largely to the availability of a strong egalitarian state educational system. "People need help to pull themselves up by their own bootstraps," he said. "The state education system gave us that help."[1]

---

1. Unless otherwise noted, all direct quotations from teachers, administrators, and policymakers were made in conversation with one or both of the authors.

The system that served Bruce Murray and his siblings so well has now been radically restructured. Those who led the restructuring believed that the move to self-governing schools and the application of market concepts to the delivery of education would greatly increase the quality and efficiency of education for all New Zealanders. Others, however, including Murray, fear that the changes are driving state schools in directions that will make it more difficult to play the role that they did for himself and his three siblings. "The gap between rich and poor is widening, and the commitment of the state to quality education for all students is weakening," he said. "It's a scandal."

To understand the changes that have been brought about through Tomorrow's Schools and the issues they have raised, one must first understand something about New Zealand and its people.

A Remote Land

New Zealand is a country of 3.8 million persons, most of whom occupy one of two islands that run 1,600 kilometers along the point where two tectonic plates converge and joust uneasily with each other in the South Pacific, making the country prone to earthquakes and volcanic eruptions. Polynesian legend has it that, like other Pacific islands, New Zealand was fished up out of the sea by the demigod Maui. The North Island is Maui's fish and the South Island the canoe from which he hauled it in. A circular fishhook remains a familiar symbol in Maori art.

Other than its precarious geology, the most significant physical feature of New Zealand is that it is not very near anything. The country lies 1,700 kilometers south of Fiji, 2,250 kilometers east of Australia, and halfway around the world from Mother Britain, the country of origin for most of New Zealand's modern-day settlers and the primary source of its cultural heritage. For practical purposes, says the historian James Belich, New Zealanders live "1,200 miles from anywhere and 12,000 from *the* somewhere."[2]

The remoteness of New Zealand explains the fact that the country has a relatively short history of settlement. The first of the Pacific Island tribes that eventually came to be known collectively as Maori did not arrive from central Polynesia until, most likely, the end of the eleventh century, which

2. Belich (1996: 450).

is about 50,000 years later than the Aborigines settled in Australia.[3] The Polynesian boatsmen named their new home Aotearoa, or Land of the Long White Cloud.

The first European known to have cast his eyes on New Zealand was Abel Tasman, a Dutch explorer who in 1642 sailed up the west coast of what he at first thought was part of South America.[4] When local tribesmen paddled out to greet him, he responded by sounding trumpets, which the paddlers mistakenly interpreted as a hostile gesture. In an ensuing scuffle, four Dutch sailors in a rowboat were killed, and Tasman hightailed it away. Europeans left New Zealand alone for more than a century, until the British explorer Captain James Cook circled the islands in the *Endeavour* in 1769. Although his contact with the country was brief and traumatic, Tasman did give the country its European name, after the Netherlands' province of Zeeland.

European immigration began in earnest in the early nineteenth century, and by midcentury entrepreneurs were aggressively promoting New Zealand to prospective settlers as an idyllic "Britain of the South" that would accommodate surplus British population and, over time, provide goods useful to British markets. New Zealanders are quick to point out that, unlike Australia, their neighbor across the Tasman Sea, their country was not settled by convicts, though some convicts who escaped from Australia found their way to New Zealand.

New Zealand maintained strong social, cultural, and economic ties to its mother country. It became a self-governing British colony in 1855 and a dominion in 1907, and it was not until 1947 that it had the functional status of a fully independent country. Most New Zealanders thought of England as home, and some older ones still do. The British queen is still the head of state, and state-owned schools are legally known as Crown schools. Over the decades New Zealanders repeatedly took up arms to fight in Britain's military conflicts, including both world wars. Its soldiers earned reputations for skill and bravery and took heavy casualties.

New Zealand enjoyed the protection of a preferred trading relationship with the United Kingdom, under which the latter provided a guaranteed market for lamb, wool, and other goods. This arrangement came to an

---

3. Belich (1996: 36).

4. Recent evidence suggests that Portuguese or Spanish navigators may have been there much earlier.

end as Britain shifted its economic loyalties away from its former colonies toward the European Economic Community, leaving New Zealand and other former colonies to fend for themselves in the global economy.

Kiwis

New Zealanders may be the only people in the world who describe themselves colloquially by their national symbol. They are known as Kiwis, after one of the numerous bird species unique to these islands. The kiwi is small, flightless, and very vulnerable—characteristics with which New Zealanders readily identify—and it is nocturnal. Few persons ever see them except in zoos.

New Zealanders form three main groups. Residents of European descent are known as Pakeha (Pak'ee-ha) and make up 80 percent of the population, while Maori account for 14 percent. The term *Maori* means non-European. It was coined by the original New Zealanders in the nineteenth century to distinguish themselves from the arriving Europeans; about 1850 it became a collective noun to describe the various tribes that had settled the islands long before the arrival of the English but that hitherto had no need for a particular collective identity. The third major group is Pacific Islanders, who began arriving during the manufacturing boom of the 1950s from Samoa, the Cook Islands, Tonga, Fiji, and other islands and constitute 6 percent of the population. Another 4 percent are Chinese, Indian, and others.[5]

The relationship between Pakehas and Maori is complex and unusual. Unlike other British colonies, New Zealand was not conquered by military force. Instead, new immigrants purchased land from Maori, who for the most part saw Europeans as useful neighbors and a source of goods such as muskets, tobacco, iron tools, and clothing. Relations between the two were formalized in 1840 in the Treaty of Waitangi, which was signed by forty-five Maori chiefs and the representative of the queen of England. Under the treaty, the Maori ceded their sovereignty of New Zealand to the queen, who in turn guaranteed them protection and granted them the same rights, privileges, and duties of citizenship enjoyed by the citizens of England. The treaty gave Maori continued possession of their land but

5. Statistics New Zealand (1997: 124). The total is more than 100 percent because persons of mixed ancestry are sometimes counted more than once.

stipulated that, if they chose to sell it, they must do so to the Crown. Although there has always been a considerable degree of intermarriage between Maori and Europeans, subsequent relations between the two groups were rocky. Disputes over land and British prerogatives led to a series of wars in the 1860s, variously known as the Land Wars, the Maori Wars, and the New Zealand Wars. Confiscation of large territories from Maori who had taken up arms against the government created resentments that continue to this day.

Maori generally accepted Christianity, and missionaries took the lead in extending education to them. Both Maori and Pacific Islanders, however, share the plight of racial and ethnic minorities in other developed nations. They lag far behind the Pakeha majority in income, educational attainment, and measures of well-being such as health.

The 1970s and 1980s brought a resurgence of Maori culture, and political activists began pushing for redress of long-standing grievances. In 1975 the Parliament passed legislation establishing a Waitangi Tribunal to investigate Maori claims against the Crown, and ten years later the act was amended to apply to all claims dating back to 1840. Substantial financial reparations have been made to Maori tribes whose lands were found to have been unjustly confiscated, and other claims are pending.

National Character

The remoteness of New Zealand has had an important influence in shaping the national character. Given their physical situation, New Zealanders have been forced to be innovative and to rely on their own devices. There is a popular saying that just about any problem can be solved with a length of number-8 fencing wire. Such pragmatism and resourcefulness helped the Kiwis dream up activities such as bungee jumping, and it brought them the America's Cup in twelve-meter sailing.

New Zealand also has a long tradition of egalitarianism. The European settlers who made the long and dangerous boat trip to this remote land shared a dislike of overt class distinctions. "New Zealand's settlers left England because of the limitations of the class system," explained John Grant, principal of Kaipara College near Auckland. "They had no desire to reinvent it once they got here." In 1873 Anthony Trollope noted a marked New Zealand reluctance to accept gratuities. "The offer of money was considered to be offensive" even among recent working-class migrants.[6] Belich says that New Zealand was marked by a "powerful and enduring colonial populism." He attributes this in part to a shortage of labor that "drove wages up, made jobs plentiful, and forced the genteel and respectable to sometimes indulge in manual work, encouraging them to acquiesce in a social revaluation of such work."[7]

As noted in the previous chapter, New Zealand was the first democracy to give women the vote. It invented the modern welfare state, and the high taxes that sustained it contributed to a situation in which there were relatively narrow gaps between rich and poor. Housing patterns are by no means as segregated by socioeconomic status as in, say, the United States. Significantly, New Zealand political leaders built the welfare state not out of commitment to some abstract left-wing political ideology but as a practical response to a political and social situation.

New Zealand's Approach to Education

These national characteristics of pragmatism and egalitarianism can be seen in New Zealand's approach to education. Its teachers are arguably less well versed in pedagogical theory than their counterparts in other developed countries, but there are many excellent practitioners, and schools are organized so that students start out with a big emphasis on the most fundamental academic skill: literacy.

When pupils enter school on their fifth birthday they find themselves in what Beth Huntington, who teaches new entrants at the Thorndon Primary School in Wellington, termed a "print-rich" environment. "We surround them with language and words," she said. New Zealand primary school teachers spend as much as half of each day on reading and writing, and the country's innovative curriculum stresses comprehension rather than rote skills. Older students guide younger ones, and there is plenty of time for silent reading of storybooks. "We allow them to develop at a rate that suits them and stress the idea that reading should be an enjoyable experience," said Huntington.

In the minds of many educators around the world, New Zealand edu-

6. Belich (1996: 330).
7. Belich (1996: 332).

cation is synonymous with Reading Recovery. This approach to reading instruction was developed by Auckland clinical psychologist Dame Marie Clay in the 1970s and has been widely replicated in the United States and elsewhere. It is a twelve-to-twenty-week intervention program under which specially trained teachers provide one-on-one help to pupils who are falling behind in their reading after one year of schooling. New Zealand primary schools routinely apply the technique to their lowest-performing six-year-olds, and research shows that the overwhelming majority complete the program reading at levels comparable to their classmates.[8]

Characteristically, New Zealanders have taken pride in having an educational system that offered a universally solid education. Up through the 1980s it was said that parents could assume that their child would get a good education at just about any state school, especially at the primary level. There were, of course, exceptions. Like any other developed country, New Zealand has its share of urban problems and struggling inner-city schools.

One negative feature of New Zealand's state educational system, however, has been the low rate at which its young people complete secondary education. The Ministry of Education's 1996 annual report conceded that New Zealand "lags behind many countries in terms of participation in secondary level programmes beyond the compulsory age."[9] In the past, low rates were partly a matter of design. School certificate examinations were traditionally scored in such a way that half of the takers failed. Although such a system may have been tolerable in an era when jobs were available for anyone with a basic education and when a generous welfare system could serve as a safety net for those with limited skills, the situation now is quite different.

New Zealand pupils begin their first year of school, as new entrants, on their fifth birthday, and they pursue twelve more years of schooling through year thirteen. Attendance is compulsory through age sixteen. The overwhelming majority, 96.5 percent, of New Zealand young people attend state schools; the rest are in private schools, which receive state subsidies ranging from 25 to 40 percent of the average state cost per pupil, depending on the age of the student. Nearly 10 percent of students in state schools

---

8. The proportion of students entering the program who completed it successfully during the 1990s has ranged between 86 and 90 percent. See Ministry of Education (1996).

9. Ministry of Education (1997a: 67).

attend what are known as state integrated schools.[10] These schools, three-quarters of them Roman Catholic, have a "special character" and are run by boards that are accountable both to the Ministry of Education and to the sponsoring body. This category of state schools was created in 1975 when the country's Catholic school system was going through a financial crisis and church leaders were threatening to force the state system to absorb tens of thousands of additional students. Although they own their own physical plants, integrated schools follow the national curriculum and are fully funded by the state for operating and new capital expenses.

One notable characteristic of the New Zealand educational system is the large number of single-sex state schools. New Zealand is an inherently conservative country, and, its fundamental egalitarianism notwithstanding, the English tradition of prestigious grammar schools lives on in the minds and hearts of many Kiwis. Prestigious all-boys schools such as Auckland Grammar and Wellington College turned out most of the country's political and other leaders in the past, and most of the highly sought after secondary schools today are single sex. Demand is particularly strong for single-sex education for girls, and all-female secondary schools currently outnumber all-male schools by twenty-eight to twenty-three in the three major urban areas of Auckland, Christchurch, and Wellington. Middle-class mothers in New Zealand seem to believe that their daughters will fare better without the distractions of males. "The belief is that familiarity breeds," observed Janice Campbell, the principal of Wellington East Girls College.

Another important feature of state education in New Zealand is the growing network of Maori schools. In response to the resurgence of interest in Maori culture in general and its language in particular, the Ministry of Education has supported the development of a range of educational institutions run by and for Maori. Preschool children learn Maori in language "nests," or *kohanga reo*, and regular primary and intermediate schools operate as immersion classrooms, known as *ruma rumaki*, that offer the chance for students to pursue part of their education in a Maori environment. In recent years the government has been encouraging the creation of schools known as *kura kaupapa* where students can receive a Maori-oriented education through secondary school. There are also eight Maori boarding schools serving about 1,000 students.

10. Ministry of Education (1997a: 31).

A Centrally Controlled System

The state school system was established by the Education Act of 1877 on a relatively decentralized basis. Much of the authority for running primary schools lay with regional boards of education that were vestiges of the former provincial educational systems, and the Department of Education, small and weak in its early years, served as little more than a conduit for funds to the elected boards.[11] Over the decades, however, as in the United States and elsewhere at the time, educational governance became increasingly centralized and hierarchical. At the top of the pyramid were the minister of education, who had cabinet rank, and a powerful department, which by 1984 had 1,700 employees.[12] The department owned the property of all state-run schools as well as the buses that transported students to them, and it supplied architectural and engineering services when needed. It dispersed operating and capital funds and developed national curriculum guidelines. It also negotiated the salaries of teachers and school administrators with their national unions and oversaw teachers' training and certification.

In practice the department continued to carry out its supervision of primary schools through the boards of education. There were ten regional boards, each with eight to sixteen members elected by representatives of the schools in their areas. These boards were charged with appointing principals and teachers in each school in their region, arranging student transportation, and providing teaching materials and equipment to schools. Funding for the boards came from government grants, with very little of it passed through to the schools as discretionary spending.

The department also maintained a corps of inspectors, who moved from school to school making sure that official policies were carried out. The inspectors, all of whom had been senior members of the teaching profession, had powerful formal responsibilities, including the grading and disciplining of teachers and the organizing of professional development programs for schools in their jurisdiction. They also carried out important informal tasks such as spotting problems, offering advice to school principals, carrying new ideas from school to school, and working out policy priorities. Since no effort was made to publicize negative findings

11. Butterworth (1993: 9).
12. Butterworth and Butterworth (1998: 41).

about particular schools, the inspectorate did not serve parents particularly well.

Secondary schools operated somewhat differently, mainly because the 1877 Education Act envisioned compulsory education only at the primary level, and it was not until 1944 that free compulsory education was extended to the secondary level. Secondary schools, along with universities, evolved separately. They were established by acts of Parliament and, in lieu of state subsidies, were endowed by gifts of Crown land. By World War I most had joined the state system.[13] Secondary schools had their own boards of governors made up of current parents, appointees of the local boards of education, and community representatives.[14] As secondary school education became more common, these boards gradually surrendered much of their independence to the department in return for financial and other support. Unlike their primary-level counterparts, however, high schools retained the right to select their own teachers and administrators. Although it was less significant than at the secondary level, primary schools also had a tradition of parental or lay participation. They had school committees of elected householders whose formal responsibilities, other than voting on members of the boards of education, were limited primarily to maintaining the school premises and organizing fund-raising activities

New Zealand's state educational system is held together by a national curriculum that, while created centrally and designed to provide overall coherence to teaching, is not as highly prescriptive as those in, say, England or France. It is perhaps best described as a set of curriculum statements, and teachers are given great latitude in how they cover the material.

In keeping with British practice, it has been traditional for New Zealand students to take a school-leaving examination at the end of their compulsory education, and over the years, as students stayed in school longer, new tests were added at higher grade levels. School attendance is now compulsory to the age of sixteen, and most students sit for a school certificate examination at the end of three years of secondary education in year eleven, or at about the age of fifteen. Year-twelve certificates are awarded on a subject-by-subject basis, and a higher school certificate is awarded to stu-

13. Butterworth and Butterworth (1998: 23).

14. Many secondary schools were attached to universities, hence the use of the term *college* to designate many of the older high schools.

dents who have satisfactorily completed five years of full-time secondary schooling, or through year thirteen. Graduates going on to further study at the university take university entrance and bursary examinations to qualify for admission and to compete for scholarships.

A notable characteristic of New Zealand schools has been the absence of any comprehensive system of national tests of student performance for students under age fifteen. New Zealand teachers are wary about the use of tests for reasons other than to organize classes or to diagnose the needs of particular students, and there is little tradition of aggregating test data or keeping them on a schoolwide, much less a national, basis. Instead of following the English model of national tests, the Ministry of Education in 1993 initiated the National Education Monitoring project, which assesses the achievement of a light sample of primary pupils in years four and eight in selected schools primarily as a source of information to teachers. The assessments cover about one-quarter of the curriculum areas each year. The first four-year cycle was completed in 1998. Other than the results of these tests, the ministry collects no data that can be used to track student performance in core academic areas over time.

Size and Location of Schools

One notable feature of New Zealand schools is that they are, on average, relatively small. The state school system, for example, has roughly the same number of students as does the state of Kentucky, but it has almost twice as many schools (2,700) as Kentucky (1,400). One reason for this is that many New Zealand schools are located in small and remote rural communities. The quality of education in the rural areas is a growing concern, and in October 1997 the Education Review Office, which is in charge of accountability in the state school system, released a report that was sharply critical of twenty such schools on the east coast of North Island. It concluded that the quality of education most of the 1,350 students in these schools receive "is not high enough to break the cycles of economic depression that are characteristic of the Coast. Nor is it sufficient to equip them adequately to participate in worthwhile economic activity in the wider community of New Zealand and elsewhere."[15]

Because the problems of New Zealand's rural schools are not directly relevant to other countries with greater population density, rural schools

15. Education Review Office (1997: 4).

Table 2-1. *Student Enrollments and Growth Rates, by Urban Area*[a]

Percent except where indicated

Area	Number of students 1997	Indicated change		Students	
		1986–91	*1991–97*	*Maori*	*Island*
Auckland	189,006	1.4	17.9	14.8	18.8
Wellington	67,664	−6.2	3.9	15.9	10.6
Christchurch	54,304	−3.1	9.9	8.6	3.2

a. Includes all students in all schools, including state schools (both Crown owned and integrated) and private schools. The Auckland area includes Auckland City, North Shore City, Waitakere City, Manukau City, and Papakura District. The Wellington area includes Wellington City, Lower Hutt City, Upper Hutt City, Porirua City, and Kapiti Coast City.

are not a focus of this book. Instead, we concentrate our attention on New Zealand's three major urban areas—Auckland, Christchurch, and Wellington—that collectively are home to about 45 percent of the country's population and where schools face problems that are more representative of those facing urban school systems in the United States and other developed countries. The Auckland area has recently experienced rapid population growth and growth in school enrollments. In addition, it has large concentrations of Maori and Pacific Islanders, especially in the South Auckland areas of Mangere and Otara. Wellington, the capital, and its surrounding communities have experienced modest population growth, but the closing of automobile assembly plants and other major employers has led to considerable disruption, especially among minority groups. In the Wellington area, minority groups tend to be concentrated less in the city of Wellington and more in the nearby city of Porirua. The Christchurch area, which comprises Christchurch alone, has the lowest proportion of Maori and Pacific Islanders.

Table 2-1 provides information on the number of students in the three urban areas in 1997. The Auckland urban area is the largest and the fastest growing. The Wellington and Christchurch areas are smaller and are growing more slowly. Increases after 1991 followed a five-year period of stability of enrollments in Auckland and a period of decline in Wellington and Christchurch, which is significant because it means that parental choice was introduced at a time when many schools had excess capacity. Now that capacity is being stretched.

The final two columns of table 2-1 show the concentration of minority students. Wellington has the highest proportion of Maori students, but

Auckland has the highest proportion of minority students overall because of its large proportion of Pacific Islanders. About one in three students in the Auckland area and about one in four in Wellington is either Maori or Pacific Island. In contrast, only about one in eight students in Christchurch is a minority.

Educational Performance by International Standards

New Zealand's state educational system has developed a strong international reputation. New Zealand teachers are widely regarded as pioneers in the development of new pedagogical techniques, especially in the teaching of reading, and their students have consistently done well on international comparisons of educational achievement.

New Zealand was among the highest-scoring countries in surveys of reading conducted in 1973 and 1993 by the International Association for the Evaluation of Educational Achievement. In the 1973 study of fifteen countries, New Zealand students had the highest mean scores in reading comprehension for ages fourteen and eighteen.[16] In the 1993 study, New Zealand nine-year-olds ranked sixth among this age group in twenty-seven countries, while fourteen-year-olds were fourth in a field of thirty-one.[17] Results from the Third International Mathematics and Science Study, released in 1998, showed that, compared with the other twenty countries participating in the study, New Zealand secondary school students "had relatively high levels of science and mathematics literacy in the final year of schooling." The mean scores for New Zealand students were 522 in mathematics and 529 in science, both significantly higher than the international average of 500.[18]

Pressures for Change

Despite its record of overall success, New Zealand's educational system, like the country's other social institutions, came under enormous pressure in the 1980s to change its ways. This pressure built up for several reasons, starting with a major economic crisis.

16. Elley (1991: 2).
17. Wagemaker (1993: 49–50).
18. Ministry of Education (1997a: 73–74).

Economic Crisis

For decades New Zealanders had been living the good life. Ties with Great Britain provided a guaranteed market for their products. Unemployment was virtually nonexistent, in part because of the strong economy and rampant featherbedding, and it was said that the prime minister could recite the names of everyone who was out of work at any given time. Although taxes were high, citizens had access to adequate medical care and one of the world's most extensive welfare systems. By the 1980s, however, the chickens were coming home to roost. New Zealand was hit hard by economic events beyond its control, notably the oil shocks of 1973 and 1979 and the loss of preferential trading after Britain joined the Common Market in 1973. Inflation and unemployment rates began to climb—the jobless rate rose from 2.1 percent in 1976 to 4.5 percent in 1981—and it was not clear whether the economy was capable of sustaining significant growth.

In the general elections of 1984 popular discontent had reached such a level that the National government was replaced by a Labour government in the general elections. Prime Minister David Lange and other leaders of the new government had not even unpacked their papers when they discovered that the previous prime minister, Sir Robert Muldoon, who had run the country in dictatorial style from 1975 to 1984 and was famously indifferent to budget deficits, had been concealing a serious balance of payments crisis. The country, it seemed, was close to bankruptcy. The new government immediately devalued the New Zealand dollar by 20 percent in July 1984 and soon afterward let it float. The following year the country was hit by a banking crisis that led the government to bail out the Bank of New Zealand. Then came the global stock market crash in October 1987, which caused numerous bankruptcies and sent the unemployment rate, which was already rising due to deregulation, privatization, and downsizing, to more than 10 percent.

This series of economic blows left New Zealanders reeling. Just about everyone agreed that there was a crisis and that bold steps were required, but few were sure what these bold steps ought to be.

Restructuring the Private and Governmental Sectors

One group of New Zealand officials was confident they knew the answers. These officials were centered in the Treasury Department and had been heavily influenced by the New Right economic ideas associated with the University of Chicago. To their minds, what New Zealand needed was a radical restructuring of its economic and social institutions around the neoliberal themes of smaller government, fiscal restraint, market liberalization and free trade, profit incentives for state-owned enterprises, and reduced government spending on social programs. The leader of this group was Roger Douglas, who became Lange's minister of finance. In July 1984 the Treasury Department published a 325-page briefing paper outlining policies that soon came to be known as Rogernomics.

To many people's surprise the new Labour government, traditionally the party of full employment and the natural heir to the social democratic belief in strong governmental involvement in economic as well as social affairs, accepted many of these ideas and restructured New Zealand's major institutions along free market lines. Controls on wages, prices, interest rates, rents, and credit were eliminated, as were export and domestic subsidies. Tariffs were reduced, restrictions on major foreign investments were removed, and new business laws that encouraged competition were passed. In 1986 the government initiated a universal goods and services tax (GST) while reducing other taxes, including those on income and corporate profits. State activities with potential commercial value—such as banks, railways, and telecommunications—were reorganized and placed under government-appointed boards of directors with a mandate to operate like private corporations. Although Prime Minister Lange personally was not an enthusiast for privatizing state enterprises, the Labour government sold off several billion dollars' worth of state assets, including the communications giant Telecom; the National government that assumed power in 1991 disposed of another several billion. Government agencies were divided into policy and operating units, agency heads were placed on performance contracts, and many activities, including policy development, were contracted out to private consultants.[19]

With economic restructuring well under way, the government turned its attention to the social sectors of the economy. The Labour government made educational reform a priority, and the subsequent National government altered the national health care system beyond recognition. Public

---

19. For additional reading on the reforms, see Boston and others (1996); and the special issue of the *Journal of Policy Analysis and Management* 16(3) (1997) on the new public management in New Zealand and beyond.

hospitals were renamed Crown Health Enterprises (CHEs) and were required to operate like private businesses and to compete with private providers for public funds.[20] The Housing Corporation, whose role had been to provide inexpensive housing for low-income earners, became Housing New Zealand and, like other former state enterprises, was instructed to show a profit. Welfare benefits were also cut back sharply.

These massive changes prompt some obvious questions. How did a country with such a strong socialist tradition make such an about-face? Why was such a change initiated by a Labour government? The answers are complex, and dealing with them in any depth is beyond the scope of this book, but New Zealanders offer numerous partial explanations. For one, the country had never faced economic and social disruptions of this magnitude, and few people had a clear vision of how to deal with them. Fixing this situation would take more than some number-8 fencing wire— and many New Zealanders were scared. When a self-confident group of policymakers came along with what sounded like a coherent plan, they were able to gain credibility.

The vocabulary used was important, for New Zealand's core problems were defined by leaders as fundamentally *economic* in nature. Much debate has ensued over the extent to which the restructuring of New Zealand's public sector institutions was driven by the Treasury Department. Its role has sometimes been overstated, but the authors of a history of Tomorrow's Schools reforms are correct in observing that, whereas treasury did not necessarily get its way in many, or even most, policy decisions, "certainly, it managed to change the whole terms of the policy debate in the public service."[21]

Put succinctly, if you ask economic questions, you get economic answers. When the debate is carried out in economic terms, it makes sense to talk about restructuring institutions and the benefits of competition, even in a field like education. One New Zealander characterized the situation as one in which a country without a strong ideological bent had its first encounter with coherent ideological thinking. Another important factor was political. The natural opposition to such policies was the Labour Party, but in this case there was no opposition because it was the Labour Party that was pushing them.

20. In 1998, they were again called hospitals.
21. Butterworth and Butterworth (1998: 35).

Concerns about the Quality of the New Zealand Work Force

The economic disruption of the 1980s made it clear to all New Zealanders that their country was part of a rapidly changing global economy that would require a work force with much higher skills than in the past. School dropouts could no longer expect to find employment, and the country could no longer afford the relatively low school persistence rates mentioned above. The rise in unemployment rates starting in 1985 focused increased attention on the role of secondary schools, especially in preparing people for the labor market.[22] Education thus came to be seen as an important element of national economic development. David Lange signaled the importance that he ascribed to education by assuming the minister of education portfolio himself following the general elections of 1987.

Closely related to general concerns about the quality of the work force was a growing recognition that the educational system was leaving some segments of New Zealand behind. Like other industrialized countries, New Zealand has concentrations of urban poor, and the schools that serve them face the same problems as inner-city schools elsewhere. Moreover, as elsewhere, student performance in New Zealand was, and continues to be, highly correlated with ethnicity and socioeconomic status.

Maori and, to a somewhat lesser extent, Pacific Island students are more likely than Pakeha students to leave school early. In 1997, the average length of stay at secondary school (normally five years) was 4.6 years for Pakeha, 4.5 years for Pacific Islanders, and only 4.1 years for Maori. In 1997 the proportion of Maori leaving school without any educational qualifications stood at 38 percent, which, though down from the more than 50 percent a decade before, is still high. The comparable figures were 26 percent for Pacific Islanders and 18 percent for all students.[23]

In addition, minorities are less likely to sit for senior school examinations, and those who do tend to receive lower scores. In the school certificate examinations, for example, the majority of papers submitted by Maori or Pacific Island test takers were graded D or E. Students from minority groups are also less likely to go on to the university. Whereas one in five of all 1996 school graduates was enrolled in a university in 1997, only one in

---

22. Butterworth and Butterworth (1998: 55–56).
23. Ministry of Education (1997a: 77f) .

thirteen Pacific Island graduates and one in fourteen Maori graduates were similarly enrolled.[24]

The Ministry of Education acknowledges "a strong link between socioeconomic status and achievement at school." A quarter of year-eleven students from low socioeconomic areas did not sit for the school certificate examination in 1997 (versus only 5 percent of students from schools drawing from privileged backgrounds). Participation rates in tertiary education rise almost linearly from 14 percent of graduates of schools serving the lowest socioeconomic students to 52 percent of those from schools serving the most advantaged students.[25]

New Zealand's urban problems are powerfully dramatized in Alan Duff's book *Once Were Warriors*, which also became a powerful and troubling movie. Duff is a controversial Maori writer who explores the dark underside of urban Maori life, with its family violence, alcohol abuse, and pervasive lack of self-esteem. When the book first appeared, in 1990, Duff was sharply criticized by Maori leaders for discussing this side of Maori life publicly, but the book has since come to be regarded as a commentary on problems that affect all races and ethnic groups, not just Maori. Duff sees education as central to improving the lot of the urban poor. Early in the novel, Beth, one of the central characters, ponders the fact that neither she nor any of her friends have books in their homes. "Why are Maori not interested in books?" she asks herself. "Well, they didn't have a written language before the white man arrived, maybe that was it. But still it bothered her. And she began to think that it was because a bookless society didn't stand a show in this modern world, not a damn show. And I live in it, don't I? And my kids."

Concerns about the Department of Education

The Department of Education evolved from a relatively decentralized system to one that was tightly controlled by a central agency working through regional boards of education. The degree of control reached the point at which board of education officials made decisions not only on matters of curriculum and textbooks but also on the number of scissors to which each school was entitled or what color to paint the gymnasium walls.

24. Ministry of Education (1997a: 79).
25. Ministry of Education (1997a: 78f).

Horror stories abound about the bureaucratic nature of the old department and the local boards. Dennis Thompson, the principal of Lyall Bay Primary School in Wellington, recalled that "mysterious packages" with school supplies would arrive out of the blue. "They sent me a new principal's chair that I didn't need, but I had a terrible time getting a second vacuum cleaner when we built a new building," he said. Brian Donnelly, who recently served as associate minister of education, recalled that, as an intermediate school principal, "I had to go to four separate departments and get a chit from Wellington to purchase a twelve dollar brush for the bus driver to use to clean his bus." Bill Sutton, the principal of the Thorndon School, recalls that schools used to get a certain quota of "points" for art supplies and that unused points could not be carried over to the next academic year. "You could not use all your points to get things you really wanted, like cartridge paper, so you would use them up on linoleum squares, which is not a particularly attractive art form," he said. "We had cupboards full of unused linoleum squares." He also told of the time when Thorndon had a safe that could not be used because the combination had been lost. "I asked the education board for a new one," he said, "but they told me that a school our size was only entitled to one safe, and we already had ours." At the same time, they refused to provide a locksmith to make it work.[26]

A series of official commissions had warned that the system had become top-heavy, ponderous, and unresponsive, that school administrators were unnecessarily restricted in doing their jobs, and that the Department of Education's outdated structures were undermining the quality of teaching and learning. By the 1980s, said educational historian John Barrington, there was a general consensus that, administratively, it was "a bloody awful system" and that changes were needed.

Another sort of dissatisfaction with the department was based on the concept of "provider capture." The concern was that it was too heavily influenced by the groups it was supervising. The department had functioned for many years under a system that placed great emphasis on harmony between itself, the regional boards of education, and the two major teachers' unions, the Post Primary Teachers' Association and the New

---

26. The story has a happy ending. Sutton used school funds to hire a locksmith to drill out the lock. The opening of the safe was covered live by a reporter from the radio station. "We found three cents and got ourselves a workable safe," said Sutton.

Zealand Educational Institute. No policy was enacted without consultation with the unions, whose leaders were viewed as professional colleagues. Judith Aitken, head of the Education Review Office, characterized it as "a well-defined tribal system in which the department was the hub of a wheel, the boards of education were the spokes, and the unions, notably the PPTA and NZEI, and others from the tertiary and early childhood educational sectors, formed the surrounding rim." Few decisions, she said, were taken without "direct collaboration and consultation with the whole family."[27]

Such coziness was anathema to critics of the old system. In its 1987 Brief to the Incoming Government, the Treasury Department argued that educational decisionmaking within the department was unduly influenced by lobbying groups such as teachers' unions and its own bureaucracy. David Lange expressed similar sentiments at a Labour Party conference in 1987: "The Department of Education is basically an education institution. Its interests as an educator color the advice it gives to the government. If the government asks the Department for advice about funding it is like asking a child how much it wants for pocket-money."[28] He and others argued that structural reforms were needed to rein in the bureaucracy and to make schools more responsive to the desires of parents and the communities they served.

The Curtain Rises

By the mid-1980s there was no sense that New Zealand's state educational system was in deep crisis. New Zealanders had confidence in the overall competence of the teaching force and local school administrators, but there were increasing doubts about whether the system in which they were operating was allowing them to do their best. Conviction was growing that New Zealand needed to restructure the way schools were governed and managed in order to keep up with the new demands that the global economy was imposing and to bring the educational system into line with the changes that were occurring in the economic and other governmental sectors.

27. Butterworth and Butterworth (1998: 40).
28. Quoted in Gordon (1992: 4–5).

In July 1987 David Lange turned to Brian Picot, a successful business-man who had founded a chain of supermarkets, to head a commission to recommend ways in which the management of state schools could be improved. In April 1988 the five-member Task Force to Review Education Administration submitted a 138-page report entitled *Administering for Excellence: Effective Administration in Education*. Thus was the curtain raised on one of the most far-reaching administrative school reform efforts ever taken by a developed country.

3 | *The Tomorrow's Schools Reforms*

THE TERM Tomorrow's Schools refers to the package of major structural changes in the New Zealand state educational system that were enacted by Parliament in 1989 and expanded upon in 1991. The most important features of the reform were to transfer responsibility for the running of primary and secondary schools from the Department of Education to locally elected boards of trustees controlled by parents and to abolish geographically based enrollment zones. Parents were given the right to choose which schools their child would attend, and schools were put in the position of having to compete for students. The major elements of the changes are summarized in table 3-1.

The process that produced the Tomorrow's Schools package was a dynamic one that began with the work of the Task Force to Review Education Administration. The reforms reflected a variety of approaches to educational reform, and the content of the package underwent considerable evolution during the design process and several distinct stages of implementation. This chapter describes the roots of Tomorrow's Schools and how they came to take the form they did.

Philosophical Currents

The Tomorrow's Schools reforms emerged from a social and political context that was shaped by three distinct philosophical currents. These

Table 3-1. *Overview of Changes after Inauguration of Tomorrow's Schools*

Area of change	Before Tomorrow's Schools	After Tomorrow's Schools
Central authority	Department of Education made policy and had operational authority over schools.	A smaller Ministry of Education primarily provides policy advice to the minister.
Governance/management	Department tightly controlled primary schools through regional education boards. Secondary schools had elected boards and somewhat more operational autonomy.	Primary and secondary schools are run by locally elected boards of trustees, a majority of whose members are parents.
Funding	Department of Education earmarked operating funds for specific purposes and paid teachers.	Ministry of Education provides block grants to schools for operating expenses and pays teacher salaries directly for most schools. Some schools have opted to receive a block grant for teacher salaries.
Accountability	Inspectors from the department visited schools, rated teachers, and enforced accountability largely behind the scenes. They also provided advice on pedagogical and other matters.	Review officers from the independent Education Review Office monitor school performance and publicize their findings. They do not provide advice and assistance.
Enrollment policy	Most students attended schools in their home zone.	Parents can choose any school, but oversubscribed schools decide which applicants to accept.
Collective bargaining	Centralized bargaining.	Centralized bargaining.
Physical property	Owned by the government. Integrated schools retained title to their physical assets.	Owned by the government. Integrated schools retain title to their physical assets.
Curriculum	Department of Education set the curriculum.	Ministry of Education sets a framework and generates curriculum statements.

currents were rooted in the history and traditions of New Zealand described in the previous chapter, but they were also heavily influenced by ideas that have been shaping thinking about educational policy in the United States and other industrialized countries over the last quarter of a century. We characterize the three currents as democratic-populist, managerial-business, and New Right–market.

Democratic-Populist Current

On one level, the call by the task force to transfer authority to the new school boards of trustees represented a significant break with the past. It can also be seen as a logical extension of a long-standing democratic-populist heritage. The previous chapter shows how New Zealanders created a society with strong egalitarian values that encouraged popular involvement in social and political institutions. Such attitudes resulted in a long tradition of parental and lay participation in governance.

This tradition of lay involvement was strongest in secondary schools, which from the beginning were run by locally elected boards of governors. These boards were set up to promote community interest in the school, to provide community feedback, to ensure that school policy was not made unilaterally by educational professionals, and to provide backing to the principal in matters of controversy.[1] Boards consisted of parents of current students as well as representatives of such community groups as alumni associations, trade unions, and other educational institutions. The boards were charged with overall governance of the school, including the management of finances and maintaining the physical property, as well as the selection of principals and the hiring of teachers. Boards had little say over curriculum, which was centrally controlled, or over day-to-day management, which was the responsibility of the principal.

At the primary level, popular participation in school governance was more diffuse. Each local school had a school committee consisting of five to nine local persons who were elected for two-year terms. Although they had the right to comment on teacher appointments and recommend suspension or dismissal of a teacher, they had little say in matters of teaching and learning. Their major formal responsibilities were to maintain the

---

1. Barrington (1981: 158–59).

school premises, to pay the caretaker, and to organize local fund-raising activities and parent volunteer programs.[2] They also took part in the election of the lay members of the ten regional boards of education through which the Department of Education wielded its authority.

Despite these formal mechanisms for giving local communities a voice in educational policy, pressure began to mount in the early 1970s for even greater parental involvement in the running of schools, for giving local schools more operational independence from the Department of Education, and for developing closer working relationships between schools and their communities. Such themes were sounded repeatedly at national educational gatherings, including the Educational Development Conference in 1972, which led to debate of such issues by 3,000 study groups over a two-year period. A 1976 report by the department, *Towards Partnership*, identified relations between schools and their communities as an area that warranted attention. Such talk, however, produced only modest changes, such as an increase in parental representation on secondary school boards. The Labour Party continued to make community participation a strong feature of its social policies in the 1978 and 1981 elections, both of which it lost; but the National Party, while paying lip service to the notion of community-oriented schools, took little formal heed of the various reports urging more community involvement in school affairs.

Another push for more community involvement came on behalf of the minority community. The mid-1980s brought growing attention to ways in which the state educational system was failing to meet the needs of significant segments of the population, most notably Maori and Pacific Islanders. It seemed to many of them that the school system, run by a large professional bureaucracy, had lost touch with the communities it served.

Most public discussion of education in the early to mid-1980s revolved ostensibly around matters of curriculum. Following Labour's victory in the 1984 elections, the new minister of education, Russell Marshall, set up the Committee to Review the Curriculum for Schools, which spent more than two years soliciting public input. The more than 30,000 responses made it clear that the gap between home and school was a major source of public dissatisfaction and that the public wanted a role in determining what would be taught in schools.[3] The committee's report, *The Curricu-*

2. Barrington (1981: 164).
3. Ballantyne (1997: 10-11).

lum Review, released in April 1987, picked up on these themes; but despite all of the effort that went into it, the main thrust of *The Curriculum Review* was never implemented. The prime minister, David Lange, took over the education portfolio himself with an agenda driven not by curricular concerns but by growing pressures to overhaul the entire educational delivery system.

The crescendo of calls for greater parental and community involvement in the running of schools, however, was not lost on members of the task force. In their report, they note that the public submissions they had received were marked by "a common theme of powerlessness—and consumer dissatisfaction and disaffection" as well as "feelings of frustration in the face of a system that too often appeared inflexible and unresponsive to consumer demand." The task force said that alienation was particularly strong among "those who had been failed by the system in the past" and noted that Maori and Pacific Island children were disproportionately represented in this failing group. "This is quite unacceptable in a society which aims for fairness and equity," it proclaimed.[4] In urging the creation of local boards of trustees and other democratic structures, the task force asserted that "the running of learning institutions should be a partnership between the teaching staff (the professionals) and the community."[5]

Managerial-Business Current

Although democratic and populist themes played a large part in the deliberations and recommendations of the task force, its fundamental mandate was to grapple with issues central to a second ideological current that saw managerial effectiveness as the key to school improvement.

At first blush it might seem that the managerial-business current had little in common with the democratic-populist current. As it turned out, they complemented each other in important respects. The notion of giving control of schools to local boards of trustees, for example, was consistent with the democratic-populist emphasis on parental and community involvement, but it also resonated with the managerial-business current as a way to improve the running of schools by locating decisions closer to the point of implementation.

---

4. Task Force (1988: 35–36, sec. 3.6.1, 3.6.6).
5. Task Force (1988: xi).

Given the fact that the Department of Education had evolved over the decades into such a cumbersome bureaucracy, it was perhaps not surprising that most of the overt pressure to reform the managerial structures came not from ordinary citizens, who had little day-to-day contact with the bureaucracy, but from professional educators, who did. David Lange also developed a passion for reform of governance out of a personal experience. As minister of education he had become frustrated at the inability of the system to discipline the governing board of Nga Tapuwae College in his home district, which had been accused of mismanagement and corruption. "It was a school from hell—a nightmare," he recalled in his interview for this book. "It had a bizarre board that had been hijacked by Maori activists. It needed to be sacked, but there was no way to do it. I made certain that the new legislation would give the minister the power to dismiss irresponsible boards."

As a businessman who had used innovative approaches to build up a successful chain of supermarkets, Brian Picot seemed a logical choice to modernize school governance and management in New Zealand. Picot himself was modest about his qualifications for the job—"I am a grocer, not a professional," he told us—but he saw relevance to schools in the fact that "I worked in a business that had a central office and lots of branches." Picot, who had a warehouse in the prime minister's district, was also attractive to Lange because he was "a businessman with a practical social conscience."[6] Picot had been strongly identified with principles of industrial democracy and had worked against apartheid in South Africa. His company, Progressive Enterprises, Ltd., motivated employees by setting up shifts with flexible hours and making more than a third of them stockholders. "They could wear badges saying 'I am a shareholder,'" he said. In addition, Picot had a clear image of the importance of extending education to all New Zealanders and of the role of the state in a democratic country. "To my mind the role of government is to balance the socioeconomic equation, that is, to assure that economic forces are counterbalanced by social concerns."

The Picot task force heard ample testimony about the problems with the existing system, including numerous bureaucratic horror stories. Picot recalled testimony regarding a school that had received a quantity of trees from its local board of education to be planted on Arbor Day. "The

6. Butterworth (1993: 66).

trees were accompanied by a letter saying that they should not go ahead with the planting of the trees until someone from the ministry came out to tell them where to put them," he said. In its report, the task force painted a devastating picture of the current administrative system as overly centralized, rule bound, wasteful, vulnerable to pressure group politics, and lacking in sound managerial expertise.

After considering a variety of ways to restructure the department, the group concluded that trying to reform the existing structure could be a hopeless task and that an entirely new apparatus was needed. "Tinkering with the system will not be sufficient to achieve the improvements now required," it wrote. "In our view the time has come for quite radical change, particularly to reduce the number of decision points between the central provision of policy, funding, and services and the education delivered by the school or institution."[7]

Significantly, Picot and his task force did *not* oppose a strong centrally directed state educational system. To the contrary, Picot believed that running a system that provided quality education to all citizens was an important and fitting responsibility of the national government. He and his group were simply pushing for good management, and one way to do this, they argued, was to devolve as many operational decisions as possible to the level at which teaching and learning took place.

The task force report also emphasized that members believed that their proposals might lead to considerable financial savings and that they wanted those savings reinvested in education and not used as an excuse for the state to reduce its commitment to public education. In agreeing to take on the job of chair, Picot had insisted that a proposed term of reference relating to cost saving be removed. "It was not our intention to set out to reduce expenditure," the members wrote. "We have, instead, operated on the basis that the Government is expecting no substantial change in the level of funding to education—apart from any additional costs resulting from the transition process."[8]

The sort of restructuring of the state educational system recommended by the Picot task force was, of course, not unique to New Zealand. Throughout the 1980s large institutions of all kinds around the world—from corporations and military commands to national health systems—went

---

7. Task Force (1988: sec. 3.7.1).
8. Task Force (1988: sec. 1.4.3).

through overhauls aimed at flattening their managerial pyramids and devolving decisionmaking. Decentralization also had become fashionable in the world of education. In the United States, which already has a relatively decentralized system in the sense that public education is run by the states rather than Washington, there has been a major push to decentralize the state educational systems through means such as school-based or site-based management. Decentralization efforts of various sorts have also been carried out in dozens of other counties, from Brazil and Chile to India and Zimbabwe.

New Right–Market Current

The Tomorrow's Schools reforms were part of the general restructuring of New Zealand's state sector that grew out of the economic crisis of the mid-1980s. The ensuing changes led to substantial reductions in government spending, the elimination of subsidies and price controls, the rolling back of government regulations, and the transformation of government "trading" departments headed by career civil servants into state-owned enterprises run by chief executive officers with fixed-term contracts. In both the private and public spheres the themes of the day were downsizing, deregulation, competition, and efficiency.

New Zealand's restructuring of its state sector was driven not only by practical necessity—the government could not continue to spend beyond its means—but by an ideological perspective variously known in many countries, especially in the English-speaking world, as New Right, or neoliberal. This perspective is grounded in a conviction that competition will improve the delivery of most services, and it draws on critiques by economists of public institutions based on a new body of theory commonly referred to as the new institutional economics. Those critiques focus on two main concepts: provider capture and transaction costs. Provider capture occurs when well-organized public interest groups "capture" agencies and twist public policies in their favor at the expense of the broader public interest. Transaction, or agency, costs arise in ensuring that the incentives of employees who deliver public services are aligned with legislated policy objectives. According to the new institutional economics, the goal is to design institutions and processes that avoid the problem of provider capture and minimize transactions costs.[9]

9. Scott, Ball, and Dale (1997: 360).

The center of neoliberal thinking in New Zealand was and remains the Treasury Department, which is headed by the minister of finance. Its primary functions are to provide policy advice to the minister, to oversee the budget process, and to scrutinize the budgets of the other departments. During the 1940s and 1950s it embraced Keynesian principles for managing the economy; by the 1980s, with the ideological pendulum swinging the other way, it was ready to import neoliberal ideas from the United States and elsewhere. As the authors of a history of the Tomorrow's Schools reforms put it, New Zealand's Treasury Department has long been "uniquely disposed to see the big picture" and stood "ready, willing and able to comment on policy on the basis of first principles."[10]

During his long tenure as the National government's prime minister through the early 1980s, Robert Muldoon had paid little heed to the Treasury Department and its warnings about the dangers of overspending. Being shunted to the sidelines, however, meant that treasury, which was staffed with bright young economists, had ample time to hone its ideas about how the state sector should be reformed around New Right principles. When the Labour Party upset the National Party in the 1984 elections, treasury was ready. It laid out its ideas in a brief to the incoming government.[11] Under the leadership of Roger Douglas, a former junior minister in an earlier Labour government, these became the basis for Labour's economic policies during its first three-year term. Prime Minister Lange made it known that, if Labour were returned to office in 1987, it would turn its attention from economic restructuring to overhauling the country's public sector, most notably welfare, health, and education. Once again, treasury was ready with a brief to the incoming government that laid out an approach for reorganizing the public sector around the central idea of performance contracting.

Volume 2 of the briefing paper characterized New Zealand's traditional educational system as both poorly managed and a victim of provider capture. Specifically, the interests of teachers and administrators were taking precedence over those of students and families. The solution, the document argued, lay in a reorganization of the system around fundamental neoliberal principles: minimize the role of the central government, separate funding from operations, encourage competition among schools, give parents and students maximum choice in determining which school to

10. Butterworth and Butterworth (1998: 35).
11. Treasury Department (1987).

attend, and introduce a management system oriented around mission statements, output targets, and performance-based pay. Significantly, the treasury document also challenged the traditional notion of education as a public good that warrants special treatment on the part of the state. To the contrary, it argued, "educational services are like other goods traded in the market place." Critics of treasury were quick to point out that the notion that education should be viewed as just another commodity in a marketplace had profound implications. As one of them asked, "If education is a mere commodity, then why should the state, and not the 'market' provide it?"[12]

The extent to which Treasury Department thinking influences government policy in education has been, and continues to be, a matter of considerable debate. Some critics on the left have portrayed the Treasury Department, working with allies such as the archconservative Business Roundtable, as an all-powerful puppeteer pulling strings from behind the scenes. Others see it as a significant, but by no means dominant, player whose recommendations are taken seriously but are rejected as often as they are accepted. The latter description fit its role in the deliberations of the Picot task force. Treasury was represented on the task force by Simon Smelt, an English economist and labor market specialist who had been one of the authors of volume 2; he served as one of two nonvoting advisers. According to one authoritative account, early on in the deliberations Picot made it clear to Smelt and at least one member sympathetic to business models that "there was a point beyond which he could not allow private enterprise models to impinge on a public system."[13] In his interview, Picot characterized Smelt's involvement as productive and the working relationship cordial, but he emphasized that the task force rejected many of the ideas that Smelt put forward.

Perhaps a useful analogy for treasury is the battery-powered rabbit in a well-known American television commercial that just keeps chugging along after rabbits powered by other brands give out. Treasury developed core ideas in the early 1980s that have remained remarkably consistent and that have been offered over and over as new public policy problems arose. Aiding dissemination has been the fact that many ex-treasury officials have moved on to senior positions in other government agencies, including as

---

12. Gordon (1992: 193).
13. Butterworth (1993: 78).

secretary of education. Eventually, many, though by no means all, of the core ideas found their way into government policy.

How the Three Currents Converged

The evolution of the Tomorrow's Schools reforms was shaped by the way in which the three ideological currents converged and interacted. Each brought its own analysis of the fundamental problem to be addressed and, by implication, of the appropriate remedy.

Proponents of the democratic-populist approach believed that the state educational system was failing to prepare a broad base of New Zealand's young people to take their place in the emerging global economy, and they attributed this problem to the fact that the system had lost touch with the students and communities it served. Such thinking was particularly strong among Maori, Pacific Islanders, and others concerned about issues of equity. To them education should be a partnership among parents, communities, and school professionals, and the way to achieve this was to build greater parental and community voice into the running of schools.

Adherents of the managerial-business current supported the idea of a strong and equitable state educational system. The problem, as they saw it, was that the current system was too large, cumbersome, and unresponsive to student needs to carry out this function effectively. To them the solution lay in importing into the state educational system managerial principles that had proved effective for corporations and other large institutions. They were open to democratic-populist ideas of community involvement in school management because they believed a decentralized system would be more efficient.

Those who advocated the New Right–market approach agreed with the managerial-business analysis that the state educational system was inefficient and needed to be overhauled. To them, however, the way to do this was not through the actions of managers but by the establishment of a competitive environment. They also argued that even if the school system were running efficiently, it infringed on the rights of parents and students to shape their own educational experience. This problem, too, would be solved by the creation of a market environment in which parents exercised choice and local schools competed for students.

To the extent that it saw the fundamental problem as essentially structural in nature, the managerial-business approach could be described as ideologically neutral. In theory, its managerial proposals were compatible with both of the other currents. Democratic-populist and New Right–market currents, however, were fundamentally at odds. Democratic populists believed in giving parents a greater role in school governance as a matter of principle, and they were comfortable with the fact that any given board might contain people with different, even conflicting, perspectives. Such a situation would make the board more representative. The New Right–market current believed that schools were best run by trained managers and that parents should exercise their voice through the market mechanism of choosing the school that their child would attend. It also viewed representative elected boards as dangerous because such a situation violated the tenet of effective schools literature—that successful schools are characterized by unity of purpose. Eventually, New Right devotees came to view the parents who served as school trustees as yet another example of a special interest group capturing an institution for their own purposes.

Although the three currents were present from the outset, their relative influence varied widely over time. The vision of education that was embodied by the Picot report and the initial enabling legislation of Tomorrow's Schools was for all practical purposes a combination of the first and second currents: mixing community involvement with management reforms. Democratic-populist ideas were gradually pushed out, and the balance of power in New Zealand's state educational system shifted to a combination of managerial-business and New Right–market concepts. Local school charters, supposedly the centerpiece of community voice, did not live up to their early billing, and the new institutions intended to promote community involvement in education were stillborn.

But we are getting ahead of the story.

Stages of Reform

Table 3-2 provides a time line of New Zealand elections and the tenure of key leaders as background for the evolution of the Tomorrow's Schools reforms. After a long period of National Party rule with Robert Muldoon as prime minister, the Labour Party won the election of 1984 and was reelected in 1987. David Lange became prime minister in 1984 and, after

Table 3-2. *Chronology of Political Leadership*

Period	Party in power	Prime minister	Minister of education
1975–84	National	Robert Muldoon	Various
1984–87	Labour	David Lange	Russell Marshall
1987–90	Labour	David Lange	David Lange
		Geoffrey Palmer (1989–90)[a]	Phil Goff (1989–90)
1990–93	National	James Bolger	Lockwood Smith
1993–96	National	James Bolger	Lockwood Smith
1996–99	National–New Zealand First	James Bolger	Wyatt Creech
		Jenny Shipley (1997–99)	Wyatt Creech

a. Kenneth Moore was prime minister from September 1990 to November 1990.

the 1987 election, also took on the education portfolio. He resigned as prime minister in 1989. After the National Party returned to power in 1990, James Bolger became prime minister and Lockwood Smith started a six-year tenure as minister of education. National was reelected in 1994 and again in 1997, although at that time it had to share the leadership with the small New Zealand First Party, a new party that represented Maori interests.

The initial Labour Party school reform initiatives began in 1984 with the work of the Committee to Review the Curriculum for Schools. By and large the committee's focus on curricular matters as the key to school reform was welcomed by the political left, but the Treasury Department sent a critical response to the minister of finance complaining that the committee had failed to address what it viewed as the all-important issues of management and parental choice.[14] When Labour won the general election in 1987 and Prime Minister Lange took over the education portfolio, he conspicuously made no commitment to implementing *The Curriculum Review*, and issues of teaching and learning fell off the radar screen. With the restructuring of the country's basic economic institutions well under way, it was time to take on the state educational system.

The Labour government decided to address all three of the major educational sectors—early childhood education, primary and secondary education, and the postcompulsory, or tertiary, sector—simultaneously, and

14. Codd, Harker, and Nash (1990: 16).

advisory panels were named for each area. The Picot task force came first, in July 1987. The Early Childhood Care and Education Working Group was set up in January 1988, and the Working Group on Post-Compulsory Education and Training followed in March 1988. The three task forces worked independently, but they were well aware of each other's work and pursued some common themes.

The early childhood group wrestled with the fact that New Zealand's system of caring for and educating preschool children was a hodgepodge of public and private arrangements ill suited to the needs of working mothers. It recommended the central funding of early childhood institutions, which would be chartered, funded, and have their performance reviewed by the state. These suggestions found their way into legislation. The report of the working group on postcompulsory schooling also found this sector to be in disarray, largely because certification processes that had evolved in the industrial era were inadequate to the needs of the new global economy. Its report argued that the government should continue to be the principal funder of postcompulsory education and training but that institutions chartered by the state should also find ways of developing their own financial bases, including moving into commercial activities.

Picot Task Force

The most important part of the Labour government's educational agenda grew out of the work of the Task Force to Review Education Administration. The Picot task force, which had five members and two nonvoting advisers, was directed to review the functions of the Department of Education "with a view to focusing them more sharply and delegating responsibilities as far as is practicable."[15] The task force was not concerned

15. Task Force (1988: ix). In addition to its chair, Brian Picot, the task force had four members. Peter Ramsay, a specialist on primary education, was associate professor of education at the University of Waikato in Hamilton, and Margaret Rosemergy, a secondary specialist, was a senior lecturer at the Wellington College of Education. Whetumarama Wereta, a Maori political scientist and statistician, was a social researcher at the Department of Maori Affairs in Wellington, while Colin Wise was a company director in Dunedin. The chief executive was Maurice Gianotti, a former school inspector then serving as an administrator in the Department of Education. The two nonvoting advisers were Simon Smelt, representing the Treasury Department, and Marijke Robinson, a Dutch-born senior adviser on education at the State Services Commission.

with curricular or other teaching matters, but members were given free rein to go back to first principles if they wished. They commissioned briefing papers, met with relevant sectoral groups, and received 700 public submissions. Picot ran the task force as efficiently as he ran his supermarkets, and it took members less than a year to do their work.

At their first meeting members of the task force agreed on some guiding principles that embraced many of the ideals of the democratic-populist and managerial-business currents. In addition to seeking to promote academic excellence, they resolved to design a user-friendly system that was flexible and responsive to consumer demands. They agreed to create a lean and efficient structure with minimal layers of decisionmaking, and presumably with accusations of provider capture in mind, they agreed to "begin with the child."

CHANGES IN THE DEPARTMENT OF EDUCATION. The first item of business was to figure out what to do with the much-maligned Department of Education. After struggling with various options, the task force, in keeping with its "blank page" approach, decided that the structures that had grown up over decades, especially the network of regional boards of education, were anachronisms beyond saving. Picot liked to say it was a case of "good people, bad system." As evidence, the task force report cited the example of a principal who as a result of "good teaching and management practices" attracted enough pupils to turn a two-teacher school into a three-teacher school. The change meant that the job of running the larger school had to be advertised, so the successful administrator lost out to a principal of a larger school whose roll was falling.[16] Picot himself was offended by chronic tolerance of poor performance and the lack of control that school administrators had over staff selection and resource allocation. As leader of a business in which it was imperative to ensure that every branch was profitable, Picot believed that the educational system should function so that every school was a good one.[17]

To achieve this end, the task force voted to abolish the boards of education, to turn the governance of each school, primary as well as secondary, over to locally elected boards of trustees, and to transform the Department of Education into a much smaller Ministry of Education, with the primary role of providing policy advice to the minister of education.

16. Task Force (1988: sec. 3.5.13).
17. Butterworth (1993: 10).

By eliminating the regional boards of education—and for that matter, any formal structure at the district level—from its proposed governance structure, the task force was left with the problem of how to supply the services that these boards had provided. Some of the boards' functions were easy to deal with; inspection, for example would become the job of an independent agency. But the task force struggled with how to deal with board functions such as the offering of curricular and managerial advice, arranging school transport, accounting, and the delivery of special education. To handle these services, the task force recommended the setting up of educational service centers that would employ former board staff members and market support services to schools on a commercial basis.

CHANGES TO PROMOTE COMMUNITY INVOLVEMENT. The primary vehicles for ensuring community involvement were the granting of governance authority to the new school boards of trustees and the drafting of school charters. As the report declared at the outset, "Individual learning institutions will be the basic unit of education administration."[18] The task force specified that the new boards should be composed of parents, but boards would have the option of co-opting nonparents in the interests of diversity or to obtain legal, financial, or other types of expertise. Boards also included the school principal and an elected representative of the teachers. The term *trustee* was preferred to alternatives such as *governor* because it implied a sense of personal commitment to the school as well as legal obligations. School trustees were to manage their school within the terms of a charter that they would write. The charter gave the local school an opportunity to specify ways in which it would tailor its program to community goals within the context of national standards for curriculum, equity, and safety. The task force specified that the charter would "act as a contract between the community and the institution, and the institution and the state."[19]

Consistent with the concept of self-governing schools, the Picot task force recommended that local schools be given the authority to manage their entire budgets, including operational expenses, routine maintenance, and most important, teachers' salaries, which typically account for about 70 percent of expenses. Under a system known as bulk funding, schools would receive lump payments to cover these areas. This meant that al-

18. Task Force (1988: xi).
19. Task Force (1988: sec. 4.3.1).

though teacher pay rates would continue to be negotiated nationally, schools would have the option of deciding on the mix of teachers they wanted at various pay levels. Thus a school could increase the size of its faculty by hiring relatively inexperienced teachers.

Community involvement in the schools was to be further enhanced by the introduction of three new institutions. The first was the education policy council, which would serve as a buffer between the new Ministry of Education and the schools. The council, which would consist of four representatives of the ministry and four "independent people" named by the minister, would advise the minister on educational issues, including "the setting of national education objectives." It would also monitor what was happening in schools in order to "evaluate the impact of current policies and to develop new policies."[20]

The second was the parent advocacy council, which would function as "an independent body which groups and individuals can go to when they have a concern which they feel is not being listened to." The council, which would have full-time staff and report to Parliament, was seen as providing help and guidance to parents. The task force recognized that under the new system parents were likely to need help beyond the services of existing agencies such as the ombudsman, the Human Rights Commission, and the Race Relations Conciliator.[21]

The third were community forums on education. These were envisioned as vehicles by which "the views of the whole community can be brought together on matters of educational importance." Such matters might range from local issues such as establishing new courses, the pooling of institutional resources, and the amalgamating of schools on issues being debated at the national level, like assessment policies. The task force saw such forums as a way of balancing the potentially conflicting interests of various stakeholders in the educational system. They would also be useful in handling situations in which decisions taken by parents connected with one school might adversely affect the interests of parents in another school. "We cannot emphasize too strongly the importance of community education forums," the task force wrote.[22]

20. Task Force (1988: sec. 6.2.1, 6.2.2).
21. Task Force (1988: sec. 6.5.1, 6.5.2).
22. Task Force (1988: sec. 5.8.4).

As a last resort in cases where a group of at least twenty-one parents believed that they were not being well served by their local schools, the task force recommended giving them the opportunity to "withdraw from existing arrangements and to set up their own learning institution." The ministry would be obligated to grant the new school a charter and to fund it like any other state school.[23]

MAINTAINING A STRONG STATE ROLE. While supportive of the notion of devolving operating authority to local boards of trustees, the task force still wanted a strong role for the new Ministry of Education. Members believed that good management practices required "an appropriate balance of responsibilities between the local level and the central government" that allowed school trustees to respond to particular needs of their community while at the same time pursuing national objectives.[24] There was never any doubt that the state would provide both capital and operating expenses and that curriculum guidelines would come from the center. Likewise, the state would be responsible for accountability through a separate Review and Audit Agency (later known as the Education Review Office), which would report to the minister of education and be responsible for inspecting schools. In contrast to the former system, under which boards of education sent inspectors into the schools, representatives of the agency would be strictly in the business of evaluating schools and school personnel. They would not have a mandate to provide advice, formally or informally, on curricular, personnel, or other matters. If the agency uncovered evidence of mismanagement, it was authorized to recommend intervention by the minister of education, including the dismissal of boards of trustees.

The governance and managerial system proposed by the Picot task force was thus fully consistent with contemporary managerial wisdom. It lodged overall policymaking and goal setting at the center while devolving most operating authority and responsibility to agencies closer to the classrooms, where education was actually delivered. As a policymaking rather than an operational body, the Ministry of Education relinquished control of functions such as picking staffs and determining discretionary expenditure, but it continued to exercise tight control of the all-important areas of level of funding, curriculum, and accountability. These changes made

23. Task Force (1988: sec. 7.7.5).
24. Task Force (1988: sec. 1.2.10).

managerial sense, but they also carried an important political message. As one group of observers pointed out, "The government has moved to relinquish 'no win' areas and consolidate its control of vital areas where losing would threaten its ability to manage the system at all."[25]

A CAUTIOUS APPROACH TO PARENTAL CHOICE. The Picot task force adopted a cautious policy on what would eventually be a pivotal issue: giving parents discretion about what schools their children would attend. Historically, New Zealand primary schools had operated without the need for formal enrollment areas because it was generally presumed that children would attend their local school. While in principle, parents could select schools outside their local area, such a practice was not common. "Before Tomorrow's Schools there was no pecking order for primary schools to motivate parents to want to look beyond their local school," said John Barrington, an educational historian at the Victoria University of Wellington.

The concept of geographic zoning at the secondary level had begun to emerge following World War II, as postprimary education was extended to almost all New Zealand children. The Department of Education embraced the idea in the 1950s as the fairest means of allocating a growing student population to various schools. In addition, area zoning served a number of educational purposes. By ensuring consistency in enrollment, it allowed schools to engage in forward planning, to maintain a stable course structure, and to avoid excessive fluctuations of rolls—with consequent disruptions to staffing. Zoning also prevented individual school boards from taking unilateral decisions on enrollment that prejudiced the interests of neighboring schools, and it promoted the orderly use of national resources such as school buildings.[26] These purposes of area zoning were generally accepted as valid.

In the 1980s student rolls began to decline, and enrollment zones took on new meaning. The Department of Education, in consultation with the teachers' unions, made a deliberate policy decision to use zoning to limit the staffing reductions in schools particularly hard hit.[27] Schools also responded to the decline by taking more students from outside their geographic zone. Under the standard enrollment policy each school had small

25. Codd, Harker, and Nash (1990: 17).
26. McCulloch (1991: 158).
27. Rae (1991: 108).

out-of-zone student quotas and could use a variety of criteria to fill these out-of-zone places. Principals in a given geographic area often negotiated informal agreements with each other on the use of such quotas.

Meanwhile, zoning became a topic of increasing ideological and political debate. Opponents of zoning argued that parents had a fundamental right to choose the school that their children attended and that zoning undermined this right. The theoretical case against zoning reflected the New Right themes of the era, namely provider capture, the benefits of competition, and the need for parents to be given incentives to take an informed interest in their children's schooling. Political figures such as Ruth Richardson, the educational spokesperson for the opposition National Party, took up the cause and made zoning an issue in the 1987 general election campaign.[28] In such a climate a growing number of parents began to send their children to schools outside their zone.

Criticism of the effects of school zoning, however, was by no means confined to the political right. Commentators on the left were concerned that the practice of zoning reinforced inequalities between different schools and different racial, ethnic, and socioeconomic groups. Their proposed solution to the equity problem, however, was not to abolish zoning but rather to use it more explicitly to help equalize the social class and ethnic mix of schools.[29] In 1987 this growing public discontent regarding school zoning policy from both ends of the political spectrum prompted Minister of Education Russell Marshall to announce a review of the school zoning regulation. The review floundered when David Lange took over Marshall's portfolio and set in process the events that led to the Tomorrow's Schools reforms.

The Picot task force agreed that the current enrollment system had outlived its usefulness. It called for the dismantling of zoning schemes but also specified that students would have the right to attend their neighborhood school. "In our view, zoning of enrollments should only have one purpose," it wrote. "That is, to ensure that every student has an absolute right to attend the nearest neighborhood school. We do not support the notion that zoning should be used to maintain enrollments in schools which might otherwise decline."[30] Significantly, the task force recommended that in the event that a particular school had more applicants

28. McCullough (1991).
29. McCulloch (1991: 156).
30. Task Force (1988: sec. 7.7.2).

than it could accommodate "a supervised ballot be held to decide which students will be enrolled."[31]

Tomorrow's Schools

The Picot task force report, *Administering for Excellence,* was released on May 10, 1988, amid considerable public fanfare, and the government wasted little time implementing its recommendations. A government policy paper, *Tomorrow's Schools: The Reforming of Education Administration in New Zealand,* was published on August 7, 1988, as a basis for new legislation on education. It was hailed by David Lange, in the covering letter, as "one of the most important proposals for educational reform ever announced by any New Zealand government."[32] The policy paper incorporated most of the principal features of the Picot task force report. It accepted the central notion that local schools "will be the basic 'building block' of education administration" and embraced its recommendations regarding governance, accountability, and enrollment policy.[33] Curriculum remained a function of the central government, as did financing, and support for schools would be distributed in the form of two bulk grants, one for teachers' salaries and another for operating expenses.

Tomorrow's Schools departed from the task force report, however, in two important respects. First, it rejected the recommendation to set up an advisory education policy council. In his interview, Lange said that this proposal put him in a "terrible dilemma." On the one hand, the council would have allowed educational policymakers to "have the counsel of wise men." On the other hand, he said, such an advisory body with no line responsibilities threatened "the heart of the political process." In his interview, Brian Picot termed the rejection of an education policy council his "greatest regret" about the way the task force recommendations were received. "We were unanimous on this matter," he said. "As the only democratic institution in between schools and the ministry, the policy advisory council was an important safety valve. Without it all the cards are stacked in favor of the bureaucrats."

The second departure from the task force's recommendations had to do with issues of equity. The task force did not dwell on the concept of

---

31. Task Force (1988: sec. 7.7.3).
32. *Tomorrow's Schools* (1988: iv).
33. *Tomorrow's Schools* (1988: 1).

equal opportunity. It asserted that education "should be fair and just for every learner regardless of their gender, and of their social, cultural or geographic circumstances."[34] There was no mention of the special needs of particular groups, and equity was essentially seen as giving everyone access to the system. *Tomorrow's Schools*, however, took a much more proactive approach to the issue. "Equity objectives will underpin all policy related to the reform of education administration," it said. It set an explicit goal of achieving "greater equity for Maori, Pacific Island, other groups with minority status; and for working class, rural and disabled students, teachers and communities."[35]

Significantly, *Tomorrow's Schools* went along with the Picot task force in affirming a strong role for the state in the provision of primary and secondary education. Some Labour Party leaders feared that the unstated long-term agenda of Roger Douglas and his allies at the Treasury Department was to move toward the privatization of education, or at least toward some sort of voucher system that would channel more public funds into private schools. Such concerns were said to be one of the reasons that Lange took on the education portfolio himself, and he was known to believe that a compelling reason to devolve the management of schools to lay boards of trustees was that it would create a powerful grass-roots lobby of 17,000 advocates for public education. Lange, however, was clearly at odds with some powerful members of his own party over such matters. He had a running battle with Douglas over the pace of restructuring, which resulted, among other things, in his famous remark about the need for a "tea break." Eventually the tensions between moderates and hard-liners within the Labour Party over a range of social and economic issues prompted his resignation as prime minister.

Parliament enacted *Tomorrow's Schools* into law in three stages, starting with the School Trustees Act of March 1989, which allowed the first elections for boards of trustees to be held that May.[36] Implementation went

---

34. Task Force (1988: sec. 1.1.4).

35. *Tomorrow's Schools* (1988: sec. 3.1.1).

36. Subsequently, the Education Act abolished the old administrative structures and authorized establishment of the Ministry of Education and other new agencies, to become operative on October 1, 1989. Among these agencies was the Education Review Office, which was equivalent to what the task force called the review and audit agency. The Education Amendment Act of 1990 set up the New Zealand Qualifications Authority and other new agencies.

about as smoothly as one might expect for changes of such magnitude. In December 1989 a small review team known as the Lough Committee was given the job of evaluating how the changeover from the old order to Tomorrow's Schools was going. The principal fruit of its work was a decision to trim the size of the Education Review Office staff from 300 to 150 persons.

In a 1997 speech David Lange looked back on the significance of the educational reforms that he and his colleagues had wrought and stressed the theme of community empowerment. "Where Tomorrow's Schools made a break with the past was in creating a system of education administration which allowed for more local participation and more local control," he said. "Standards in education would not be uniformly imposed from the center but would allow for local differences and allow schools to shape themselves in ways which met the distinctive needs of the local community. In this local responsibility lies the greatest potential for good of Tomorrow's Schools, and perhaps its greatest risks."[37]

National Takes Over

With the coming of the 1990 general elections the political situation changed abruptly. A new government took office, with James Bolger as prime minister and Lockwood Smith as minister of education. With the National Party now in the driver's seat, those favoring New Right approaches to schooling had an easier row to hoe.

The new National government wasted little time in backtracking on ideas dear to the heart of the democratic-populists. One of its first actions was to pass the Education Amendment Act of 1991, which limited the powers of community forums on education to deal with conflicts between boards of trustees of nearby schools. National also abolished parent advocacy councils with the argument—specifically rejected by the Picot task force—that disputes between parents and the educational system could be handled by existing structures such as the ombudsman and the Human Rights Commission or by direct contacts with the ministry.

By far the most important change wrought by the 1991 legislation was the decision to abolish enrollment zones and to give parents the right to

37. Speech to School Trustees Association Conference, Nelson, August 30, 1997.

choose the schools that their children would attend. In keeping with the philosophy of self-governing schools, the act specified that schools that had more applicants than places had the right to design their own "enrollment schemes," or admissions policies. Students were no longer guaranteed a place at their local school. The only limitations on schools were that they could not discriminate in ways that violated the Human Rights Act and that, in disputed cases, the ministry had the authority to direct a school to accept a particular student. Thus the enrollment procedures endorsed by *Tomorrow's Schools* providing for a "supervised ballot" lasted only one year.

The effect of this ruling was to change the culture of public education in New Zealand. Whereas enrolling children in a primary or secondary institution other than the neighborhood school had always been a quiet option, it now became the norm. Parents were encouraged to shop for the best educational situation for their children; indeed, the failure to do so almost became a sign of parental neglect. As for the schools themselves, competition became the name of the game, especially at the secondary level.

One element of the reform package proved difficult to implement and remains a contentious issue to this day. Both the Picot task force and *Tomorrow's Schools* called for bulk funding of both teachers' salaries and operating grants, but some officials within the ministry were concerned that bulk funding would widen performance disparities between schools. Most important, it was an issue on which the teachers' unions dug in their heels.

The two unions—the New Zealand Educational Institute, representing primary school teachers, and the Post Primary Teachers' Association, representating secondary school teachers—had for the most part played the role of interested bystanders in the Tomorrow's Schools design process. The task force had solicited their views along with those of other interested parties, but it was eager to maintain the sort of detachment from educational professionals that it found lacking in the old Department of Education. Prime Minister David Lange had strong views about provider capture, as did the National government that assumed power in 1991. Union members were initially excluded from participation in the working parties created in 1989 to implement the reforms, but they fought successfully to win places at the table and are thought to have exercised influence on some matters of funding and operations.[38] Preferring to stand

38. Butterworth and Butterworth (1998: 119).

in opposition, the Post Primary Teachers' Association did not take up all its allocated positions.[39]

The teachers' unions watched the reform process unfold with mixed emotions. They welcomed the task force's talk of partnerships between schools and communities, but they were suspicious of turning control of schools over to boards of educational amateurs. They clearly had much to lose with the demise of a department that viewed them as professional colleagues in running schools and its replacement by a ministry with few operational responsibilities. Teachers were conspicuously excluded from membership in the education policy council proposed by the task force. The unions found important consolation, however, in the fact that industrial relations continued to function in much the same way as before the Tomorrow's Schools era. As two historians put it, "The rejection of bulk funding, the retention of national employment contracts for teachers, and the central determination of staffing schedules have meant that the teacher labor market remains remarkably old-fashioned, without the flexibility the reforms intended."[40]

Although there was little that the unions could do to resist the forces that were undermining their traditional role in policymaking, the push for bulk funding was quite a different matter because it impacted directly on their jobs, salaries, and working conditions. Teachers feared that schools that received a fixed amount to cover all teachers' salaries would be tempted to discriminate against older staff members at the highest pay scales in order to hire a greater number of younger teachers at lower salaries. They also argued that pooling teachers' salaries at a level to be determined by Parliament would make it too easy for a future government to cut overall spending for education and that bulk funding would push the Ministry of Education even further toward the role of a "purchaser" of education, thus playing into the hands of New Right proponents who saw education as just another commodity in the marketplace.

The Lange government made no effort to implement the controversial policy, and even Lockwood Smith, National's minister of education, was unable to garner sufficient support to do so. On his initiative, the legislation requiring bulk funding was changed so that schools could choose whether they wanted it or not, and he turned his attention to other issues.

39. Butterworth and Butterworth (1998: 158).
40. Butterworth and Butterworth (1998: 229).

The National government was returned to office in the 1993 general elections, and Lockwood Smith continued to push for what his party regarded as the unfinished agenda of Tomorrow's Schools.

Three Strands

The state educational system that emerged in New Zealand as a result of the reform efforts of the late 1980s and early 1990s—and that continues to exist to this day—is notable for bold innovations, such as turning control of schools over to parents, depriving the Ministry of Education of operational authority, and introducing parental choice. These changes were complex and often highly technical. When all is said and done, however, they can be understood as built around these three defining strands, or fundamental organizing principles. We define the three strands as self-governing schools, schools as agents of the state, and the notion that schools exist in a competitive marketplace.

Each of the three strands has historical and conceptual roots in one or more of the three ideological currents discussed at the beginning of this chapter. The concept of self-governing schools, for example, is compatible with both the democratic-populist emphasis on community involvement and the managerial-business belief in devolving operational authority, and it is a prerequisite for setting up the competitive environment favored by the New Right–market approach. On the other hand, most democratic-populists would reject the assumption of the latter approach that putting schools into competition with each other will improve the quality of teaching and learning.

None of the three strands is unique to New Zealand. All three concepts have been embraced, or at least debated, by policymakers in the United States and other developed nations. We find them a useful way to organize our analysis of the Tomorrow's Schools reforms and to use as a basis for considering lessons for other countries. In part 2 we discuss each of these strands in depth. Following is a brief summary of them:

Self-Governing Schools

The single most definitive characteristic of public educaton in New Zealand is that the individual school is, as *Tomorrow's Schools* puts it, the "basic building block" of the system. As a result of the reform process a governance system that was already partially in place at the secondary level was extended to primary schools and was enhanced at the secondary level. This concept of a network of relatively autonomous primary and secondary schools contrasts sharply with the traditional notion of a hier-archical system managed from the top with the schools subject to the control of the regional boards.

The principle of self-governing schools is built on the assumption that the educational system will be most effective and productive when local schools, as the places where teaching and learning actually take place, are free to make personnel, pedagogical, and other decisions and when these decisions are informed by the needs and wishes of the communities they serve.

There are some important problems associated with this first strand, starting with the huge issue of what to do when the actions of a particular self-governing school appear to undermine the interests of other schools and, by implication, the broader interests of the system as a whole. Closely related is the question of whether the community served by a self-govern-ing school should be defined narrowly as current parents or whether a broader definition is in order.

Schools as Agents of the State

The second defining strand of state education provided the basis for scrapping the old Department of Education, which had operated primary schools through regional boards of education and had exercised consid-erable control over secondary school governing boards, and replacing it with a Ministry of Education whose primary responsibilities were in the policymaking area and whose operational powers were sharply curtailed.

As a result of the Tomorrow's Schools reforms, New Zealand can be said to have switched from a model of governance in which the Depart-ment of Education ran the schools through its regional boards to a con-tractual model of governance. The Ministry of Education sits at the center of the system and, despite the devolution of operating authority, retains significant power. It affirms the state's interest in sustaining a system of compulsory education, works with the minister to set overall policies, and establishes the parameters by which self-governing schools operate. It also carries out important functions such as administering the educational funds authorized by Parliament, managing property, developing curriculum guidelines, and working with the Education Review Office to hold local schools accountable for their performance. The State Services Commission has also devolved authority to the ministry to negotiate salary contracts with teachers and administrators.

When it comes to the actual delivery of educational services, however, the ministry's role is indirect. The ministry enters into a contract with 2,700 self-governing schools to carry out its policies. Local schools in this sense function as agents of the state. This second strand, of course, is the necessary complement to the first. The yin of self-governing schools combines with the yang of central direction in order to make the system work.

Although this contractual model seems theoretically sound, the way it was implemented, and the way it subseqently evolved, posed some problems. The nature of the contract went through considerable evolution, and central authorities ended up having little authority or inclination to articulate and defend collective interests in situations in which decisions by their agents appeared to undermine broader interests. These problems turned out to be fateful ones.

A Competitive Environment

The final strand underlying the system that emerged from the Tomorrow's Schools reforms is the notion that the quality of education will be enhanced if schools operate in a competitive marketplace. If schools are forced to compete for the allegiance of students and parents, the argument goes, they will have the incentive to operate more efficiently and to improve the quality of the programs they offer. Student and parent "customers" in turn will benefit not only from the enhanced quality of schools seeking their business but from the fact that they have more offerings from which to choose.

One sure way to set up a competitive environment is to abolish enrollment zones for local schools and to implement a policy of parental choice. The *Tomorrow's Schools* policy paper adopted a low-key version of parental choice: abolishing enrollment zones while specifying that students had a right to attend the nearest school and providing for supervised lotteries for places in oversubscribed schools. With the Education Amendments of 1991, the National government ratcheted up the stakes of educational competition by eliminating all centrally determined zones, ending the requirement of selection by lottery, and giving popular schools virtually unlimited control over which students they accepted.

National's faith in the virtues of educational competition had consequences that sharply altered the directions in which the Tomorrow's School reforms evolved. The new emphasis on competition as a reform mechanism dramatically changed the culture of schooling in New Zealand, especially at the secondary level, in that it forced administrators to devote increased attention to marketing activities and, since schools were now competing against each other, put strains on traditional professional collegiality.

New Zealand thus became a laboratory for testing the extent to which principles deduced from the economic marketplace are relevant to the delivery of public education.

Effects of the Tomorrow's Schools Reforms

II

4 | *Self-Governing Schools*

COLIN DALE is a veteran primary school principal in Auckland who became intrigued with the concept of multiple intelligences developed by Harvard University psychologist Howard Gardner. In 1990, just as the Tomorrow's Schools reforms were kicking in, Dale was named principal of Gladstone Primary School in Auckland, and he decided to create a learning environment that, in keeping with Gardner's ideas, would systematically promote the full range of pupils' intelligences. "Schools typically focus on a narrow band of logical and linguistic skills," he explained. "We teach these, but we also address other important intelligences, like spatial, kinesthetic, and interpersonal ones."

Dale's efforts resonated with teachers, parents, and students alike. Enrollment at Gladstone soared from 415 students in 1990 to 744 in 1998, making it the largest new entrants-through-year-six primary school in the country. It now encompasses a school of performing arts and four other minischools, and it has rich academic offerings that include instruction in seven languages. Gladstone runs an extensive after-school program and pays for students who have self-esteem problems to take part in a ten-week program at the University of Auckland. The board of trustees recently purchased three adjoining properties to help meet pressing needs for new space.

Dale attributes Gladstone's success to the managerial freedoms accorded by the Tomorrow's Schools reforms. From the outset Gladstone was among the minority of schools that accepted the Ministry of Education's offer to take its funds for teachers' salaries in the form of a bulk grant. This choice gave the school somewhat more money for teachers' salaries—the ministry's carrot to encourage schools to opt for bulk funding—so Gladstone now has a full-time technology tutor, a strategic planner, and two Japanese language teachers. Under a beefed-up professional development program, the school even pays to send three teachers abroad for training every year. "No one is restricting us," said Dale. "The potential is now there to do whatever you want. It's all about meeting needs and performing. If you get it right, people will flock to you."

Gladstone Primary qualifies as a poster school for the governance strand of Tomorrow's Schools, and policymakers point to what Dale and his colleagues have done as vindication of the argument that self-governing schools can accomplish great things. Gladstone, however, is by no means typical. Many other schools have struggled to handle the autonomy thrust upon them by Tomorrow's Schools, and some have collapsed under its weight. Problematic issues raised by self-governance range from increased workloads for teachers and administrators to conflicts between the interests of a self-governing school and those of nearby schools.

The concept of self-governing schools is the bedrock on which the Tomorrow's Schools reform package rests. The Picot task force, whose mandate was in the area of governance and management, proposed a state educational system built around self-governing schools, and most of the changes enacted by Parliament in 1989 were directed toward this purpose. The 1991 reforms aimed at promoting parental choice and competition among schools pushed the reforms in a new and quite different direction; but they, too, were built on the premise of school autonomy. Unless schools are free to manage their own affairs, they cannot really be said to be competing in an educational marketplace.

Autonomy for local schools is also the middle part of what Howard Fancy, the secretary of education, refers to as the tight-loose-tight governance structure toward which the Tomorrow's Schools reforms are pointing. Under such an arrangement, the goals and missions of the schools are clear (that is, tight), the schools have significant responsibility for how they operate (the loose part), and schools are then held tightly accountable to the center for outcomes. Such a structure contrasts sharply with the former loose-tight-loose arrangement, whereby the government closely controlled the day-to-day operations of schools but was relaxed about specifying the goals and, in the absence of measures of student learning, in enforcing accountability.

New Zealand does not yet have a fully developed tight-loose-tight system of school governance of the sort that Fancy envisions, mainly because the goal-setting and accountability functions are not as tight as the model would have them be. In this chapter we focus on the "loose" part of the scheme.

Shift to Lay Governance of Schools

Implementing the concept of self-governing schools required a gigantic leap of faith. In 1989, when New Zealand embarked on its bold restructuring experiment, no one knew whether it would be possible to transfer control of an entire state educational system from the professional administrators who had run it for more than a century to a corps of 15,000 untested lay volunteers and 5,000 teachers and principals. Since no other country had ever done anything quite like this, there were no road markers to follow, and unanswered questions abounded. Would a sufficient number of parents agree to stand for places on boards of trustees? Could schools in low-income areas muster the expertise to govern a school? What if religious fundamentalists or other special interest groups attempted to take over a state school to promote their own interests? Secondary schools had experience with lay governance, but was such experience transferable to primary schools? "It was a huge gamble," recalled David Lange in his interview for this book. "Quite frankly, we were not at all sure that we could come up with anywhere near the 2,700 boards we needed."

The Tomorrow's Schools legislation provided for an Implementation Unit to oversee the transition to the new system, which was scheduled to become fully operational on October 1, 1989. The unit's first and most visible tasks were to organize elections of boards of trustees for the 2,686 primary and secondary schools existing at the time and to oversee the drawing up of charters for each school. It could then turn to the task of designing a policy-oriented Ministry of Education to replace the old Department of Education.

The architects of Tomorrow's Schools realized that carrying out successful elections for the founding boards of trustees was crucial to establishing public confidence in the entire reform package. The Implementation Unit consequently invested substantial sums in publicizing the elections through newspaper articles and advertisements and radio and television spot announcements. The advertisements sought to encourage parents not only to vote but to stand for election themselves. The ads stressed the theme that joining a board of trustees was a good way to support your local school and to become personally involved in your child's education. Schools promoted the elections by distributing short biographies and personal statements by candidates and by holding candidates nights, during which parents could question candidates and hear them speak. Subsequent elections in 1992, 1995, and 1998 have also been well organized and publicized. In the most recent election, the ministry, working through a contract with the New Zealand School Trustees Association, placed nearly 4,000 radio advertisements and 1,000 television spots.

To organizers' great relief, the initial elections in April 1989 were by most measures successful, and this triennial ritual has now become a normal and accepted part of the state educational system. The first election attracted ample candidates for the more than 13,000 elected seats available for parents, and all but a few schools succeeded in electing at least three parents to a board, which is the minimum required by the ministry for a board to be considered functional. Since the advent of Tomorrow's Schools, only a handful of schools were unable to muster a sufficient number of parents to form a board. In such situations, the ministry appoints a commissioner to run the school and organize a new election.

Boards also have the right to co-opt additional members in order to enhance representation from particular groups or to obtain needed expertise in areas such as finance or legal matters. Ministry data show that men and women are almost equally represented on boards of trustees, with men slightly more numerous among elected trustees and women among those who are co-opted. Although ethnic balance has improved since 1989, Maoris, Pacific Islanders, and Asians are still underrepresented in comparison with the school population.[1] In many cases members of minority groups are co-opted.

The problem of attracting a sufficient number of candidates to fill the five elected seats typically available for parents on each board was eased somewhat by a provision of the Education Amendment Act of 1992, which

1. Ministry of Education (1997a: 29).

gave people who did not have children at a given school the right to put themselves forward for election to that school's board. Although it has had relatively little impact on the overall composition of the boards, some schools aggressively took advantage of this option. In her review of the first seven years of Tomorrow's Schools at the primary level, Cathy Wylie observes, "It appears that there is either little interest among people who are not parents of children at a school in standing for election—they have always been able to be co-opted or appointed—or that parents may be less keen on electing non-parents."[2]

Many of the initial concerns about the election process turned out to be unfounded, including the fear that special interest groups might attempt to gain control of a school to promote their own agenda. At a college near Wellington one man ran for the board in order to improve the quality of the school's cricket team and then, having accomplished his purpose, stopped coming to meetings. The deputy principal of a primary school in Auckland said that schools would occasionally elect board members who were out to "get at" teachers. By and large, however, such problems were remarkably rare and tended to involve zealous individuals rather than organized groups. As Rob Willetts of the Post Primary Teachers' Association, put it, "People discovered quickly that it is very difficult to impose your views on a whole school." There was some concern early on about teachers running for positions as parent representatives in schools where they both taught and sent their own child, but the 1992 legislation forbade this practice.

School boards have often been divided over local issues, such as whether to mount a new Maori language program, to ask for the principal's resignation, or to opt for bulk funding of teachers' salaries. By and large, however, school boards have remained remarkably removed from partisan politics, and joining a school board in New Zealand has not been seen as a first step toward a political career. By specifying that staff members would be entitled to elect only one representative to the board, the architects of Tomorrow's Schools made it virtually impossible for teachers' unions to gain control of the boards. In general, board members agree to run because they are interested in the quality of education that their own and other children receive. Turnover tends to be high in rural areas, where there is a tradition that "we all need to take a turn," while service on the

2. Wylie (1997: 59).

board of high-quality urban schools is seen as prestigious. In some cases parents view service on a board as a way to get training in how to run an organization, and some members see it as a way of developing business contacts. The ministry likes to describe the boards in low-income areas as a powerful form of adult education.

Despite the overall success of the election process, several problems have developed. Perhaps not surprisingly, the enthusiasm that surrounded the selection of the first trustees in 1989 has waned, in part because parents now have a better grasp of what it means to serve as a trustee. Ann Pattillo, a consultant who has organized elections for the New Zealand School Trustees Association, suggested that the public relations blitz for the first elections understated the amount of work involved. "The message was that being a trustee is easy and fun," she said, citing a television advertisement that showed a picture of a child followed by a picture of a school and then proclaimed: "If you can manage one of these, you can manage one of these."[3] The first group of trustees, however, faced the task not only of running a school but of creating a governance structure, and the workloads turned out to be heavy. "By the next time around, in 1992, there was a lot of turbulence and turnover as overworked founding trustees moved on," she said. "People got the perception that being a trustee was a thankless task." Subsequent publicity has stressed that being a trustee is important work, which, while demanding, can be carried out by ordinary people. This message seems to have been effective. In 1998, according to the Ministry of Education, 16,831 people stood for election for 2,675 schools, up from 16,200 in 1995.

Another problem is that school officials are by no means universally enthusiastic about carrying out contested elections. Many principals have found that their lives are easier and school morale higher if the number of candidates is the same as the number of seats available. Dennis Thompson, principal of the Lyall Bay Primary School in Wellington, recalled that in one election fourteen persons ran for seven board seats, and "the seven who were not elected felt affronted." One common tactic for avoiding contested elections is to work out an arrangement whereby candidates who agree not to run will be co-opted by the board after the election. An added incentive for schools to avoid elections is that they receive a fixed allotment of funds from the ministry to cover the costs of the election. If no

---

3. Gordon (1992: 187).

election campaign is necessary, they can use the funds as they wish. In 1998, 65 percent of schools required elections, while 28 percent had the correct number of candidates, and 7 percent had fewer candidates than vacancies.[4]

The Ministry of Education and New Zealand School Trustees Association (NZSTA) vigorously oppose the efforts of schools to avoid elections. For one thing, a declining number of candidates could be interpreted by some politicians as a reason to curtail the independence of boards. During the 1998 elections the NZSTA operated a telephone hot line to handle complaints about the process, including instances in which potential candidates were actively discouraged from running.

How Schools Have Used Their New Autonomy

Despite the government's inability to implement bulk funding for teachers' salaries, the Tomorrow's Schools reforms dramatically increased the operational autonomy of the schools. This new autonomy was manifested in a multitude of ways, including enhanced operational flexibility, greater responsiveness of schools to the wishes of parents, new opportunities to turn around struggling schools, and new academic missions.

Operational Flexibility

Although doubts and controversies abound regarding many aspects of the Tomorrow's Schools reforms, there is no question that virtually everyone involved in New Zealand schools—parents, teachers, and administrators—welcomed the new operational autonomy granted to local schools. In the course of our travels and research for this book we encountered literally no one, not even the most vocal critics of the new fiscal and enrollment policies, who wanted to go back to the old highly regulated system. "There is no doubt that the increased autonomy at school level has been attractive to many principals and trustees," writes Cathy Wylie, who has closely monitored the changes at the primary level in a series of surveys and reports for the New Zealand Council for Educational Research. "It has allowed faster decisions, and has allowed—where their budgets

4. Ministry of Education.

permit—the direction of funds in areas which are relevant to those at the school. So schools have been able to purchase computers, develop programs, strengthen a bilingual Maori unit, hire a consultant for school-wide staff development, or hire a part-time teacher or teachers' aide."[5]

The most dramatic governance changes occurred at primary and intermediate schools, which prior to Tomorrow's Schools had operated under the thumbs of the regional boards of education. Administrators at these schools are quick to cite examples of ways in which they have seized upon the chance to decide for themselves how to allocate their operational funds. Trustees at the Thorndon Primary School in Wellington found ways to save money on insurance and classroom furniture and redirected the savings to subsidize tutors for students in need of extra help. The Wycliffe Intermediate School in Napier used some of its funds to purchase services from outside organizations, such as Tough Love and a Tu Tangata program that brings adults from the community into the school to provide one-on-one support for students. Ferguson Intermediate School in Auckland, which serves predominantly Maori and Pacific Island students, used its newfound flexibility to teach many of its classes on a single-sex basis and to put students in classes with teachers of the same sex. "We found that girls were shy about giving answers with boys in the room, and boys were reluctant to do so if they thought that girls would giggle at them," explained Jenny Lynch, the principal.

Principals especially welcomed the new authority to hire teachers suited to the particular needs of their school rather than having to accept whoever was sent by the local board of education. Margaret Ngatai is the principal of Rowley Primary School, which serves a low-income community in Christchurch. Three-quarters of the 150 pupils at Rowley are Maoris or Pacific Islanders, and many arrive at school with quite limited life experiences. Ngatai recalled the experience of taking pupils to a park outside town and finding one child crawling on her hands and knees. "She had never walked up a hill," she said. "Being able to select teachers and other staff members sensitive to the needs of such children is important. We can choose people with compassion, people who understand the children in our school and give them support."

Secondary schools have long experience with governing boards, and they have always had the right to select their own staff members. They,

5. Wylie (1994).

too, gained welcome new flexibility in managing operational funds. The Papanui High School in Christchurch used discretionary funds to hire a full-time social worker and to set up a health center that, among other things, assists students in obtaining contraception devices. "We could not have done this before Tomorrow's Schools," explained Marge Scott, the principal. "We would have had to ask for permission, and it probably would have been denied." Wellington College, a boys' school that has turned out numerous national leaders, redesigned its managerial structure and re-wrote job descriptions in order to attain a different mix of administrative skills and to give the principal more time to focus on academic policy. Graeme Marshall, the principal of Hutt Valley High School near Wellington, estimates that the amount of discretionary funds that he and his board control has multiplied tenfold since Tomorrow's Schools. "We put a lot of money into building up classrooms and labs," he said. "I'm also in the position of telling the ministry that some of the policies they suggest are not useful and that we won't implement them."

Impact of Parents

Despite the fact that one of the stated goals of the reform was to in-crease parental involvement in the schools, the evidence is mixed on whether this has occurred. Parental involvement with schools in New Zealand has traditionally been quite high, especially at the primary level, and Wylie's surveys for the New Zealand Council for Educational Research show that this high level has persisted since 1989 with little change. As of 1997, Wylie found that only 29 percent of trustees of primary schools were generally satisfied with the level of parental involvement in their schools and that the proportion of trustees seeking more such involve-ment has been growing since 1993.[6] In addition, she found that only a third of the teachers in primary schools thought the reforms had had a positive impact on their relations with parents, with roughly half saying it had no impact. Principals had a slightly more positive view, with about half saying they thought the reforms had had a positive impact on the relationship between teachers and parents.[7]

Many principals and teachers report that the Tomorrow's Schools re-

6. Wylie (1997: 100).
7. See tables 8-8 and 8-9 in this book.

forms have caused parents to become more assertive in articulating their children's needs and even in questioning school policies, and they say that such attitudes have caused them to more responsive to parental demands. "Tomorrow's Schools gave parents and caregivers permission to challenge what is happening in school," said Sister Frances Feehan, principal of the Saint Francis de Sales integrated school in Wellington. "They question teachers a lot more." Angela Stone, the principal of Waitangirua Intermediate School near Wellington, where most students were Maori and Pacific Island, agreed. "Many of our parents had bad experiences during their own schooldays, and to them schools have been very alienating places," she said. "Slowly, slowly these parents are becoming more comfortable about coming into the building, and they are now beginning to ask questions about what we are doing."

By formalizing parental responsibility for the running of schools, the reforms have fostered a culture in which parents and other members of the community have a recognized place in them. At Tamaki College, located in low-income South Auckland, Maori parents and other caregivers have become involved as tutors in the school through the Community Iwi Liaison Project.[8] "The general attitude in the past was that the parent's job was to get the child to school and the school would take care of the rest," said one of the parent volunteers. "Now we realize we have to become involved."

Parents tend to be most vocal about issues regarding discipline and health and safety, and their influence has often been felt in practical areas, such as student attire.[9] The tradition of wearing uniforms developed in English grammar schools, and intermediate and secondary schools in New Zealand adopted the custom. Many parents view the wearing of distinctive clothing by students as the mark of a quality school, and the number of schools with uniforms has increased substantially since the advent of Tomorrow's Schools at both the primary and secondary levels. Tamaki College, for example, initiated such a policy several years ago and then, in response to parental complaints about the image the students were conveying, opted for a more expensive uniform.

Parental pressure can lead to the formation of new academic programs and policies. At Kaipara College, located in farming country west of

8. Iwi is the Maori word for tribe.
9. Wylie (1997: 100).

Auckland, parents successfully pushed for a horticultural program that had engendered little enthusiasm from the staff. Kaipara parents also forced the school to restore a policy of streaming students by academic ability that had been terminated by teachers and administrators. In this latter case, parental power emanated not so much from the new governance structure as from the school's knowledge that parents can choose to send their children elsewhere. As Peter Lee, the principal of Upper Hutt College near Wellington, put it, "Our teachers are only too aware that if they don't look after parents' wishes, they won't have kids to teach and they won't have jobs."

Turning around Declining Schools

Some principals have used the elbow room accorded them under Tomorrow's Schools to bring about dramatic rescues of schools in decline. Iain Taylor, for example, a brash young school administrator whose credentials include a master's degree in business administration, took the helm of Ponsonby Intermediate School in Auckland in the fall of 1994 only to learn shortly after his arrival that the school was slated by the Ministry of Education for closing. Enrollment had fallen to an untenable eighty-three students; the school's previous low-income residents were moving out of the neighborhood, and the school had little appeal to the middle-class and upper-middle-class parents who were replacing them. Taylor, who was only twenty-eight years old at the time, began knocking on doors in the neighborhood, asking if the residents had any intermediate school-age children and, when told that these children were going elsewhere, inviting himself in to tell about his plans for the school. He also conducted surveys of current and potential parents to learn what they wanted in a local school. "They wanted us to concentrate on academics and watch their kids from 8 a.m. to 6 p.m.," he said.

Taylor opted for bulk funding and used the added funds and the resultant financial flexibility to reorganize Ponsonby's staffing structure. He cut out one of the two deputy principal positions, spreading its responsibilities among other senior staff members, and saved NZ$40,000 by handling the school's books himself (in 1998, NZ$1 was worth slightly less than U.S.$0.50). No relief teachers were employed the first year, and secretarial services were cut to the bone. Savings were used to hire four teachers more than the twenty-four that the school was allotted by the ministry. Taylor also set his sights on the curriculum. He established a policy that no classes would be larger than twenty-three students and cut the number of subject areas from seven to five, in part by eliminating social studies, which, he said, "in New Zealand is nothing but socialistic claptrap." He started up after-school programs in music and overall academic enrichment. All of these changes were trumpeted in newspaper advertisements and columns under his byline.

Taylor's energy and boldness paid off. Enrollment at Ponsonby has grown steadily, to 445 in 1998, and some students commute from more than twenty-five miles away. But he is also controversial. Supporters hail him as a boy wonder of New Zealand education and point to Ponsonby as an example of what all schools ought to be able to do under Tomorrow's Schools. Critics say that, since the school was in a newly gentrified area, it was a turnaround waiting to happen, and they scorn his personnel policies. All but four of the faculty members at the school work on year-to-year contracts, and Taylor has no qualms about not renewing the contracts of teachers who he believes do not have the right attitude, such as one who declined the opportunity to coach a sport after hours. Taylor believes that allowing schools to be self-governing and forcing them to compete for students is a way of "leveling the playing field" of state education. "Teaching is the last bastion of the left in New Zealand," he commented. "Everything is aimed at a common denominator." It is a fair question to ask whether Taylor's approach would work at schools in quite different circumstances, such as those facing the effects of sustained poverty, much less for the system as a whole. What is not in question is the fact that, for better or for worse, Tomorrow's Schools gave Iain Taylor the opportunity to do "his thing."

New Academic Missions

Other schools used self-governance to think about their mission in entirely new ways. Aranui High School in Christchurch serves the sort of students who were traditionally among the 50 percent who were expected to fail their school certificate examinations. "People seemed to think that failure was good for the spirit," said Graeme Plummer, the principal. Seventy percent of Aranui's 1,100 students read below national norms when they enter. Several years ago Plummer and his staff conceived the idea of capitalizing on students' love of athletics and set up the Aranui Sports

Academy. Thirty-five students, including ten girls, were allowed to spend half their time developing their athletic skills and the rest on academics, which included an emphasis on relevant topics such as physiology. The program attracted national attention when the Aranui rugby team began beating teams from the schools in the wealthy western suburbs, which traditionally dominated the sport. Aranui's capture of the local championship was the more remarkable because its players had grown up playing rugby "league," a working-class variation of the sport, and had had to learn new rules and strategies to compete in rugby "union." The team also lacked good equipment, and substitutes sometimes had to put on the shoes of the players they replaced.

Plummer said that all but five of the original thirty-five members of the academy have either found jobs or are continuing their education. "We have a winner," he said. "By finding something that kids were passionate about, we were able to build up their self-esteem and give them transferable skills, like working in teams and showing up on time." Aranui High School has now built on the success of the Sports Academy by setting up similar programs in the performing arts, hospitality and tourism, early childhood education, and construction trades; these now serve about 200 students. Plummer sees the academies as a fruit of Tomorrow's Schools. "It's not just that we had the flexibility to set up these programs," he said. "The reforms have sharpened awareness of our obligations to students and parents. We feel as if we own our school community, so we run it better."

Some boards of trustees of primary schools have even used their self-governing authority to alter the grade structures of their schools. The first and most celebrated example of this involved Seatoun Primary School in the eastern suburbs of Wellington. Within a matter of months of the Tomorrow's Schools beginnings, the newly elected board, responding to parental pressure, voted to add grades seven and eight so that Seatoun pupils could stay on for two more years rather than going on to the nearby Evans Bay Intermediate School or to private schools. The school's unilateral action was controversial and raised important policy issues.

Classifying Self-Governing Schools by Decile

As one might expect, the extent to which the nearly 2,700 state schools in New Zealand succeeded in taking advantage of the operational autonomy afforded them under Tomorrow's Schools varied enormously from school to school. To a considerable extent these differences reflect the varying internal cultures of schools and personal qualities of their leaders. Some of the examples cited show how critical the energy and vision of the school principal can be in helping a school to maximize its institutional potential.

Other important explanations of differences have to do with conditions that are to a large extent beyond their control. Perhaps the most important of these constraints has to do with the characteristics of the students in the school. The mix of students matters because children from disadvantaged backgrounds come to school less ready to learn than children from advantaged backgrounds and thereby impose greater educational challenges on the schools. In addition, less-advantaged parents are in a weaker position than more-advantaged ones to provide assistance to the school in the form of money or services. Student mix thus has an important effect on the ability of schools to make effective use of their autonomy.

In 1995 the Ministry of Education introduced a system of classifying schools by deciles as a means of reflecting the greater educational challenges imposed on schools by disadvantaged students. The new indicator system was intended primarily to provide an objective means of identifying which schools deserved more funding from the Ministry of Education so that more public funds could be directed to them. The decile system, however, also provides a useful means of classifying schools for other analytic purposes.

The task for the ministry was to develop a measure of a school's mix of students that was transparent and relatively simply to calculate, seemed fair, and had face validity in that it generated rankings consistent with the public's understanding of each school. The resulting decile ranking of schools, which developed in 1994 for the 1995 funding cycle and updated in 1997, appears to meet all of those expectations and has in general been well accepted by the public.

The indicators incorporate information about the ethnic mix of the students in a school—the proportion who are Maori or Pacific Islander—and five socioeconomic characteristics. These consist of the percent of households in the lowest 20 percent of the distribution of household income, the percent of parents with no school qualifications (that is, who did not pass the school certification exam), the percent of parents receiving income support, the percent of parents in lower occupational groups, and the average number of persons per bedroom. Information on the ethnic breakdown of the students was available directly from school enrollment data. The five socioeconomic variables were estimated from census mesh-block data based on the home addresses of each school's students.[10] The ministry sorted all 2,700 schools across the country from low to high by each of the six variables and divided them into tenths, or deciles, so that each school had a decile ranking for each characteristic. In the interests of simplicity and clarity, the ministry chose to weight each characteristic equally by adding the rankings for all six variables. It then sorted the schools once again into deciles and assigned each school an overall decile ranking from 1 for the lowest to 10 for the highest.

Table 4-1 provides information on the average values for each of the components of the 1997 index for four illustrative deciles for all schools in New Zealand's three major urban areas: Auckland, Wellington, and Christchurch. By their construction as indicators of educational challenge, the measures all decline as one moves from decile 1 to decile 10 schools. Consider, for example, parental education. The table indicates that while about 52 percent of the parents of children in decile 1 schools left school with no educational qualification, only 15 percent of parents in decile 10 schools have no educational qualification. Of particular interest are the characteristics of the parents with children in the low-decile schools. They are disproportionately low income and recipients of income support; less than half have educational qualifications; they hold low-skilled jobs and tend to live in crowded housing; and most striking of all, they are heavily minority. About 85 percent of students in decile 1 schools in the three urban areas are Maori or Pacific Islander.

The table provides some additional background information on the numbers of schools and students as well as average sizes of schools across deciles. Decile 10 schools were typically larger than decile 1 schools, and more students and schools were in decile 10 than in decile 1. Deciles are based not on the distribution of schools in urban areas but rather on na-

---

10. For small schools, all students were included. For large schools, a one-in-three random sample of students was used. To avoid any efforts of the schools to manipulate that sample, the ministry provided the software to do the randomization. Mesh blocks are the smallest geographic unit for the census. The 1995 rankings were based on 1994 school enrollments and 1991 census data. The renormed rankings for 1998 were based on 1997 enrollments and 1996 census data.

Table 4-1. *Characteristics of Students in Urban Schools, by Illustrative Decile, 1997*[a]

Characteristic	Decile			
	1	4	7	10
Percent low-income[b]	22.2	16.4	12.4	8.9
Housing crowding (people per bedroom)	1.51	1.36	1.24	1.17
Percent of parents with no educational qualification	51.9	33.1	24.3	15.0
Percent of parents receiving income support	37.9	22.7	14.8	6.6
Percent of parents in lower occupation groups	30.8	18.5	12.6	5.5
Maori and Pacific Island students (from roll)	85.2	33.2	16.3	5.2
Primary and intermediate schools				
Number of schools	94	54	42	110
Number of students	27,641	15,608	14,507	38,430
Average school roll	294	289	345	349
Secondary schools				
Number of schools	10	15	8	20
Number of students	5,773	12,826	7,521	26,548
Average school roll	577	819	940	1,327

Source: Data provided to the authors by the Ministry of Education.

a. Entries in rows 1–5 are estimates based on information by school on the decile ranking for each component as well as the median values for each decile of each component for all schools in the country. Because the variation within each decile is greater at the tails of the distribution, these estimates are more accurate for the middle deciles than for deciles 1 and 10. Entries in row 6 are based on actual enrollments.

b. Percent of households in the lowest 20 percent of the income distribution, where income has been adjusted for the number and age of persons in the household.

tional distributions. Because urban areas typically generate higher wages and incomes than rural areas, it is not surprising that decile 10 schools are overrepresented in urban areas relative to the country as a whole.

Self-Governance and Local Fund-Raising

In keeping with the spirit of local self-reliance, self-governing schools are not only given considerable leeway in spending their operations grant from the state, but they are allowed—indeed, encouraged—to supplement these operational grants by raising additional resources on their own. Local fund-raising played a limited role in New Zealand state education long before Tomorrow's Schools, but such activities took on additional importance following the reforms. The principal sources of local revenues are student activity fees, fund-raising events, trading activities, and foreign fee-paying students.

Student Fees

Although state schools in New Zealand are nominally free, most primary and secondary schools post fees that parents are asked to pay when their children enroll. The fees range from nominal amounts to as much as NZ$500, and the money is used for a variety of purposes, including student activities, teachers' aides, computers, and enrichment programs. Rate adjustments are typically made for families with more than one child in the school, and to maintain the fiction of free public education, schools are prohibited from making fees compulsory. As one might expect, the proportion of parents paying these "voluntary" fees varies widely. High-decile schools serving wealthy communities typically succeed in getting the vast majority of parents to pay the stated nontuitions of several hundred dollars, while principals working in low-income areas accept the fact that parents can afford only nominal amounts. The decile 1 Rowley Primary School in Christchurch sets a fee of NZ$15 for one child and NZ$20 for two; Margaret Ngatai, the principal, reports that "we get about 70 percent payment with a lot of reminding." Some low-decile schools have given up even setting a fee because mailings to parents cost more than they yield. Students often incur additional costs for taking part in extracurricular activities such as rugby.

School-Based Fund-Raising Activities

Although they hold the usual fairs and sausage sizzles to raise money, New Zealand schools have been characteristically creative in devising other fund-raising schemes to raise money. Many rent out their facilities for use by community groups in the evenings and on the weekends. The Cannon's Creek School in Porirua, outside Wellington, leases its facilities to a church on Sundays. Porirua College raises money by running tours for visiting American teachers who want to learn about the New Zealand educational system. Several major corporations have worked out partnerships programs that assist schools while enhancing their public images. The national phone company, Telecom, contributes a portion of its receipts from long-distance calls to schools designated by customers.

The prize for the most unusual relationship with a corporate sponsor probably goes to what used to be known as the Bairds Primary School, a decile 1 school on Bairds Road in Auckland. In 1993 Bruce Plested, the managing director of Mainfreight, a large transport company, instructed his assistant to find a school that might have a use for some sports equipment that the company no longer needed. She picked Bairds randomly from the phone book, and soon the company began making small donations of books, a computer room, and other equipment to the school. When the school decided to offer uniforms to children, it put a flying "M" on the shorts and track suits, and in 1995 the school persuaded the Ministry of Education to change its name to Bairds Mainfreight Primary School. Kerry Crossman, the principal, said that the change has "secured their future interest in us" but adds that there are no specific obligations on the part of either party.

Under Tomorrow's Schools, fund-raising from foundations and other outside donors has become an important—and time-consuming—part of the principal's job, especially in low-decile schools. "I keep a data base of potential donors and do a lot of writing away for funds," said Margaret Ngatai. Last year she raised NZ$3,000 for scholarships so that children from low-income families could take part in extracurricular activities.

Foreign Fee-Paying Students

Perhaps the most striking form of local revenue enhancement by New Zealand schools is the enrolling of foreign fee-paying students. Secondary schools send representatives, often the principal, on recruiting missions to Asia and, more recently, to Brazil and other countries in Latin America in search of students able to pay hefty fees. The revenue from such students can be sizable—usually well over NZ$10,000 for room, board, and tuition. Anecdotal evidence suggests that such students are underwriting a high proportion of the investment that New Zealand secondary schools are making in computers and other technological improvements.

Papanui High School in Christchurch is a good example of the system. In 1998 Papanui's student body of 1,073 included 60 foreign fee-paying students who, in addition to tuition, pay for food and lodging in local homes. The school has added six teachers to the faculty to take care of the foreign students: the school's financial statement for 1997 listed gross revenues of NZ$580,000. The government also does well in the deal. It charges schools NZ$900 per student as a management fee for processing student immigrants as well as the usual 12.5 percent goods and services tax on their tuition.

The schools that aggressively pursue foreign fee-paying students tend to be those with student bodies that are racially and ethnically diverse and in the middle of the decile rankings. Prestigious schools serving the wealthiest families can get the local funds they need without the hassle of recruiting international students, and they would have difficulty explaining why they were allocating places to such students rather than to New Zealanders eager to attend. Schools at the other end of the socioeconomic spectrum have less appeal to foreign students. Middle-decile schools like Papanui need the revenue from foreign students, have the capacity to absorb them, and since they already have a diverse mix of students, offer a social setting in which such students are likely to feel relatively comfortable. Single-sex schools, especially those for girls, tend to have a recruiting advantage because many foreign families view them as safe places for their daughters.

Although reliance on foreign fee-paying students will undoubtedly continue to be important for many schools, some New Zealand educators have reservations about the process. Bruce Murray of Tawa College has refused as a matter of principle to divert any places in his oversubscribed school to foreign students as long as there are local students who seek them. Ann Brockenshire, deputy principal at the Hillmorton High School in Christchurch, which had thirty-eight foreign fee-paying students in 1998 and hopes to increase the number, said that she regards the program as educationally beneficial but added that it takes a huge amount of her time. "The money becomes important; that's why I recruit overseas," she said. "But I also wonder what my spending a month in a hotel in Brazil has to do with our kids' education."

Magnitude of Local Fund-Raising

How important is this local fund-raising and what are its principal sources? Table 4-2 provides answers to these questions for urban primary schools for illustrative deciles. Both gross and net figures are presented to

Table 4-2. *Locally Generated per Pupil Revenues, Urban Primary Schools, by Illustrative Decile, 1996* [a]

NZ dollars

	Decile			
Revenue source	*1*	*4*	*7*	*10*
Trading				
Gross	84	40	33	56
Net of costs	15	9	6	2
Fund-raising				
Gross	58	77	115	187
Net of costs	53	62	105	174
Activities				
Gross	35	51	24	58
Net of costs	15	23	6	26
Fees	0	5	0	4
Foreign students	0	0	1	0
Other				
Gross	4	8	6	10
Net	4	7	6	10
Total				
Gross	178	180	179	314
Net	79	106	124	228

Source: Averages calculated by the authors based on data provided by the Ministry of Education.
a. Entries are average revenue per pupil, with *pupil* defined as the number of students used for the calculation of public funding for each school. Includes only contributing primary schools, that is, those offering years one through six, with student rolls greater than 100 students.

highlight the fact that some of the gross revenue is offset by the costs of raising that revenue. In the category labeled *trading,* for example, gross revenue greatly exceeds net revenue because relevant activities, such as lunch canteens or sales of various items, have large costs associated with them. Indeed most of the trading activities are not intended to generate a profit for the schools. Although the guidelines from the Ministry of Education direct the schools to report the gross revenue as local funds, the net figures are the more meaningful. Similarly, the activities fees charged by many schools are offset in part by the costs of providing those activities. The small or zero amounts for fees suggest that most schools account for the "voluntary" fees they charge as activity fees rather than pure fees. Net

Table 4-3. *Locally Generated per Pupil Revenues, Urban Secondary Schools, by Illustrative Decile, 1996*[a]

NZ dollars

	Decile			
Revenue source	1	4	7	10
Trading				
Gross	106	149	119	236
Net of costs	2	4	4	46
Fund-raising				
Gross	54	58	27	123
Net of costs	54	31	27	116
Activities				
Gross	176	438[b]	136	228
Net of costs	140	350[b]	67	182
Fees	0	3	185	20
Foreign students	0	40	115	47
Other				
Gross	103	57	113	79
Net	34	6	60	57
Total				
Gross	439	743	696	732
Net	163	423	458	469

Source: Averages calculated by the authors based on data provided by the Ministry of Education.

a. Entries are average revenue per pupil, with *pupil* defined as the number of students used for the calculation of public funding for each school. Includes only secondary schools offering years nine through thirteen. These schools account for about three-fourths of all the secondary schools in the illustrative deciles in the three urban areas.

b. This average is high because many schools in this decile apparently included revenue from fee-paying students in this category rather than in the separate category for that revenue source (confirmed by telephone inquiries and consistency with low revenue from foreign students for these schools).

revenues vary greatly, from NZ$79 per pupil in decile 1 schools to NZ$228 for those in decile 10, and account for 2.8 percent of funding for decile 1 schools and 9.1 percent for decile 10 schools.

Local funding plays an even more important role in the funding of secondary schools, averaging NZ$163 per pupil for decile 1 schools (3.1 percent of funding) and NZ$469 for decile 10 schools (11.8 percent of funding; see table 4-3). Although we are relatively confident about the accuracy of the total figures, the breakdown among categories appears to include some errors. In particular, activities fees for decile 4 schools appear surprisingly high. Based on telephone inquiries to the business managers of several decile 4 schools that reported large numbers in this category, we determined that much of that revenue should have been reported as revenue from foreign fee-paying students. A similar confusion may also arise in decile 7 schools, for which it appears that the revenue from foreign students may in some cases have been reported as revenue from fees.

Despite the difficulty of sorting out the categories, the conclusion is relatively clear: many middle-decile schools supplemented their public funding with significant amounts of revenue from foreign fee-paying students. Such revenue from those students helped these schools to raise on average almost as much money per pupil as decile 10 schools raised. Of course, the averages hide great variation, with some schools getting considerable revenue from this source and others in the same decile generating none. In contrast, decile 1 schools had much less opportunity to raise revenue in that or any other form and ended up with net local funding equal to only about 35 percent of that raised by decile 10 schools.

Burdens of Autonomy

The movement to self-governing schools was generally well received, and some schools took full advantage of their new independence to strike out in bold new directions. Such schools, however, are only part of the story. A substantial number of schools found the burdens placed upon them to be heavy and, in a few cases, crushing. These problems fall into two broad categories, the first having to do with the governing capacity of boards and the second with increased workloads for teachers, administrators, and trustees.

Capacity to Govern

It was understood from the outset that many of the 17,000 new school trustees would require some training in order to carry out their new duties. Toward this end the government set up and funded the New Zealand School Trustees Association (NZSTA) to provide training and information for school boards and to represent the interests of trustees at national conferences and in discussions with the ministry. The NZSTA, which since 1992 has had the contract to run the triennial school board elections, distributed handbooks and other materials to board members. Written materials were also published by the primary teachers' union and other professional organizations and by the Education Review Office.

As a general rule, schools serving predominantly middle-and upper-income constituencies have had no trouble mustering board members with the requisite governing skills. Most trustees in such schools are sophisticated enough to organize the search for a principal, read a budget, and engage in strategic planning, and they understand subtleties such as the distinction between governance and management. "We have a lot of cultural capital to draw on," said Graeme Marshall of Hutt Valley High School just outside Wellington. When board members in such schools lack specific skills, such as legal or financial expertise, they usually have little difficulty co-opting parents who do have them, and principals have no reluctance using the human resources at their disposal. When she decided that the school needed to do some market research to get a better handle on what its constituency was thinking, Margaret McLeod of Wellington Girls College enlisted a parent who worked at Telecom to design the study and another parent who ran her own consulting firm to set up the data base and carry out the analysis.

Obtaining legal expertise can be important for self-governing schools, which under Tomorrow's Schools bear a level of liability they did not have when the Department of Education was running the system. For example, several schools have found themselves facing substantial court-imposed damages to settle cases brought by employees who argued that they had been improperly dismissed. In such cases the ministry has made a public point of declining to come to the financial rescue of the board. In practice, however, as with a well-publicized case at Timaru Girls High School, which might otherwise have gone bankrupt, the ministry has found ways to assist schools discreetly.

The situation is quite different in low-decile schools, where the sort of cultural capital that middle-income schools take for granted is largely missing. When Ashley Blair, principal of the Cannon's Creek School, a decile 1 school in Porirua, needed to install a bookkeeping system, he had to hire an accountant to make recommendations. "The theory is that we will have that sort of expertise on our board, but no one in the school community has these skills," he explained. Margaret Ngatai of the decile 1

Rowley Primary School in Christchurch managed to recruit a government official to serve as her board chair, but she conceded, "This is very unusual for this area." When the 1998 elections came around, Cannon's Creek School recruited the socially and politically well-connected founder of a nearby alternative school for teen-age parents to be the new chair. Critics wondered, however, whether, since she was not a resident of the community, her perspective and expertise was being acquired at the cost of sensitivity to community views.

A lack of technical expertise among board members at low-decile schools is only one aspect of the issue of governance capacity. Another is the fact that boards frequently lack the sophistication that would allow them to challenge decisions by the principal. "Boards of low-decile schools don't feel confident to deal with the principal as an equal," said Howard Fancy, the secretary of education. "They don't know how to ask the hard questions." In some cases, they do not know enough to ask simple questions. At a recent meeting of a decile 1 school in which the board was called upon to approve the school budget, the principal had to explain in his presentation that there were two sides of the document, one for income and one for expenses. That same principal told us it is "almost embarrassing" to have his board vote on his annual salary, an amount of money that it would take some board members years to accumulate. Terry Bates, principal of the Southern Cross Campus, which encompasses three schools in South Auckland, praised the intelligence and dedication of his board but added, "There is no way that I will get a robust appraisal of how I am doing." Principals in low-decile schools are candid in acknowledging that they are in a position to dominate their boards. When the trustees of Tamaki College in South Auckland were confronted recently with the need to decide how to deal with teachers who might participate in a threatened industrial action, David Hodge, the principal, conceded, "I'll have to instruct the board on how to handle it."

The Education Review Office acknowledged that "trustees with limited expertise are less likely to understand the nature of their governance role." Such trustees, it said, "may fail to put in place appropriate systems for monitoring the performance of the principal and managing the delivery of the curriculum, which are critical factors in determining the quality of education received by students."[11] The Education Review Office has iden-

11. Education Review Office (1998: 10).

tified cultural differences as a contributor to the problem. Specifically, it says that "boards of trustees with a majority of Pacific Island representatives were unlikely to feel comfortable with any approach that was perceived to be challenging the principal's authority."[12] Others define the cultural dimension more broadly, noting the historical legacy that until recently one of every two students emerged from school without credentials. "Half the population were academic failures and came to loathe schools," said Philip Capper of the Center for Research on Work, Education, and Business. "Now we're telling these same people to go manage them."

The Education Review Office documented the extent of these failures in a 1998 study that analyzed reports that its review officers had filed for 236 decile 1 and 231 decile 10 schools. As shown in table 4-4, 24 percent of the low-decile schools were judged inadequate in terms of their compliance with the legal requirements of Tomorrow's Schools, versus only 5 percent of the high-decile schools. Similar patterns were documented in the areas of personnel relations, administration, overall leadership, and instruction and assessment. The only category area in which decile 1 schools were rated higher than decile 10 schools was "positive educational provision for Maori students." Only 4 percent of the low-decile schools, in contrast to 9 percent of the high-decile schools, were judged inadequate on this measure.[13]

The Tomorrow's Schools reforms give the minister of education the right to dismiss boards of trustees for poor performance and to appoint commissioners to run the school until such time as a new board is elected. The minister took such a step thirty-two times between 1993 and 1997, including instances in which boards were initially unable to form.[14] In several cases the minister ordered a restructuring of schools with governance problems. The Southern Cross Campus in Auckland was created to coordinate three schools—a primary, an intermediate, and a high school—that were having difficulty functioning on their own.

12. Education Review Office (1998: 10).
13. The table from which these figures and table 4-4 are drawn includes a number of categories not reported in table 4-4. Our criterion for including a category was that at least 10 percent of either decile 1 or decile 10 schools were judged inadequate.
14. Ministry of Education (1997a: 30).

Table 4-4. *Inadequate Performance, by Type of School*
Percent

Area of performance	Decile 1 schools	Decile 10 schools
Compliance		
Compliance with legal requirements	24	5
Curriculum		
Provision of balanced curriculum	21	6
Effective delivery of national curriculum: knowledge	21	6
Effective delivery of national curriculum: skills	17	6
Effective assessment of student achievement	27	8
Effective monitoring and reporting of student progress	15	5
Personnel		
Effective fulfillment of good employer requirements	12	3
Effective performance management of staff	26	7
Administration and management		
Effective financial management	8	1
Effective self-review	36	13
Other evidence of excellence or improvement		
Effective leadership and vision	11	1
Informed and effective governance	18	3

Source: Adapted from Education Review Office (1998: app. 2).

Workload

Another problematic area is workload. In giving schools the responsibility of governing themselves, the Tomorrow's Schools reforms handed over to them the burden of carrying out many of the administrative tasks that had been handled by the Department of Education and the boards of education. For the first time primary school principals had to deal with matters such as budgeting, hiring, and relating to boards of trustees, while teachers found themselves with new responsibilities such as the increased record-keeping associated with new accountability mechanisms. In addition, self-governance imposed whole new areas of activity on schools, brought on by the enhanced needs to raise local funds, to market themselves, and to maintain better contact with parents. Carrying out these tasks was complicated by the fact that during the 1990s the Ministry of

Education was also developing a new curriculum framework whose implementation required extra time and effort on the part of teachers. "Self-management works because of the high workloads taken on by principals, the increase in teachers' workloads, the voluntary time given by trustees, and the additional money which schools have raised," observed Wylie in her seven-year report on self-managing schools for the New Zealand Council for Educational Research.[15]

In her survey of primary school trustees Wylie found that the average number of hours they devoted to their responsibilities each week in 1996 was 3.4 hours, slightly less than the 4.2 reported for the first year of the reforms.[16] The bulk of the additional workload was borne by principals and teachers.

PRINCIPALS. The workload of principals increased noticeably when the reforms first went into effect in October 1989. Some of the new demands were related to the transition and were thus temporary. For example, schools were obligated to draft charters and work out formal policy statements in dozens of areas ranging from discipline to the rights of pet animals in the classroom. Other tasks, however, became a permanent part of the job. Wylie concluded that primary school principals' workloads "rose substantially the year after the shift to school management and stayed at that level."[17] The average work week for such principals in 1996, she found, was 58.8 hours.[18]

Principals at individual schools frequently cited administrative overload as a problem. "Our workload is phenomenal," said David Hodge, the principal of Tamaki College. "Seventy-hour weeks are not uncommon. We are all trying to compensate for the support services that are not there anymore." Brent Lewis, the principal of Aotea College near Wellington, agreed. "I get up at 5 a.m. and work evenings," he said. "They're trying to run a modern system without realizing what they have transferred to the schools. Being a principal is now more akin to being a city councilor—dealing with interest groups and the Rotary Club. A lot of people I know are looking to get out of the job."

When Wylie surveyed primary school principals in 1996 she found that 94 percent of them had received some professional training within the

---

15. Wylie (1997: 175).
16. Wylie (1997: 92).
17. Wylie (1997: 81).
18. Wylie (1997: vi).

previous year, usually on their own time and with some financial assistance from their board. The most common area of training dealt with how to conduct staff appraisals; other areas high on the list were curriculum, management and administration, school self-reviews, and the general role of the principal. She noted that over the course of her seven-year study principals had shown growing confidence in their ability to handle some key areas, such as financial planning, administration, and staff appraisal.[19]

Nevertheless, principals frequently complain that they are being asked to do things for which they have no previous experience and for which the ministry has provided little professional support. "Lack of training is a big fault of the system, " said Margaret McLeod of Wellington Girls College. "I've had to learn a lot of new skills by myself on the job." One area in which they seem to feel particularly uncomfortable and ill-prepared is management of their school's physical property. "I'm basically a teacher," said Dennis Thompson, the principal at Lyall Bay Primary School. "Dealing with property is a huge area. I sometime feel as if I have been dropped into the deep end of something for which I had no training."

TEACHERS.   Workloads have also increased among teachers since the advent of Tomorrow's Schools. A survey of 160 primary and intermediate schoolteachers in the Wellington area found that in 1994 teachers were working 54.5 hours during the week and another 6 hours on the weekend.[20] In primary schools throughout the country, Wylie found that primary teachers' working hours rose steadily from an average work week of 45.8 hours a week in 1989 to 48.3 hours in 1996.[21] A major reason, she observes, is that "teachers have not cut back on their extra-classroom responsibilities to accommodate the new administrative demands." Seventy-seven percent of teachers responding to her survey said they were spending more time doing student assessment in 1996 than in 1989.[22] To the extent that teachers are devoting more time to their school's educational program, the Tomorrow's Schools reforms and the new curriculum that coincided with them can be thought of as salutary.

However, 60 percent of teachers also reported spending more hours on administrative work than in the past, and Wylie found "clear signs that

19. Wylie (1997: 63–64).
20. Livingstone (1994)
21. Wylie (1997: 86).
22. Wylie (1997: 87).

this continuing high workload is having a negative impact on morale" of both principals and administrators.[23] She concludes that high workloads are "associated with decreased job satisfaction, deterioration in the quality of life outside work, and the attribution to the reforms of more negative than positive impacts. The original satisfaction of having control over funding allocations and other decisions has worn off, exposing rather more clearly the administrative work which came with the reforms. The administrative work seems to principals and teachers to have too great a weight in their work, eroding the time and energy they have for the core work of schools, teaching and learning."[24] Wylie reports that 53 percent of the teachers who had been teaching in 1989 experienced a decline in job satisfaction between 1989 and 1996.[25]

Data are not available on teachers' resignations for the first few years of Tomorrow's Schools. One would expect resignations to have risen during that period as teachers not suited to the new working environment chose to leave the profession. However, the data in table 4-5 show that resignations continued to rise during the mid-1990s. In particular, resignations rose through 1995 for primary schools and through 1996 for secondary schools. Despite the subsequent slight decline, the resignation rate for secondary schools and for all schools was still slightly higher in the 1996–97 period than in the 1992–93 period. Teachers leave public schools for various reasons. For the 1992–93 period, about one in eleven resignations were for personal and health reasons and another one in eleven were so the teacher could move to a different occupation. By 1996–97, in contrast, almost one of five resigning teachers cited the desire to shift to another occupation as the main reason for quitting. Thus the good news of the slight decline in the resignation rate in 1996–97 is offset in part by the evidence that teaching is becoming a less desirable profession relative to other occupations.

Many principals and teachers lament the loss of some of the services previously provided by the regional boards and inspectors of the Department of Education. These inspectors were for the most part experienced educators who were in a position to offer advice in areas ranging from curriculum to personnel relations and, in some cases, to intervene to solve

23. Wylie (1997: vi).
24. Wylie (1997: 93–94).
25. Wylie (1997: 88).

Table 4-5. *Loss Rates of Regular Teachers in State Schools, 1992–97* [a]

Percent

Type of school	1992–93	1993–94	1994–95	1995–96	1996–97
Primary	11.8	13.2	15.0	13.8	10.7
Secondary	8.8	10.9	12.5	12.9	10.6
All schools	10.5	12.2	13.9	13.5	10.8

Source: Ministry of Education.
a. Entries show percentage of teachers who resigned from permanent positions in a given year.

problems. "If I was having trouble with a staff person, I could call up my inspector and arrange for a transfer that would make everyone happy," said David Stanley, principal of Russell School near Wellington. It should be noted that the Picot task force expected many inspectors and administrative staff from the department and boards of education who lost their jobs when the boards were dismantled to regroup and offer their services to schools on a commercial basis. Since the implementation of Tomorrow's Schools, a number of companies have sprung up to offer schools help in areas such as accounting, property maintenance, and bulk purchasing, but the broad range of private support services envisioned by the task force did not take place.

Tensions and Contradictions

The reforms had barely been implemented when it became evident that a number of fundamental tensions—even contradictions—had been built into the new system. These included ambiguities in the roles of trustees and principals and the potential for head-on conflicts among various stakeholders in the system.

Ambiguous Role of Trustees

One of the first tensions to manifest had to do with the role of school trustees. In keeping with the democratic-populist current and the strong views of the Picot task force regarding the importance of community participation in the running of schools, Tomorrow's Schools stressed the theme of partnership. "The running of the institution will be a partnership be-

tween the professionals and the particular community in which it is located," it stated. "The mechanism for such a partnership will be a board of
trustees."[26] Wylie reiterates the importance of such cooperative attitudes
in her seven-year report on primary schools: "The ethos of partnership
among school staff, and between school staff and the school board, has
also been an important lubricant for school self-management."[27]

While school trustees were partners in the collective effort of running
schools, however, they also had duties that raised potential conflicts. For
one thing, they had obligations to the Ministry of Education to carry
out national educational policies in areas ranging from curriculum to
health and safety. They were also the legal employers of teachers and
administrators.

The inherent ambiguities of the role of trustees were dramatized in
1996 when the union representing secondary schoolteachers and administrators, the Post Primary Teachers' Association (PPTA), was negotiating
a new national teachers' contract with the ministry. As part of its negotiating strategy the PPTA began an industrial action known as "rostering,"
under which teachers refused to teach one grade level each day. Schools
remained open, with teachers in the classrooms, but students in the grade
that was affected on a particular day were sent home. The question then
arose: Should teachers who participated in the rostering action be paid or
not? The ministry took the position that boards of trustees should dock
the pay of the participating teachers. Some boards declined to do so.

Lockwood Smith, minister of education at the time, was furious at what
he regarded as an abdication by local boards of a fundamental responsibility they bore as the teachers' employers. Trustees, however, saw their
role in more complex terms. To be sure, they were the legal employers of
teachers and principals. But under the Tomorrow's Schools philosophy
they were also supposed to function as partners with the community and
the educational professionals in carrying out the job of educating children. In the event that the two roles came into conflict, there was little
doubt that most trustees would come down on the side of partnership. "I
spend a lot of time in school talking to people," said Stan Phillips, a farmer
who is a board member of Kaipara College. "I get to know them. I play
rugby with them on weekends. I don't see myself as their boss." John Grant,

---

26. *Tomorrow's Schools* (1988: 1).
27. Wylie (1997: 175).

the principal of Kaipara and a PPTA leader, suggested that such reactions were predictable. "Boards spend their time working with teachers," he said. "The government did not realize that parents looking out for their own kids would see their relationship with teachers as primary. In the eyes of the community, boards of trustees run the school, but they are not the real employer." Wylie came to a similar conclusion in her surveys at the primary level: "Principals and trustees are in agreement that being an employer is not the key aspect of the trustees' role."[28]

Philip Capper of the Center for Research on Work, Education, and Business in Wellington sees the rostering dispute as indicative not only of ambiguity in the role of trustees but of "a fundamental tension in Tomorrow's Schools between centralized funding and community decisionmaking." He suggested that "if the unions play it right, they can use their partnership with parents as a means of getting money from the central government." Sensitive to such issues, the ministry took a hard line in 1998 when the PPTA once again threatened a rostering action. Minister of Education Wyatt Creech stated publicly that if boards of trustees once again paid teachers who participated in the action, the law would be changed to ensure that boards could not repeat their failure to deduct pay from striking teachers.

Ambiguous Role of Principals

Related conflicts also developed in the roles played by principals. The partnership theme running through Tomorrow's Schools evokes the image of principals working alongside teachers, parents, and other members of the community as part of a collegial effort to educate children. In the case of small schools with fewer than eight teachers, this is usually the situation. About half of primary schools in New Zealand have teaching principals, who spend the bulk of their time in classrooms and thus relate to teachers as both peers and employers. No secondary school has a teaching principal as a matter of course, although many high school principals choose to teach a class either to keep in practice or to help out with scheduling difficulties.

Since the National Party took the reins of power in 1991 the ministry has sought to clarify the functions of principals and to eliminate any am-

28. Wylie (1997: 177).

biguity between their roles as partners and bosses of teachers by empha-
sizing the latter. The government apparently feels that, as in the rostering
incident, boards of trustees cannot be trusted to carry out ministry policies and that principals would be more reliable if they were given the appropriate authority and a job description that made it clear that they were
executives, not partners. Accordingly, the ministry has taken a number of
steps aimed at bolstering the concept of the principal as the chief executive officer of the school. It has offered financial incentives to principals
who agree to fixed-term contracts and performance objectives, and there
has been talk of changing education legislation so that the teachers' legal
employer would be the principal rather than the board of trustees. Teachers would thus be accountable to the principal and the principal to the
board.

Such changes have been vigorously resisted by the unions and the New
Zealand School Trustees Association, which view them as part of a broader
effort to replace democratic institutions with a managerial and market-
oriented approach to education. "We see these efforts to undermine the
authority of boards as a government agenda, not an education agenda,"
said Janet Kelly, the former executive director of the NZSTA. "We can work
through any management concerns that the ministry may have, but they
are pushing a particular model that is not suitable at all for small schools
with teaching principals. How can you be a CEO and part of a teaching
team? When Tomorrow's Schools was first introduced the fear was that
principals would be threatened by lay boards. Over the years this concern
has disappeared. Schools have developed good partnerships between principals and boards. The government's ideas would undermine these relationships." Others, however, abruptly dismiss the idea that there is any
problem in principals having ambiguous relationships with teachers. "Anyone with hiring and firing responsibilities has to maintain collegiality as
well," said Peter Bushnell, deputy secretary at the treasury. "Welcome to
the real world."

Tensions between Individual Schools and the Broader Community

In affirming the principle of self-governance for individual schools,
Tomorrow's Schools to a large extent left open the question of what would
happen if the interests of one school happened to clash with those of other
schools or the system as a whole. In such cases the plan provided for the

minister of education to convene a community forum on education so that interested parties could make their views known, but it offered little guidance on the principles to be followed in balancing the interests of the various stakeholders.

The issue of conflicting interests was enjoined in May 1989, even before the Tomorrow's Schools reforms were scheduled to go into effect, when the newly elected board of Seatoun Primary School announced its decision to recapitate, that is, to add two grades to the school. At the time, Seatoun offered instruction to new entrants through year six, after which pupils who wanted to continue in the state system normally went to Evans Bay Intermediate School. In contrast to Seatoun's almost idyllic setting, Evans Bay is located in a light industrial area near the airport, and the sound of airplanes taking off and landing is a constant fact of life. Its student body is also much more diverse, both ethnically and socioeconomically, than the primary school's upscale clientele.

Seatoun's decision to become its own intermediate school was greeted with dismay by Evans Bay, whose viability was threatened by the loss of Seatoun students who would be staying put rather than moving on to Evans Bay. The move was also opposed by other primary schools in the area, which pointed out that if Evans Bay were to close, they would be deprived of an intermediate school option and would be forced into upward grade expansions of their own. Critics also accused the generally upscale Seatoun parent body of racial or socioeconomic discrimination.

In response, the Seatoun board argued that its parents were primarily concerned with maintaining "continuity" in their children's education and that racial or socioeconomic issues were irrelevant. The board also pointed out that many parents in New Zealand had serious reservations about the educational and social value of intermediate schools. Ramon Parbhu, the principal of Seatoun, said that the potential negative impact on Evans Bay of Seatoun's offering an intermediate-level education had always been minimal "since at that time nearly half of our graduates used to go to private schools anyway as a way of avoiding the state intermediate school." He also noted that the principal of Evans Bay had actually helped Seatoun make the change by agreeing to offer the technology courses that are required of intermediate schools and would have been difficult for Seatoun to mount. "Our parents were simply the first out of the box to figure out that they could do this sort of thing under Tomorrow's Schools," he said.

In October 1989 Minister of Education Phil Goff advised the Seatoun board that it needed his permission to recapitate and that, before making a decision on the matter, he was obligated to appoint someone to convene a community forum on education for the eastern suburbs. He named Mary O'Regan, selected from a list prepared by Seatoun parents, and she organized a series of four public meetings between April and July 1990. In her report to the minister as convener of the forum, O'Regan argued that the question of whether Seatoun should be allowed to recapitate hinged on the definition of the "community" that schools are mandated under Tomorrow's Schools to serve.

The Seatoun board's definition was the "immediate school community," she said. "According to these interpretations they believed their actions were entirely in line with the new educational philosophy, which promoted local solutions to local issues. They had a clear mandate from their own community and wished only to act on that." Other interpretations were broader and included "all those who may be affected by the action of a school." Under such a view, "the right of one school to exercise 'choice' was seen to have the potential to limit the choices of others. In this context it was considered that any decisions made should be preceded by a thorough analysis of the likely impacts in terms of overall community choice."

O'Regan argued that the two definitions of *community* grew out of two quite different educational philosophies, one competitive and the other cooperative, and she suggested that Goff's decision should hinge on which of the two philosophies he endorsed. "If the *free market* or competitive approach to education provision is endorsed," she said, "Seatoun School should be granted the right to recapitate. If the coordinated, cooperative approach to education provision is endorsed . . . schools in the Eastern Suburbs should be given the opportunity to continue the process which has begun during this Forum with a view to exploring ways in which the existing educational resources of the Eastern Suburbs can be most effectively used to provide the widest possible range of options in terms of educational provision." She added that following the latter course would not preclude recapitation by Seatoun at a later date.[29]

Six weeks later Goff convened a meeting of the boards of trustees of the affected schools to announce that he was opting for the narrow interpretation of *community* and would thus make no efforts to resist Seatoun's

29. Mansell (1993: 74–78).

recapitation. "I come from the position that under *Tomorrow's Schools* we're trying for maximum choice for parents [and that] the decision needs to be made locally," he said. "The convener's report goes into ideological or philosophical differences, between co-operation among schools or a free market. But I don't think in those terms, so that is not very useful to me. The choice is really to allow Seatoun its choice now or to go on talking about it. My decision is that Seatoun School should be permitted to cater for [year-7 and year-8] pupils for 1991. This confirms my priority for parental choice." However, Goff backed off from totally embracing the free market by adding that in the event that parents no longer had an intermediate school option for their children, permission to recapitate would not be granted.[30]

Since Seatoun, nine other primary schools in the Wellington region have recapitated.[31] Lockwood Smith, who became minister of education following National's victory in the 1991 general elections, routinely approved subsequent recapitation moves by primary schools. It was not until Wyatt Creech replaced Smith in 1996 that the ministry began expressing doubts about rubber-stamping such proposals. "The ministry has become conscious that there is a wider community to be considered, not just the local one," said David Carpenter, liaison officer at the Lower Hutt Regional Center of the ministry of education.

One consideration in shaping ministry policy, Carpenter said, is growing public distrust of intermediate schools in general. "A lot of parents in this area don't like them," said Carpenter. "They think children pick up bad habits in big schools, and they prefer full primary schools in the hope that good habits will brush off." Carpenter noted that, with four large full primary schools and several smaller ones now available, parents in Wellington have a choice of whether to send their children to an intermediate school or a full primary.

The official adoption of the idea that the community served by schools did not extend beyond the current body of parents had significant implications down the road. Tomorrow's Schools had lodged control of schools in parents not only as a way of fighting the self-serving influence on policy of educational professionals but as a way of putting schools in closer contact with their constituents and addressing the problem of parental pow-

30. Mansell (1993: 79–80).
31. Information from David Carpenter, Lower Hutt Regional Center.

erlessness, which had been identified by the Picot task force as a key issue. These democratic concerns gradually lost ground to concepts of education shaped by the marketplace. By giving Seatoun parents a green light to pursue their own interests without regard to the interests of other schools, the ministry affirmed, both implicitly and explicitly, the ideals of competition and choice and the assumption that the common good would be enhanced when individuals were free to pursue their own perceived self-interest.

Not all such disputes have involved upper-middle-class parents seeking to insulate their children from particular people or settings. The Ferguson Intermediate School in South Auckland, which serves low-income students, began offering the first two years of high school as an addition to its program. The arguments used by its principal, Jenny Lynch, are similar to those heard at Seatoun nearly a decade before. The pressure, she said, comes from parents who are dissatisfied with the instruction offered at the two nearest high schools. "We haven't had a negative effect on their rolls," she said, "because the students were not going to go there anyway." While it waits for a ministry decision, Ferguson has added the grades indirectly through an agreement with another school.

Balancing the conflicting interests of various educational stakeholders is a major philosophical policy issue generated by the Tomorrow's Schools reforms. The issue became critical in the mid-1990s when it became evident that the market model was working to the advantage of some groups of parents and schools and to the disadvantage of others.

Decline of Democratic Populism

We characterize the Tomorrow's Schools reforms as reflecting three philosophical currents: democratic-populist, managerial-business, and market-competition. The initial blueprint was mostly a combination of the first two, but with the decisions of the National government in 1991 to abandon zoning and to push parental choice, the balance shifted abruptly toward the second and third currents. Efficient management remained an important priority, but the rhetoric of community participation gave way to the language of the marketplace. It also soon became clear that the state was not about to abdicate its interest in education simply because the schools were now self-governing.

Controversy over Charters

The most obvious signal of the decline of the democratic-populist current can be observed in the fate of school charters, which were intended to be a key component of the Tomorrow's Schools reforms. Initially conceived as representing a three-way partnership between the state, the school, and the community, charters were also intended to be the vehicle through which individual communities would impress their values on the schools. As an explicit statement of a school's educational mission and objectives, the charter would then serve as the basis for both the local community and the ministry to hold the school accountable for results. Early in the reform process, however, the charters were transformed in ways that minimized their function as expressions of community interest and expanded their use as an instrument of state control.

The concept of school charters takes center stage in the Picot task force report, which describes them as the "lynchpin" of the new structure of compulsory education. Charters would provide each school with "clear and explicit objectives" reflecting "both national requirements and local needs." They constitute a "contract between the community and the institution, and the institution and the state."[32] Under this three-way contract the various parties would have different responsibilities but relate as equals. The state would fund schools and provide national guidelines, while boards of trustees would make local policies and run the schools. The *Tomorrow's Schools* policy paper adopted this language verbatim. "The charter of each institution will be approved by the Minister, on the recommendation of the ministry," it states. "It then becomes a contract between the state and the institution, and between the institution and its community."[33]

Given the importance of contractual relationships to other parts of the public sector reform efforts in New Zealand at that time, it is not surprising that *Tomorrow's Schools* maintained the language of the three-way contract. But the language papered over some built-in ambiguities and tensions. How much control over missions could be handed to schools given that primary and secondary education was compulsory? Could the charter ever be a contract in the sense of imposing enforceable responsibilities and obligations on all parties? How would it be enforced? Could

32. Task Force (1988: xi).
33. *Tomorrow's Schools* (1988: sec. 1.1.7).

the government commit itself to provide sufficient funding for a school to achieve the objectives in the charter? Working out such details was the task of the implementation group, which circulated a draft framework for charters in March and a final version in May 1989 that addressed the ambiguities by substantially altering the design laid out in the earlier documents.

The March draft made it clear that local school communities would have little or no say over about 80 percent of the contents of the school charter because, to protect the government's interest in educational outcomes, the government was planning to require that every charter include a commitment to the national educational guidelines. To the dismay of some, these guidelines placed a much heavier emphasis on the state's equity objectives and the provision of special programs for Maori students than on promoting educational quality.[34] In the May version, this emphasis was altered to require that all charters also include the "paramount principle," which states that the needs of children and their learning should be paramount.

Significantly, the May 1989 framework changed the three-way contract to a bilateral agreement between the board of trustees and the minister of education, leaving no formal governance role for the local community. Each board of trustees was to administer the school in accordance with its charter, and the minister was to provide funding for the school to meet the requirements of the charter. This change served two purposes. First, it clarified the lines of accountability that would have been confusing in a three-way agreement. Second, it ruled out the possibility that parents or community groups could contest the agreement because they were not signatories to it. The May framework also replaced the term *contract* with the term *agreement*. Although this change had the effect of limiting the obligation that the ministry had to local schools, the May framework made it clear that central authorities were obligated to provide sufficient funding to meet the needs of local schools. It stated, "The Minister of Education upon approving this Charter undertakes to provide services and funding to a formula to be determined by the Minister from time to time, to enable the Board of Trustees to meet the requirements of the charter."

Partly out of concern about the ministry's insufficient capacity to negotiate and approve 2,700 new charters in a short period of time and partly because the Picot task force had overestimated the ability of local boards

---

34. Codd and Gordon (1991: 27).

to develop meaningful charters that were explicit enough to be used as accountability documents, the charter framework was changed once again in January 1990. First, the relationship between the two parties, downgraded to an *agreement* in the May 1989 document, was further redefined as an *undertaking*. Second, the new document removed the ministry's legal obligation to provide adequate funding, thus turning the former partnership into what amounted to a one-way obligation of boards to the state. In another major shift, the paramount principle, which lawyers in the ministry had warned would leave the ministry open to litigation, was deleted.[35] These changes were debated within the government, with no participation from educational and community groups, and they initially went unnoticed.

Thus in a few months the charter went from being a three-way contract or partnership to a two-way agreement to a one-way undertaking. As Liz Gordon, an academic critic who subsequently became a member of Parliament as a member of the small left-wing Alliance party, wrote shortly afterward, "The state had taken the first step in regaining the power that had been given away in the Picot Report, . . ."[36] The ground had been laid for moving from a system in which communities worked alongside central authorities to set and implement goals for state schools to one in which boards of trustees essentially acted as agents in carrying out purposes established by the state. "This principal-agent relationship clearly lies at the heart of the charter changes announced in January 1990," wrote Gordon, "and is a marked departure from the model of community power that constituted one of the central principles of the educational reforms."[37]

Opposition to these changes developed once their significance began to be appreciated. It became apparent that some boards were going to refuse to sign charters that entailed commitments on their part but not on that of the government. Negotiations were carried out between the ministry and the New Zealand School Trustees Association, and a set of changes was announced in April 1990. The negotiated agreement addressed boards' concerns about one-way obligations not by strengthening the obligation of the ministry but by weakening that of boards. A final change

35. When the national education guidelines were broadened in 1993, the emphasis on equity goals was reduced somewhat in favor of educational excellence.

36. Gordon (1992: 195).

37. Gordon (1992: 196).

removed the regulative power of the charter with a clause that read: "In governing this school, the board of trustees will take all reasonable steps to ensure that the school meets the goals and objectives of this charter within the resources and time available to it, in accordance with section 64 of the 1989 Education Act." Boards of trustees were thus relieved of any obligation to accomplish objectives that the state declined to finance adequately.

"The principal-agent relationship had remained secure, at the expense of the power of the charter as a document on which educational practice and outcomes could be evaluated or challenged by the community," wrote Gordon. "In reality, the charter moved from being a blueprint for action to a statement of educational ideals which could not, without resources, be achieved."[38] As a result of these changes, the controversy over the charter itself largely disappeared.

Starting in June 1989, writing a charter had become a major activity for newly elected boards of trustees. In some cases the drafting process was a rewarding activity for the boards and their school communities; it was comprehensive and thorough, although at times frustrating because of the uncertainty associated with the ongoing changes in the government's charter framework. In many other cases, however, inexperienced and untrained board members, overwhelmed by their other new responsibilities, deferred to school principals and let them play pivotal roles in the writing of the charters. In addition, many boards confined their attention to those sections of the charter that they were required to complete rather than working through the implications for them of the many state-imposed requirements.[39] As a result, not only have school communities played a smaller role in the charter development process than had been envisioned, but charters have also ended up more bland and general and have not played the core role within the schools that was anticipated.[40]

Demise of Other Populist Institutions

While the role of charters was being redefined, other populist institutions built into the early iterations of the reforms never got off the ground.

38. Gordon (1992: 196).
39. Mitchell and others (1993: 58–60).
40. The conclusion about the role in schools is based on Wylie's surveys of trustees, teachers, and principals. Wylie (1997: 149).

The *Tomorrow's Schools* policy paper provided for the setting up of an independent Parent Advocacy Council, appointed by the minister but reporting to Parliament, to "promote the interest of parents at all levels of education." Specifically, it was charged with serving as a "last resort" to help individuals and groups who felt that the system was not hearing or responding to their needs, including parents who wished to educate their children at home or to set up a separate school.[41] The council lasted only eighteen months before being abolished on the ground that parents needing such support could be served by other government agencies such as the Human Rights Commission.

A similar fate awaited the community forums on education, one of which played an important role in the Seatoun controversy. In recommending a new educational system built around individual learning institutions, the Picot task force had recognized that "a wider community forum will be required so that the views of the whole community can be brought together on matters of educational importance." Such an institution would, among other things, "discuss and if possible settle local conflicts of interest." This section of its report concluded, "We cannot emphasize too strongly the importance of community education forums."[42] *Tomorrow's Schools* embraced the idea, stating that "community education forums will be set up to act as a place of debate and a voice for all those who wish to add their concerns—whether students, parents, teachers, managers or education administrators."[43] It also made a few modifications to increase ministerial control of the process, including the right to draw up the terms of reference for the convener.

The Education Act of December 1989, however, which established the legal basis for the reforms, made no specific mention of community forums on education. It stated only that "the Minister shall not change the designation of schools without first appointing a community education convener" and giving this person a reasonable time to organize meetings and offer advice to the minister.[44] The Seatoun controversy, however, proved to be the high point of community forums on education. In 1991 the National government passed legislation abolishing them completely.

---

41. *Tomorrow's Schools* (1988: 22–23).
42. Task Force (1988: sec. 5.8.4).
43. *Tomorrow's Schools* (1988: 2).
44. Mansell (1993: 21).

They were replaced by the Education Development Initiative with the much narrower mandate of providing some assistance and encouragement from the ministry for groups of schools that want to consider amalgamating. Since merger discussions usually involve administrators, not parents, the concept of public forums was dead.

Toward Schools as Agents of the State

As is evident, the concept of self-governing schools was only the starting point of the Tomorrow's Schools reforms. The original notion was that the Ministry of Education and local communities would be partners in running the state educational system, and success would be ensured by good management practices, including the location of as much decisionmaking as possible close to the delivery of services.

The Tomorrow's Schools governance reforms were remarkably successful on several levels. They broke up a controlling educational bureaucracy that many believed had become overly bureaucratic, inefficient, and out of touch with the needs of local communities, and they opened up channels for community input into the running of schools through election of parent-dominated boards of trustees. It turned out that most schools were able to handle self-governance reasonably well, and there is evidence that some of the traditional walls between schools and parents have broken down, especially in low-decile schools. At the same time, the new provisions for self-governance created an enormous workload for teachers and principals, and they seriously overestimated the governance and managerial capacity of most schools, many but by no means all of them low decile. They thus created situations in which the ministry was forced to intervene and to acknowledge that the system was not working for some schools.

The concept of self-governance was evolving even before the ink was dry on the legislation. The Picot task force favored self-governing schools as a way of both increasing community involvement in schools and fostering good management. The task force did not anticipate the demise of the parent advisory councils and the community forums on education, nor did it foresee the reduced role of charters. Further changes occurred with the election of a National government, which placed more emphasis on individual parental choice than on collective action as a way to ensure that schools reflected parental preferences. National was also conscious that the center has clear purposes in setting up and financing a state system of compulsory education and that the "partners" did not always have the same interests.

The changing conception of the school charter and the demise of other populist institutions originally built into the Tomorrow's Schools reforms illustrates the tension between a model of autonomous, self-governing schools working to achieve community objectives within very general government guidelines and a model in which the central government views the schools as agents empowered to work on the state's behalf toward the state goals that justify making primary and secondary education compulsory. In her study of primary schools over the first seven years of reform, Wylie observes, "We see in school boards the meeting of two of the reforms' contrary currents: the 'citizen' model, pushing for more parental involvement in schools, through partnership, and the public sector reform model, with its emphasis on hierarchical accountability and contractual relationships."[45]

Thus the evolution of charters provides a useful introduction to the second strand of the Tomorrow's Schools reforms. This strand recognizes that, despite their new operational autonomy, schools continue to serve as agents of a state that has maintained significant power through the tools of articulating a national mission, providing funding, and requiring accountability. These constitute the first and third elements of the tight-loose-tight formulation. To this model of schools as agents of the state we now turn our attention.

45. Wylie (1997: 177).

5 | *Goals and Accountability*

IN THE DAYS BEFORE Tomorrow's Schools, when the Department of Education was running the New Zealand school system, no one had any doubt about how central authorities related to local schools. Working through its regional boards of education, the Department disbursed funds, tightly controlled the allocation of those funds, and used a system of inspectors to oversee and work closely with the individual schools. These inspectors dispensed advice as well as criticism and thus played an important role in shaping the successes and failures on which they reported.

The introduction of self-governing schools changed all this. By giving local schools a role in goal setting and by drawing a sharp line between policymaking and operations, the Tomorrow's Schools reforms dramatically altered the relationship between the center and individual schools. New Zealand's self-governing schools are still part of a centralized state educational system on which they are dependent for their resources and to which they are accountable for their performance. Writing new rules to govern the new relationships between the center and the periphery has been an ongoing task. In this chapter we discuss the way these relationships have been worked out with regard to goals and accountability. The following chapter takes up the other key aspect of this relationship: funding.

Both the old and the new systems were built on the premise that the state has an obligation to establish and maintain a system of compulsory education for all children. By transferring operating responsibilities to the schools, Tomorrow's Schools made schools the primary units responsible for carrying out the interests of the state. Hence the concept of schools as agents of the state, which we identify as the second of the three strands that shaped Tomorrow's Schools.[1]

The concept of schools as agents of the state was implicit in the Picot task force report and the *Tomorrow's Schools* policy paper, although language such as a "three-way partnership" among state, schools, and local communities served to diffuse the point. Government leaders realized early in the process of reform that the state did not want to leave itself vulnerable to boards of trustees that might be of a mind to contest state policies and actions. Thus as the state withdrew from its traditional role of operating schools, it filled the void with a system that protected the power of the state to pursue its goals for education while delegating significant but limited power to local boards of trustees.

We describe New Zealand as evolving toward a tight-loose-tight form of school governance. The previous chapter focuses on self-governing schools (the loose part). We now turn to the government's role in setting the goals and missions of the schools (the first tight) and in holding them accountable (the second tight).

National Goals and Objectives

Although New Zealand has a national curriculum and national tests at the school-leaving level, its objectives for individual schools are quite general and leave significant leeway for schools to define their own outcome

---

1. Economists and other social scientists have developed a large body of literature investigating the principal-agent relationship, that is, a situation in which one person or organization (the principal) uses agents to carry out its goals. The challenge for policymakers is to set up institutional frameworks and incentives to motivate the agents to work on behalf of the principal while at the same time minimizing transactions costs. In much of that literature, the focus is on the design of contracts that will elicit the desired behavior given that the objectives of the agents are typically not fully consonant with those of the principal. In the case at hand, the state is the principal and the schools are the agents. The following discussion does not draw explicitly on the formal theory of principal-agent models but is in the spirit of such models. See Williamson (1985); Moe (1984).

objectives, albeit within the context of the national goals and guidelines. The government's role is to establish a policy framework or environment within which schools can pursue locally determined purposes while at the same time furthering the government's broad program for education.

National Education Guidelines

The fundamental goals and objectives for New Zealand's educational system are spelled out in a three-part document entitled the *National Education Guidelines* (NEGs), which emerged in its current form in 1993. These guidelines, which must be incorporated into all school charters, consist of national educational goals, national curriculum statements, and national administration guidelines.

NATIONAL EDUCATIONAL GOALS AND NATIONAL ADMINISTRATION GUIDELINES. The national goals are quite broad and include such ambitious objectives as high achievement for all students, equality of educational opportunity, and development of the knowledge and skills needed by New Zealanders to compete successfully in the "modern, ever-changing world." They also call for the advancement of Maori education through special initiatives and respect for the diverse ethnic and cultural heritage of New Zealand people.[2] The administration guidelines spell out general responsibilities for the boards of trustees in the areas of student achievement, employment and personnel matters, finance and property issues, and provision of a safe physical and emotional environment for students.

NATIONAL CURRICULUM. More explicit operational goals are specified in the national curriculum, which spells out what the government wants children to know and to be able to do. Such a curriculum has always been an important component of the country's system of compulsory education. When the Labour Party gained power in 1984, for example, it focused its initial reform effort on the curriculum. Although welcomed by the left as a major reform effort and bolstered by considerable popular input, that effort was abandoned in 1987 in favor of the governance and managerial reforms proposed by the Picot task force. Not until the early 1990s did curriculum reform return to the front burner.

---

2. Ministry of Education (1993). These guidelines broadened the earlier guidelines and balanced the state's concerns with equity and the education of Maori with a greater focus on educational excellence.

In 1993 a new curriculum framework called for curricula to be offered in seven subject areas—languages (both English and others), mathematics, science, technology, social sciences, the arts, and health and physical well-being—and in eight sets of essential skills. The framework was to be followed up by new curriculum statements in each of the seven areas. These statements began to be released in the early 1990s, but even by 1998 not all of them had been completed. In contrast to earlier iterations of the national curriculum, the 1993 version attempted to focus on the expected outcomes of learning rather than the specific topics that teachers were to teach.[3] The new framework was also the first to include technology as one of its components.

Significantly, the new curriculum policy is quite flexible and not highly prescriptive of what the schools need to do. A few schools have creatively redefined the seven curriculum areas. The previous chapter describes how Gladstone Primary School appropriated the ideas of Harvard psychologist Howard Gardner for its curriculum and how Iain Taylor, the energetic young principal of Ponsonby Intermediate School, organized teaching at his school around five areas rather than seven. Wellington Girls College has chosen not to teach New Zealand history because, as one teacher explained, students find it more interesting to talk about South Africa or English kings and queens.

QUALIFICATIONS FRAMEWORK. The qualifications framework spells out the system for recognizing student achievement. The noncompulsory school certificate exams are given in various subjects to students at age fifteen, which, until recently, was the school-leaving age. After this age was increased to sixteen in 1993, the rules were changed so that failing grades on one or more parts of the school certificate exam could keep a student from moving to higher-level courses but would not force the student to leave school. In addition to the school certificate exams, there are tests for the sixth-form certificate exams (typically taken at age sixteen) and exams for a higher certificate (typically taken at age seventeen). Students going on to a university take the bursary, or scholarship, exams, which are offered by subject area. These national exams are the clearest statement of New Zealand's educational standards.

The approximately 17 percent of students who leave school without passing the school certificate exams end up with no formal academic

---

3. Butterworth and Butterworth (1998: 212).

qualifications, and many others leave school with little opportunity to go on to higher education. In response to growing demands from the labor market for students with some level of postsecondary education and training, support emerged for a qualifications framework that would allow people with limited school qualifications to participate more fully in the workplace and to have opportunities for further education and training. To achieve that end, as well as to ensure a qualifications framework that would make the country internationally competitive, the 1990 Education Amendment Act established the New Zealand Qualifications Authority (NZQA), with the mandate to set up and review a unified qualifications structure that would encompass both the educational and training sectors.

The new qualifications framework became Lockwood Smith's baby. Minister of education from 1990 to 1996, Smith took special interest in a framework that would provide what he called a "seamless web" of knowledge and skills as students, including those not well served by a traditional academic focus, moved through various academic and vocational offerings. The idea was that students would be able to earn unit qualifications in the upper grades of secondary schools that would be recognized by employers and by other providers of training and that would accumulate over time. Although such a system lent itself to vocational subjects, in which skills such as how to create a parallel electrical circuit were relatively easy to identify, the ultimate goal was to develop unit standards for all subjects, including academic subjects like history. According to Smith's vision, the qualifications earned through the academic track would eventually be fully merged with qualifications earned elsewhere.

During Lockwood Smith's tenure as minister of education, considerable energy and resources were devoted to developing the new voluntary system. The concept made sense for vocational courses and was strongly supported by teachers and administrators in low-decile schools, where the students were most likely to benefit from the new credentials. However, it was vigorously opposed by educators in high-decile schools, who raised philosophical issues relating to the nature of merit and excellence. It also aroused the ire of teachers in the humanities, who argued that instructional goals such as teaching students to analyze a Shakespearean play did not lend themselves to being divided into discrete units. Teachers also complained about workload issues, especially when they found themselves dealing with a new qualifications system while maintaining the old one.[4] Although the system is still in place, it has not taken hold to the extent that some of its supporters had hoped and is unlikely to lead to a unified system of qualifications. Plans for extending it to the traditional academic track are now being put aside.[5]

System Performance

Somewhat paradoxically, while the government sets national curriculum frameworks and runs national secondary school exams, it has little information for determining how well the system as a whole is performing. None of the national tests at the school-leaving age are mandatory, and no nationwide tests are currently required at the primary level. About 40 percent of primary schools administer a ministry-sponsored progressive achievement test to judge the performance of their students; but they do not report scores to the ministry or to any other national body, and the national norms are now somewhat dated. Only recently has New Zealand begun moving toward an assessment system to provide information on the system's performance over time. In addition, other measures of system performance such as the percent of students leaving school with no educational qualifications are hard to interpret because of the 1993 change in the school-leaving age.

Despite their national curriculum guidelines and school certificate exams, the New Zealanders have been reluctant to introduce detailed prescriptions of educational outcomes at a systemwide level, especially at the primary level, for fear that they will focus too much attention on testing and lead to a narrowing of the curriculum. Instead of providing detailed goals, Howard Fancy, the secretary of education, argues that the central government should be providing a policy framework that encourages schools to specify their own objectives and to suggest procedures for meeting them—for which they can then be held accountable.[6] As part of this

4. One side benefit of the system is that it provides opportunities for many teachers to get some professional development by serving as moderators for NZQA seminars. In chapter 8 we use information on the distribution of teachers serving as moderators across schools to draw some inferences about the distribution of teachers' quality.

5. An article in *New Zealand Education Review* declared that unit standards would be dumped for "conventional" school subjects, according to secret plans for senior school qualifications. See Hotere (1998: 1).

6. Howard Fancy, communication with authors, October 1998.

framework, however, he agrees that more nationally comparable data on school outcomes would be useful. Such data, combined with research that helps establish benchmarks, should, according to Fancy, gradually reduce the divergence in expectations across schools.

Holding Schools Accountable

Central to any decentralized managerial system is accountability, the second "tight" in a tight-loose-tight governance structure. Because in New Zealand the educational goals of the center are broadly defined and are not easily measured, and because of the philosophy that schools should have leeway to determine their own goals and objectives, accountability poses a variety of challenges in the New Zealand educational system.

In most people's minds, accountability is synonymous with the well-publicized reports on schools of the Education Review Office (ERO). Periodically, the ERO sends a team of outsiders, all former teachers, to each school. The teams have one to five members, one or two being typical for primary schools. The team visits classes, pores over documents and records, discusses a draft report with the schools, and then issues a final public report laying out both the school's strengths and any deficiencies that need to be addressed.

The style of the ERO teams and the substance of their reports differ dramatically from those of the inspectors who were charged with enforcing accountability for the old Department of Education. Inspectors were for the most part respected educators who, in addition to carrying out formal responsibilities such as allocating resources and evaluating and grading teachers, provided important informal services. They offered advice on curricular or personnel matters, set up in-service training programs, and could use their contacts to solve tricky problems, such as arranging for the transfer of a teacher who was not getting along with his or her principal. Although the nature of their jobs was such that the inspectors inevitably provoked anxiety among principals and teachers—they had, among other things, the authority to get people fired—they were also seen as having an avuncular side, and the harshness of their judgments was tempered by the fact that they functioned behind the scenes.

By contrast, review officers from the ERO were given only the monitoring function so they could provide independent evaluations uncompromised by their involvement with the schools. In addition, their reports are public documents and thus have the potential to make or break a school's public image and, as a direct result, its capacity to attract students in the new educational marketplace. Educators live in fear of damaging reports from the ERO, and the devastating effects of some such reports in the past has led to the coining of a new verb. A principal on the receiving end of such a report is likely to declare, "I was ERO'd."[7]

How the Education Review Office Came About

Developing a system with clear lines of accountability and effective mechanisms for enforcing them was a central goal of the Picot task force. One pillar of the new accountability system was supposed to be the school charter, which would serve as a benchmark against which schools could be judged. However, the charter failed to emerge as the definitive document envisioned by the members of the task force, a fact that contributed to the uncertainty about precisely what the schools should be held accountable for.[8]

The other pillar of the new accountability system was external monitoring. The task force, and subsequently the policy paper *Tomorrow's Schools* called for an independent review and audit body that would monitor not only the performance of the individual schools but also the quality of the policy advice provided to the Ministry of Education. The task force proposed that the new agency report directly to the ministry, that it review each school at least once every two years, and that it focus on how

---

7. The New Zealand approach to accountability is most similar to that used in England, where the Office for Standards in Education (OFSTED) performs functions similar to that of the ERO. Although the OFSTED differs in that it contracts out its inspections to private inspection teams, its inspectors spend more time in classrooms than ERO reviewers, and it reviews against clear national norms, it is similar in its independent monitoring function and its focus on making managers manage. This approach differs from that used in Victoria, Australia, which can be described as "letting" rather than "making" managers manage. See OECD (1995).

8. That uncertainty continues. An official review of the ERO by a committee chaired by Margaret Austin recommended that every school be required to include in its charter a three-year strategic plan along with annual statements of performance indicators and that the plan and the indicators be used by the ERO for evaluation and audit purposes. Austin Report (1997: 7).

well each school was meeting the "clear and specific aims and objectives, expressed as outcomes" specified in each school's charter.[9]

As discussed above, the new agency would differ in fundamental respects from the inspectorate that was the principal force for accountability in New Zealand schools from 1877 to the advent of Tomorrow's Schools. Whereas the inspectors carried out a variety of operational responsibilities, the new agency's sole function was to provide an arm's-length evaluation of how well the schools were performing. In recommending such a setup, the task force in effect abandoned a professional model of accountability aimed primarily at helping teachers deal with the teaching and learning process in favor of a more management-oriented model that would minimize the possibility of monitors being captured by the groups they were evaluating. Under the management approach, the focus is on good management practices; the major purposes are to inform boards about how well they are doing, to provide the government with information on the performance of schools, and to provide information to groups outside the system.[10]

The new agency got off to a halting start. The initial idea was that the agency would audit both the financial and the educational programs of the schools (including early childhood centers) and that it would also evaluate the quality of the policy advice that the ministry was giving to the minister of education. Early on, however, the financial function was reduced, full responsibility for financial auditing being placed with the auditor general, and the agency was stripped of its mandate to review the policy advice of the ministry.[11]

Despite a large operating budget with provision for 306 employees, the new Education Review Office initially accomplished little and had trouble determining its direction. One reason for the confusion was the decision by the first head to establish ten relatively autonomous regional offices, each with thirty employees who in many cases were carryovers

---

9. Task Force (1988: 60).

10. Willis (1992).

11. Before its start-up, the new office was called the Review and Audit Agency, but the name was changed at the last minute to the Education Review Office. The financial function was reduced in part because the failure to implement bulk funding for teachers' salaries meant that schools has less financial flexibility than had initially been intended. Butterworth and Butterworth (1998: 126–28).

from the old Department of Education. This move sent a signal that things might not be too different from the past. A 1990 review by the Lough Committee, which was set up to review all the reforms, was highly critical of the ERO and called for major restructuring and a reduction of its NZ$24 million budget by 40 percent. After a year without a permanent head, the new agency finally began to develop a sense of identity and purpose under Judith Aitken, who was hired as its chief review officer in 1992. Aitken came to the job with some background in teaching, but most of her training and experience was in public administration and strategic planning.

Evolution of the ERO Strategy

The law that established the Education Review Office provided only sketchy direction about how it should operate and what it should do. It gave power to the chief review officer to send teams into schools to obtain information and to write reports about what they found, but the agency had no authority to enforce its recommendations. The new chief review officer had a lot of flexibility to put her own stamp on the organization, which is exactly what she has done.

With a background in public management, Aitken brought a more formal approach to the review process. She began with the premise that everything done by the ERO would be public. No longer would the agency mimic the old inspectorate by working informally and privately with individual schools. Instead, it would release its findings to the media and use the pressure of public opinion as a policy tool to motivate change. She also altered the character of the review teams that would visit each school. While recognizing the importance of some practical experience in education, Aitken worked to develop a professional corps of review officers who would play a quasi-judicial role in monitoring how well teachers, administrators, and entire schools were performing. Unlike the inspectors of old, they were not to see themselves primarily as professional colleagues.

The real challenge for Aitken was to determine what the ERO should be monitoring. Her solution was to introduce two distinct types of audit: assurance and effectiveness. The assurance audits, which began in 1992, were designed to ensure that the boards of trustees were meeting their legal obligations to the Crown as specified in the school's charter, including the National Education Guidelines, and in other agreements between the state and the schools, such as the school's property agreement.[12] The relatively narrow emphasis on legal compliance meant that this type of audit focused on the link between the boards of trustees and the schools, with little attention to impacts on students or educational outcomes. The ERO wanted to know whether the boards were implementing the various policies required under the law, such as teaching the national curriculum. As Aitken told us in an interview, such a focus on compliance was essential during the early years of the Tomorrow's Schools reforms, when lay boards were still learning what was expected of them. During 1992–93, only 12 percent of the boards of trustees were operating in a fully lawful way. By 1998 the proportion was up to 90 percent.

In 1993 the ERO added the second type of audit—the effectiveness audit—to its arsenal as a means of shifting attention toward student achievement. According to official documents, an effectiveness audit is "an evaluation of student achievement and the impact of the teaching services and management practices within a school on that achievement." Such a description is a bit misleading, however, since, in the absence of national compulsory tests, the ERO has no reasonable way to compare student achievement in one school either with other schools or with national standards.

Instead, effectiveness audits are primarily process oriented and pose two specific questions to local boards of trustees: What do you expect the children in the school to learn? How will you know that learning has occurred? Thus the effect of the ERO is to encourage schools to focus on student achievement and to implement practices, such as better systems of assessing students, that would allow the trustees and the principal to gain a better sense of how much students are learning. While the reviewers spend time in classrooms and comment in their reports on the quality of teaching in schools, they lack the authority of the inspectors of the former system to evaluate individual teachers.

In 1998 the ERO began to consolidate the two types of audit into a single combined accountability review with the purpose of assisting in improving the quality of education for students. The new reviews are sup-

---

12. Early in the implementation process the working party rejected a proposal that the ERO have a role in approving school charters on the grounds that the charter should be a contract between the ministry and the schools and that, if the ERO was to provide an independent audit of the school, it should not be a party to the contract.

posed to pay less attention to the compliance issues that were so central in the early days of the Tomorrow's Schools governance reforms, to give more attention to academic outcomes, and to put more emphasis on the schools' own self-review reports. Such self-review programs are required of boards of trustees under the national administration guidelines, but they have not been very well developed.

How Schools View ERO Activities

The site visits by ERO teams and the public reports that they produce elicit a wide range of reactions from educators, parents, and board members in the affected schools. In a survey of principals of primary schools that went through ERO visits in 1995–96, Cathy Wylie found that 51 percent said that the review process had been on balance a positive experience, while 49 percent described it as more negative.[13] The average amount of time spent by the principal in preparing for the visit was 26.6 hours.

Not surprisingly, vigorous criticism—frequently outrage—has come from schools that have received negative reports that they believe are unfair. In 1995, for example, the ERO wrote a scathing review of Tangaroa College in South Auckland, a decile 1 school that had been losing students and that had experienced a good deal of internal staff turmoil. Jim Peters, a relatively new principal at the time, welcomed the report on the ground that "the report said some things that needed to be said" and that he could use it to generate pressure to change. He set out to address some of the issues and was confident that, when the ERO returned six months later to update the situation, the school would be portrayed as one that, for all its problems, was getting its act together. "But then they came back and dwelt only on the things that still had to be done," he recalled. "Instead of being recognized for what we had accomplished, we got roasted by the media again for what we had not done." Kay Hawk, one of two Massey University researchers who carried out a major study for the Ministry of Education of schooling in low-decile schools, agreed with Peters's assessment of the situation. "ERO blew it," she said. "By not talking at all about what had

---

13. Wylie (n.d.). This study was based on responses to reviews by principals who are members of the New Zealand Principals Federation who had had an ERO review in 1995–96. The sample is reasonably representative, with some underrepresentation of city schools and of very small schools.

been done over the last six months they did a lot of damage." In other situations as well, she added, "ERO has hurt schools that were actually improving."

In the early days of Tomorrow's Schools, the principal objective of the ERO was to make sure that schools had put in place procedures and policy documents that the ministry required of schools to ensure that they were governing themselves properly. Because drawing up the more than two dozen policies required was a time-consuming task for educators and trustees, a cottage industry developed in which principals, sometimes for a fee, would fax to colleagues the documents that they had drafted on topics such as how the school was protecting animal rights. A major emphasis was also placed on whether teachers were keeping adequate records on student achievement. Not surprisingly, principals criticized the ERO teams for nit-picking and creating unnecessary paperwork. Teresa Lilley, deputy principal of Mount Albert Primary School in Auckland, recalled that one of her teachers was criticized by the ERO "for not having procedures on feeding goldfish."

Most schools, especially those without significant enrollment problems, have now more or less learned to take ERO visits in stride. Jill Stanley, principal of the decile 2 Porirua School near Wellington, said that since she and her teachers routinely keep rather detailed records of student performance, they do not have to spend much time preparing for ERO visits. "It's basically a question of tidying up the records we already have," she said. She prefers current accountability methods to the former system because inspectors used to make snap judgments when evaluating teachers; she suggested that the system benefits "when someone comes in and exposes a badly managed school and forces changes to be made." On the other hand, she said, "ERO reports never told me anything I didn't already know."

The Wylie study found that 75 percent of primary school principals viewed ERO team members as either reasonably or highly professional; yet only 32 percent felt that the review team had sufficient understanding of the particular needs of their school, and 24 percent thought the team had no such understanding. A general view among teachers and principals seems to be that ERO reports are not particularly helpful on really important issues relating to teaching and learning. "Teachers find the ERO people very off-putting," said Dennis Thompson, principal of Lyall Bay Primary School in Wellington. "Some of the people are not familiar with primary education. They come in the classroom not sure of what they are looking for, and some of the statements they make are not well founded. There is nothing that the school gets out of the process. We have had three glowing reports, and the only recommendation from the most recent one told us that the gate on the swimming pool swings the wrong way."

One paradoxical effect of the ERO has been to create a certain nostalgia for the old inspectors. "We used to have one attached to the school, and he got personally involved in what was going on," recalled Ashley Blair, principal of Cannon's Creek School in Porirua. "He had educational vision and was my mentor. He didn't just carry out a cold and impersonal inspection."

Another review of the ERO, this one sponsored by the Post Primary Teachers' Association, also found mixed responses. Respondents complained that schools sometimes put their efforts into compliance rather than genuine school improvement. They reiterated complaints that review teams do not put enough emphasis on what goes on in classrooms and suggested that the resulting media reporting feeds a negative view of the teaching profession.[14]

ERO as the Conscience of the System

As a review agency that is independent of both the Ministry of Education and the schools and that reports directly to the minister of education, the Education Review Office has no direct impact on the policies proposed and implemented by the ministry.[15] Indeed, Parliament specifically prohibited the agency from offering comments on the quality of the advice that the ministry provided to the minister, a function that was part of its original mandate under Tomorrow's Schools. Instead the ERO affects ministry policy only indirectly.

Aitken has chosen to use the power and visibility of the ERO specifically to challenge national educational policies and to focus public attention on large structural problems encompassing groups of schools. Her

14. Auckland Uniservices Limited (1997). This review is based on an analysis of documents supplemented by school and regional case studies and a survey of schools. The overall study design is not clear.

15. More precisely, it reports to the minister responsible for the Education Review Office, who could be the associate minister of education, as it was in 1997 and 1998.

method was to publish a series of high-profile reports on different aspects of the state educational system. Between 1996 and 1998, the ERO released three reports on groups of schools in the urban area of South Auckland, on the East Coast, and in Northland. In doing so, the ERO sought to balance its narrow purpose of evaluating individual schools with the goal of addressing larger structural problems. As Aitken put it in a conversation with the authors, "It has been a struggle to get the ministry [of education] to understand that the school is not a great unit to focus on. Compare the successful firm. It has a lot of vertical and horizontal linkages to other firms."

The first and most controversial of these reports, and the one of most interest for this book because of its urban angle, focused on the forty-five schools in the two South Auckland suburbs of Mangere and Otara, most of which served highly disadvantaged and overwhelmingly minority student bodies.[16] The ERO concluded that 42 percent of the schools in these areas were performing very poorly or were underperforming and that 27 percent were in the highest category of risk because they had required at least one follow-up review by the ERO. Low-performing schools, according to the ERO, are typically those in which there are failures of governance by the board of trustees or failures in management by the principal. Despite the many negative individual ERO reports on specific schools in South Auckland, the schools were not improving.

Believing that the problems facing many of the schools were too large to be addressed by the schools alone, Aitken convinced her divided agency to make a public political statement that would embarrass the ministry into action. The August 1996 report in effect described the South Auckland schools as a disaster area characterized by rampant failure in governance and management. Trying to be constructive, the ERO couched its policy recommendations in ways that it hoped would be acceptable to a ministry not oriented toward intervention. For example, it called for the establishment of a strategic development center that would serve as a broker for the management services needed by the South Auckland schools, exit incentives for poor teachers, and recruitment incentives for new, higher-quality teachers.

The report was met with outrage in South Auckland. The local principals, including principals at schools that the ERO proclaimed to be rela-

16. Education Review Office (1996).

tively successful, were distressed at the agency's apparent insensitivity to the severity of the educational challenges they faced, many of which they linked to middle-class flight that was well beyond the power of schools to control. The two teachers' unions and the principals' association were also enraged at what they viewed as unfair criticisms of schools and teachers. Parents, too, thought the report was unfair and charged that it inappropriately singled out their schools for criticism. In addition, academics criticized the report on grounds similar to those raised by the principals: that it failed to take sufficient account of the context in which the schools operate and focused its recommendations too much on management issues.[17]

The ERO report had a major impact on discussions within the ministry and ultimately prompted the government to establish a NZ$19 million program aimed at assisting troubled urban schools. Contrary to the hopes of the ERO, however, the ministry did not adopt any of its proposals related to recruitment of teachers, opting instead for a focus on management and community engagement.

Subsequent reports of this type focused on twenty very rural schools in the East Coast and seventy-eight schools in Northland. Like South Auckland, these areas have high proportions of minority and low-income students. Unlike South Auckland, many of the problems faced by these schools emerge from their geographic isolation, the poor state of their regional economies, and the multiple roles that even very small schools play in local communities. The East Coast report has encouraged the ministry to consider new ways of organizing school resources in that area, which might involve new forms of shared administration.[18]

ERO as Promoter of Good Educational Practices

Under Judith Aitken, the Education Review Office has also come to see itself as the provider of general information on education to help schools do their jobs more effectively. It uses the information it gleans from its individual school reports to distill what works and what does not work in the teaching and learning process. Some of its periodic reports were written for principals and teachers and for members of boards of trustees

---

17. Thrupp (1997a).
18. Howard Fancy, interview with authors, Victoria University of Wellington, April 17, 1998.

who must oversee them (*Professional Leadership in Primary Schools; Core Competencies for School Principals; The Capable Teacher*). Others were addressed to parents (*Choosing a School for a Five-Year-Old; Choosing a Secondary School*), while still others were focused on general issues related to teaching and learning (*Addressing Barriers to Learning; Students at Risk*). All are public documents available on the Internet.

An official review of the ERO in 1997 praised these publications and reported that they are regarded highly and are helpful in describing best practice and in generating debate on a variety of issues.[19] An alternative perspective on these reports appears in a 1997 analysis of the ERO commissioned by the Post Primary Teachers' Association, the union for secondary school teachers. The authors criticize the ERO for promoting a "good practice" model of schooling that is conservative, rather than a "best practice" model, which they argue would be potentially more progressive.[20] They also assert that while the ERO claims that its reports are asocial and apolitical, they define the concept of a good teacher and a good school through middle-class lenses.

These two viewpoints highlight one of the tensions that inevitably arises in a decentralized system. On the one hand, the government says it wants schools to be innovative and creative. On the other, there is no doubt that many schools could benefit from some guidance about what approaches might make sense. The danger is that, in giving that guidance, the government may be thwarting innovation by sending signals about what it expects the schools to do.

Would National Tests at the Primary Level Improve Accountability?

As head of the Education Review Office, Aitken is quick to express her frustration at the absence of test data that would allow the ERO—and for that matter, principals, teachers, and boards of trustees of local schools—to compare the performance of students against national norms. No such information is typically available until students reach the age of fifteen and take the school certificate exam, and even that test is not mandatory. For many students, failure on that exam comes as a brutal reality check, one that has particularly serious consequences these days, given the dis-

19. Austin Report (1997: 7).
20. Auckland Uniservices Limited (1997: 5).

appearance of jobs for school dropouts. Aitken believes that students should be evaluated earlier so that schools will have greater incentives to meet their needs along the way.[21]

Aitken is not alone in pushing for more national testing. Both political parties have recently supported some form of national testing at the primary level, and the government has put forth a specific proposal to be implemented in 1999.[22] However, any such proposal must overcome Kiwi educators' long-standing and serious concerns about national tests, including fears that they will narrow the curriculum and will lead to invidious and inappropriate comparisons among schools

BACKGROUND: THE NATIONAL EDUCATION MONITORING PROJECT.   As part of his commitment to curriculum and assessment reform, Lockwood Smith proposed early in his term as minister of education in 1990 that New Zealand follow the lead of England, which had recently introduced a system of mandatory national testing at four points during a student's schooling.[23] Smith wanted such tests to provide information for three purposes: diagnosing the progress of individual students, evaluating the performance of schools, and monitoring the educational performance of the nation as a whole.

In late 1991 six experts on assessment paid a visit to the minister and convinced him that New Zealand should not follow the lead of England, which at that time was experiencing an extensive backlash from its required testing.[24] They recommended instead that assessment of individual

---

21. Judith Aitken, interview with authors, Wellington, April 1998.

22. A Labour Party announcement that it might introduce reading, science, and math tests for all ten-year-olds induced the government to announce that it was about to release a similar proposal, which it did in May 1998. Interestingly, an article about the two proposals carried the following negative headline, "Tests to Measure Schools' Failure," *New Zealand Education Review*, March 25, 1998, p. 1. As of this writing (late 1999), this proposal for national testing has not been implemented. Instead, it was replaced with a pilot project to test nine- and eleven-year-olds in 125 schools.

23. In 1989, the fourth Labour government set up a working group, called Project Able, to recommend an assessment system to monitor the effectiveness of the New Zealand school system on student learning and to assess the effectiveness of individual schools with particular attention to the country's dual cultural heritage. That effort was derailed with the change in government in 1990. See Willis (1992) for an insightful evaluation of the working group's efforts.

24. Terry Crooks, interview with authors, Dunedin, April 22, 1998. Crooks was a member of that delegation and subsequently the head of the National Monitoring Project.

students be left in the hands of teachers and that New Zealand establish a national monitoring system based on a random sample of schools and of students within schools. The downside of this proposal from the minister's perspective was that it included no data on outcomes by school. He believed such information was needed both because the government had an obligation to monitor schools and because such information would be helpful to parents in deciding which school would be best for their child. Nonetheless, he essentially accepted the proposal and established the National Education Monitoring Project.

The project started in 1993 and finished the first cycle of testing two years later. The assessments, which are very hands-on and include team projects, generate a mountain of information, including information from videos, on students in year four (ages eight to nine) and year eight (ages twelve to thirteen). Students are also asked about their attitudes toward the various subjects. Each year the project covers about one-quarter of the curriculum, with one-third of the tasks kept constant from year to year to allow measurement of changes in student performance over time. Overall reports of how students perform various tasks provide detailed information to educators about the strengths and weaknesses of New Zealand students' understanding of various parts of the compulsory curriculum and permit comparisons among certain subgroups of the population.[25] Because the first four-year cycle is still in progress, longitudinal data on whether the system is improving are not yet available.

FILLING THE GAP WITH MANDATORY NATIONAL TESTS.   A May 1998 policy paper circulated for discussion by the National Party government makes the case for mandatory national tests at three levels in primary schools. First, it argues that such tests would be useful to teachers. Without such tests, teachers waste a lot of time developing their own assessment devices, and when they do they are unable to determine how their expectations for student performance compare with national expectations. Of particular concern is the performance of children at risk. Without a national assessment system, says the paper, teachers in a school serving

---

25. Across subgroups of the population, the findings are not very surprising. In reading, for example, results were poorer for students in low-decile than in high-decile schools and were poorer for boys than for girls; the gap between Maori and non-Maori performance was more marked for reading than for other curriculum areas. Ministry of Education (1998b: 73).

disadvantaged students are unable to compare the performance of their children to similar children elsewhere in the country. Second, such tests would be useful to boards of trustees and principals responsible for ensuring that school programs are effective. Third, the government could use the test results to formulate national policy and policy for specific groups and to monitor its effectiveness. The government is also concerned about the relative underachievement of Maori and Pacific Island students.[26] Interestingly, as a treasury official pointed out to us, the document makes no reference to the need of parents for information of this type, perhaps because of the ministry's concern that parents may misuse the test results. This official believed, however, that some information for parents is better than none.

The ministry is, in fact, quite concerned about the misuse of test results, and not only by the parents. Officials fear that either parents or schools might place undue weight on average test results as a measure of school effectiveness when, in fact, the tests would measure only a small fraction of the important school outcomes. The government is particularly concerned about the possibility that newspapers will report the results in the form of "league tables" that rank the schools by their average results. Because test results tend to be highly correlated with the socioeconomic backgrounds of the students, the publication of such tables could exacerbate the movement from low-decile to high-decile schools. To forestall the publication of league tables, the government intends to avoid presenting the results for each school in numerical form. Instead, it is talking about using a graphical form that obscures the precise numbers while still providing a useful visual picture of how the school is performing both absolutely and in relation both to schools with similar mixes of students and to the nation as a whole.[27] Despite the government's intentions, a subsequent ERO report on testing suggested that league tables were inevitable.[28]

Test results could also be misused by the ERO as it evaluates the performance of schools. For low-decile schools in particular, the danger is that in evaluating the test results, the ERO might fail to take sufficient account of the magnitude of the educational challenges faced by a school with

26. Ministry of Education (1998a: 12–16).
27. Ministry of Education (1998a: 25–26).
28. Gerritson (1998: 1).

low-performing students. Ample precedent for this concern can be found in its South Auckland report, which dismissed socioeconomic explanations for the poor performance of some low-decile schools on the ground that other low-decile schools were doing well. Critics say that the ERO disregarded evidence that the better-performing schools served a somewhat more advantaged group of students and may have had other factors working in their favor.[29] The best way to address this problem would be for the government to test every student every year and to use those results to estimate value-added measures for each school. To date, however, there has not been much talk in New Zealand about estimating value-added measures of school effectiveness.

Although the final form of the testing policy is not yet known, it seems likely that New Zealand will soon introduce some form of national tests at the primary level. From Aitken's perspective such tests will be a welcome and a necessary addition to the tools available to the ERO, and they will allow that office for the first time to focus on student outcomes as measured by test scores. Because the new tests will be given only at selected grades, however, interpretation of the test results will be confounded by the changing mix of students in those classes over time.

Schools as Agents of the State: Assumptions

At least four assumptions or strongly held views appear to underlie the way the government has been implementing the decentralized management of the country's school system and defining the relationship between the center and local schools. While one of them was explicitly part of the original conception of Tomorrow's Schools, the others became more explicit as the reforms took shape under the guidance of a politically conservative government.

The first assumption is that schools can get along without the government-provided advice and support systems that were available in the former system. The second is the government's belief that good school management and governance are the key to educational success. Third is the view that public information is a powerful and effective policy lever. Fourth, and perhaps most important, is the view that the government has

29. Thrupp (1997a: 153).

no responsibility to provide special support for struggling schools. In response to intense public pressure, the government is now rethinking the validity of this last view.

Limited Assistance and Support for the Typical School

School officials complain that almost completely absent from the new system is the advice and counseling that had often been provided by the regional school inspectors. The ERO was set up as a monitoring agency, not an agency to provide advice and guidance. In its 1994 annual report, the ERO explicitly acknowledged that schools and educational professionals were increasingly calling for more advice and believed that they had few sources to which to turn. The ERO's response is interesting. First, it noted that schools do have means of getting advice now from various sources. The only difference now is that much of that advice is no longer free.[30] As long as schools can figure out what advice they need and are prepared to pay for it, they can get it.

Second, the report argued that in fact the ERO does provide advice—to individual schools in the form of recommendations for action and to schools in general in the form of its reports on good school practices.[31] To some extent that is accurate. However, with respect to "advice" in the school reports, schools might well not interpret something labeled as "actions required to meet legal obligations and undertakings" as the type of wisdom they need and seek. More like advice is the second category of "suggested developments" that appears in some ERO reports. Reviewers have urged boards, for example, to implement staff appraisal policies, to establish long-term maintenance plans, and to ensure that the mathematics program addresses all requirements of the national curriculum. With respect to the general information on school practices, schools may still lack the school-specific advice and personnel actions that might help them address sticky internal conflicts.

An official review of the ERO in 1997 confirmed that because the ERO is an evaluation and audit agency, it "would be inappropriate for the Edu-

---

30. Some free advice is also available in the form of advisory services provided by the colleges of education and financed by the government. However, this advice is limited and has not been very effective. Butterworth and Butterworth (1998: 130).

31. Education Review Office (1994: 13–14).

cation Review Office to have an advice and guidance function or to be involved in enforcement."[32] However, in partial recognition of the general problem, the report recommended that, as a normal part of its reporting procedure, the ERO include a section on the sources of advice and guidance available in the local area. More significantly, it recommended that the Ministry of Education "establish a range of actions to assist schools where action is required to improve the management and delivery of education."[33]

Good Management as the Key to Educational Success

For all the reasons discussed above, including the absence of outcome measures, the ERO has placed a tremendous amount of emphasis on management and process issues in its review of individual schools. Not surprisingly, as illustrated by the report on the South Auckland schools described above, it has maintained that emphasis in its reports on groups of struggling schools. That report enumerates failures of the following types: governance failure (as evidenced by inactive or ineffective trustees), management failure (in the form of incomplete management systems and lack of professional leadership within the schools), ineffective management of teachers' performance (including the inability of the boards to discipline teachers), and failures of resource management. To be fair to the ERO, the report also includes some failures related to teaching, but even in this category it focuses on managerial and process issues such as the quality of teachers' planning, systems for assessing students, and whether the national curriculum is being delivered.

This focus on governance and management reflects the ERO's belief that such factors are key determinants of educational quality. In its 1993–94 Annual Report, the ERO stated: "The quality of school governance and management is a reliable indicator of the quality of educational services provided. . . . Poorly governed and poorly managed schools which employ relatively low-performing staff do not provide an effective environment for children's education."[34] Implicit in this statement is the view that improving school governance and management is both a necessary and a sufficient condition for improving school outcomes. The view that good

32. Austin Report (1997: 9).
33. Austin Report (1997: 11–12).
34. Education Review Office (1994: 6).

management may be necessary, or at least desirable, is probably accept-able to most people, although one could point to schools that are poorly managed by ERO standards but still provide a stimulating learning envi-ronment for children. Indeed, even the ERO's own report on South Auckland provides some support for the alternative view that good man-agement is not necessary. The report states that in 45 percent of the schools in which governance or management weaknesses were identified, the ERO considered the quality of teaching to be of a reasonable standard.[35]

More problematic is the idea that good management is sufficient to ensure that a good education is being delivered. This concern is particu-larly valid for South Auckland schools, where the educational problems faced by the schools are overwhelming because of the high concentra-tions of difficult-to-educate students they serve and because of the ob-stacles they face in recruiting and retaining high-quality teachers. Although to its credit the ERO highlights their recruiting and retention problem and makes some recommendations to address it, most of its recommen-dations have a more technocratic and management focus.[36] The proposed strategic development center, for example, would provide only short-term management assistance and would bring with it additional compliance and accountability requirements.[37] The ERO's focus on management, the reader should be reminded, should not be attributed to that agency alone. Instead, it mirrors the views of the Treasury Department and the Ministry of Education.

This focus on managerial performance has some clear downsides, es-pecially for schools serving low socioeconomic status students. The power of the ERO reports is such that even if the schools are providing a reason-able quality of teaching, public highlighting of the management prob-lems weakens a school's reputation and may exacerbate its problems by encouraging even more flight from the school. In addition, the efforts necessary to comply with the government requirements may put even greater stress on already overworked principals. Most important, how-

35. Education Review Office (1996: 13).

36. It is difficult to determine the extent to which the choice of policy recommenda-tions reflects the ERO's beliefs alone or rather the orientation of the ministry. As Judith Aitken reported to us, the ERO tried to couch the recommendations in ways that the ministry might find acceptable. Aitken, interview with authors.

37. Thrupp (1997a).

ever, the focus shifts attention away from the real causes of the failures and the policy recommendations that might have a chance of successfully addressing them.

Public Information as a Policy Lever

One of the first changes that Aitken made in the operation of the ERO was to make all reports public and to encourage the local newspapers and television stations to publicize them. Given that the ERO had no enforcement power, she viewed public information as the main policy tool available to her to induce the schools to improve. Schools would be more likely to try to ensure positive ERO reports, she reasoned, if they knew they were going to be affected by what they contained. Public reporting would have an impact on them in at least two ways. First, it would affect schools' reputations and, more important, the professional reputations of school officials. For ambitious principals and teachers, being at a school with positive ERO reports would have major benefits. Second, it could have an impact on how attractive the school was to potential students and their parents.

But are the outcomes of such a public process always the appropriate ones? Do the public reports always elicit the desired behavior? And are they fair? To the extent that the reports focus on the symptoms of much larger problems outside the control of the schools, they may do a disservice to the school's officials. That helps explain the tremendous anger of South Auckland principals at the release of the report on South Auckland schools. In addition, the distinction between managerial effectiveness and teaching quality can be important. The danger is that a school—and the principal and teachers within it—gets a bad rap in the press because of managerial ineffectiveness despite the fact that it is providing a reasonable level of educational services.

Two reviews of the ERO come to opposite conclusions about the relative benefits and costs of the use of public information as a policy lever in this context. A 1997 report commissioned by the teachers' union highlights the concerns of teachers that arise from the fact that media reporting tends to be fragmentary and crisis oriented. The effect is to highlight the negative, to create a compliance mentality in the schools, and to contribute to a perception of schooling in crisis. In addition, public reports on failing schools, many of which are low decile, are likely to exacerbate the decline.[38] By contrast, the official review of the ERO fully endorses its legal obligation to make all final reports available to the media. At the same time, it proposes procedural changes designed to minimize some of the adverse effects that have occurred in the past. These changes would include a longer time for schools to respond to the initial report so they can be ready with an action plan to address the report's recommendations. The final version would include not only the school's action plan but also an introduction prepared by the schools describing the context in which it operates, brief details of significant achievements since the last review, and issues on which the school is working. These proposed changes are intended to maximize the chances that a negative report will lead the schools to improve their practices while minimizing the chances that the public will respond by giving up on the school.

Lack of Support for Struggling Schools

Many schools, especially low-decile schools, are struggling under the burdens of self-governance. It is reasonable to ask what provisions the government has established to ensure that struggling or weak schools get the special support they need to carry out their roles as agents in an effective manner. Strikingly, there appears to be little room in New Zealand's conception of decentralized school governance for the buttressing of weak schools.

In essence, New Zealand chose an essentially noninterventionist strategy on the ground that schools should be able to function autonomously within the appropriate overall policy environment. While the government recognized early on that some schools may need some prodding to improve school governance and management and, in extreme cases, to have their boards replaced by an appointed commissioner, the government has been reluctant to accept the possibility that the problems may go deeper than management. Treasury officials appear to be the most adamant on this issue and the most unsympathetic to the plight of struggling schools. If schools cannot compete effectively in the new educational marketplace, there must be a management problem; any attempt to solve the problem by buttressing the school could prove counterproductive in the long run by promoting inefficiency in the provision of education.

---

38. Auckland Uniservices Limited (1997: 7).

The Ministry of Education has begun to acknowledge the nature and magnitude of the problems faced by many schools in areas like South Auckland and to develop strategies for intervening. Even in situations in which it recognizes that the system is failing, however, the ministry has taken the approach that good management will solve the problems, an approach about which we have some serious reservations.

6 | *Funding of Schools*

From the outset of the Tomorrow's Schools reforms no one questioned the idea that the state should continue to fund primary and secondary schools in New Zealand. The only major issues were how state funds were to be allocated among schools and who would control the way they were spent. In this chapter we look at the ways in which the move to self-governing schools altered the funding arrangements between the government and local schools.

The Picot task force argued that if self-governing schools were to be in a position to exercise their new responsibilities, they needed maximum control over their spending. It thus proposed that state funds be allocated directly to schools in the form of a block grant, which schools could spend as they wished. The new funding arrangement of Tomorrow's Schools would be elegant in its simplicity: the state would provide the money and the schools would spend it.

Such an arrangement differs significantly from the former system, in which the Department of Education either tightly controlled specific components of school spending or reimbursed schools for their actual spending. The task force had heard abundant testimony about how such an arrangement led to wasteful and inefficient spending, especially in primary schools. The compartmentalization of funding by budget category meant that a school facing a major illiteracy problem could not, for example, shift funds from its book budget to a tutoring project. Chapter 2 mentions "mysterious packages" that would arrive at schools from the Department of Education containing school supplies that were neither ordered nor needed. In those budget areas, such as utilities, for which the department fully reimbursed primary schools for their actual spending, schools had little incentive to use resources efficiently. The task force found that primary schools on average spent 30 percent more for heat, light, and water than secondary schools, which had a different funding arrangement, and that, for the same reason, maintenance costs per square meter in primary schools were 82 percent higher.[1]

The proposed separation of the funding and spending functions in education was fully consistent with the spirit of other public sector reforms occurring in New Zealand at the time. Those reforms were designed to establish explicit contractual relationships between the government and the agencies from which it was purchasing services, ranging from air traffic control to health care. Under the new arrangements, the government would contract with agencies to provide certain outputs for a given amount of funding, and the agencies would be free to determine the best way to provide the mutually agreed upon quantity of services.[2]

One problem confronting Tomorrow's Schools was that education did not fit neatly into this new output-oriented contractual framework. The educational outputs that the government cared about were not easily measurable. Moreover, schools were supposed to define additional outputs valued by their school communities. This lack of precision about what the central government was purchasing made it virtually impossible—and fiscally risky—for the government to behave as if were purchasing the paving of a street. Thus instead of agreeing to provide enough money "to enable the board of trustees to meet the requirements of the charter," the government reverted to the wording of the 1989 Education Act, which simply established "the legal responsibility of the Minister to provide" funding for schools. For all practical purposes, the boards of trustees of local schools were simply instructed to do the best they could with the resources available to them in fulfilling both their local goals and the mandatory national educational objectives.

Many at the local school level believe that the resulting funding arrange-

---

1. Task Force (1988: 33).
2. Boston and others (1996).

ment is neither adequate nor equitable. Moreover block granting to schools of the funds for teachers' salaries turned out to be highly problematic and has taken nearly a decade to be implemented in a substantial number of schools. The controversy over bulk funding of the salaries grant illustrates the tensions that arise in a decentralized educational system.

How Schools Are Funded

Consistent with the recommendations of the Picot task force report, the *Tomorrow's Schools* policy paper called for schools to be funded by a bulk grant with two components, one for teachers' salaries and the other for other operating expense, with each component based on its own separate funding formula.[3] While full bulk funding was written into the new legislation, serious resistance by the teachers' unions and a variety of political considerations induced the government to delay implementing the salaries portion of the block grant.

Funding for schools has thus been divided into two main parts. Each school receives an operations grant to be used for budget lines that do not involve teachers' salaries. In addition, it receives an entitlement to hire a specified number of teachers, who are paid directly by the Ministry of Education. Schools supplement this public funding with additional funds from local sources. Because the government continues to own the facilities, the government pays directly for large capital projects.

The Salary Component

Each school's allotment of teachers is based on its student roll, differentiated by grade level. Through this mechanism, the ministry establishes a minimum number of teachers for each school based on policy decisions about the appropriate student-teacher ratio for students at various grade levels.[4] Schools then make their own decisions about whom to hire, and the salary for each teacher they select is then determined by a national

---

3. *Tomorrow's Schools* (1988: sec. 1.3.1).

4. As of February 1, 1996, the teacher-student ratios were as follows: 1:23 for school years one through three; 1:29 for years four through eight; 1:25 for years nine and ten; 1:23 for year eleven; 1:18 for year twelve; and 1:17 for year thirteen. Ministry of Education (1995).

salary schedule negotiated by the teachers' unions and the government. Payments to the teachers are made electronically directly by the ministry.[5]

Two features of this method for funding teachers are worth highlighting. First, the cost to the ministry of maintaining faculties varies across schools depending on which teachers the schools hire. A school that is able to attract experienced teachers receives more overall salary funding than a comparable school that hires less-experienced teachers. Senior teachers like this system because the schools have no financial incentive to replace them with less-experienced teachers with a lower salary scale. Second, schools have a strong incentive to hire their full allotment of teachers each period. Schools cannot bank teachers' pay for a subsequent period, so failure to hire their entire allotment of teachers means that part of the allotment is wasted. Schools have some flexibility in hiring additional staff beyond the entitlement, using their operations grant—and many schools do so—but the small size of the operations grant does not give them much leeway.

The Operations Grant

The operations grant is designed to provide funding for all other components of a school's budget, from books and swing sets to the salaries of nonteaching staff. Although the schools are empowered to use the money however they wish, the amount of money each school receives is a cumulative amount based on a series of formulas that apply to the individual components of the operations grant, a fact that creates some tensions. The majority of the funds are distributed based on student rolls, but some components take into account other school characteristics, such as size of property, entitlement to teachers, and number of Maori students in language programs.

For primary schools the major components of the operations grant and their shares of the total are as follows: basic funding, also referred to as per pupil funding, 56.4 percent; base funding, 7.4 percent; targeted fund-

---

5. The ability to make all the payments electronically is central to making the whole system work. The Ministry of Education deposits money for salaries directly into teachers' bank accounts and funds for schools directly into schools' bank accounts. Eric Pederson, senior manager, Early Childhood and Schools Resourcing, interview with authors, Wellington, March 16, 1998.

ing for educational achievement, 8.9 percent; maintenance and minor capital works, 8.9 percent; and relief teachers' funding, 7.1 percent. Other components include such categories as funding for heat, light, and water; vandalism; Maori language programs; and special education. For secondary schools, the categories are similar, with the addition of special programs to provide career information.[6]

PER PUPIL FUNDING AND BASE FUNDING.   The per pupil funding component is based on the assumption that the appropriate level for a school's operations spending depends mainly on the number of students in the school. To account for the fact that older students typically require more equipment and other resources than younger students, the per pupil funding amounts are set at four levels, with the funding for the oldest students about 50 percent higher than that for the lowest levels.[7] The base funding component recognizes the diseconomies of scale in small schools, many of which are tiny and located in remote rural areas. The two elements of the formula provide opposite incentives. For all but the smallest schools in urban areas, the per pupil funding component dominates and provides an incentive for schools to attract more students under the plausible assumption that the additional operational costs associated with the additional students are less than the average costs per pupil. For small rural schools, the base funding component provides a disincentive for schools to merge, a point that has been noted with some concern by policymakers in Wellington.[8]

TARGETED FUNDING FOR EDUCATIONAL ACHIEVEMENT.   Perhaps the most noteworthy aspect of the funding system is that it explicitly directs additional funding to the schools facing the most significant educational challenges. The targeting is based on the decile rankings of schools (described in chapter 4). Recall that the rankings categorize the schools according to six variables that researchers have found to be correlated with achievement. Low-decile schools have far greater concentrations of children from low socioeconomic backgrounds and minority groups. To offset the educational challenges faced by those schools, they receive significantly more targeted funding for educational achievement (TFEA) than high-decile schools.

6. Pole (1997: 4–5).
7. Pole (1997: table 10-4).
8. Pole (1999: 246).

When set up in 1989, the operations grant did not include this formula-based compensatory component, although even then it was anticipated.[9] The TFEA program was introduced in the mid-1990s to rationalize a set of ad hoc programs that had evolved to provide funds to schools serving disproportionate numbers of disadvantaged students. Resources under those programs typically required burdensome annual reapplications and were often distributed because of the arguments made rather than demonstrated need.[10] As a result, some of the neediest schools received no assistance. Also, as is so often the case with such programs, the targeting of the funds had been diluted as political considerations widened the pool of eligible schools.

Under the leadership of Nicholas Pole, its respected and savvy senior manager of data management and analysis, the Ministry of Education developed and implemented the decile approach to classifying schools. This approach was based on careful research that identified empirical links between student achievement and various socioeconomic and ethnic characteristics of students. The goal was to develop objective measures of school need that would not be subject to political tinkering, that would be relatively simple, and that could serve as the basis for block grants that would not impose any additional administrative burdens on the schools. The decile system has generally been well accepted and has served as the basis for distributing TFEA money since 1995.

As anyone who works with school funding formulas might expect, however, the distribution of these funds has not been free from political pressure. It is one thing to develop an objective measure of need for classifying schools. It is another to determine how to distribute the funds across categories, especially in a zero-sum situation in which more funds for some categories means less money for schools in a higher category. In sharp contrast to the typical ministry approach, Pole consulted fully with the relevant interest groups and persuaded them to buy into the methodology and to support his proposal that the available funds be channeled to schools in the lowest three deciles. However, Lockwood Smith, the minister of education, found that degree of targeting to be politically unacceptable because too many schools received no funding. He changed the distribution so that schools in deciles 1–6 would obtain funding, albeit in a sharply

9. Funding Working Group (n.d.: 23).
10. Pole (1999: 237).

Table 6-1. *Targeted Funding for Educational Achievement, per Pupil, by School Decile, 1998*[a]

NZ dollars

Decile	Amount
1	281.00
2	168.00
3	94.33
4	55.50
5	42.84
6	34.68
7	26.52
8	17.34
9	10.71
10	0.00

Source: Ministry of Education (1998c).

a. The amounts for deciles 1 to 4 represent averages of amounts for three subcategories within each decile.

declining manner. By 1998, the distribution was expanded up the decile rankings even further to include schools in all deciles except for the highest (see table 6-1). While Pole would have preferred to concentrate the funds on the lowest deciles, he still takes pride in the fact that the schools in the lowest deciles receive much more assistance than high-decile schools.

Local Funding

Schools are also encouraged to raise additional revenue from local sources. Those sources include fees from parents, net revenue from fundraising activities, and revenue from foreign fee-paying students. The ministry typically reports gross revenue from these sources as local revenue and the cost of raising such funds as expenditures. As a source of funding, the appropriate measure is net revenue, which is gross revenue minus the cost of raising the funds, since that is the amount available for funding other parts of the school budget.

Funding for Special Education

Funding for special education is still evolving and has emerged as one of the most controversial aspects of school finance. Like most developed countries, New Zealand has increasingly come to believe that children with special educational needs are best served by programs that integrate them as much as possible into the regular classroom.[11] To make funding consistent with the goal of inclusion, while at the same time recognizing the large needs of some children, New Zealand's current policy, called Special Education 2000, established a new funding program with two components, one to fund the additional costs associated with students with moderate special needs and one for the costs of students with severe needs.

The first component provides block grants to schools and is intended to give the school the flexibility necessary to meet the special needs of their students in whatever way they believe is best. Since 1997 this grant has been distributed to all schools primarily on the basis of a school's total roll, with the amount of the per pupil grant varying inversely with the decile ranking of the school. Thus, for example, in 1998 all schools received base funding for special education of NZ$1,000 plus a per pupil amount that declined from NZ$51 in decile 1 schools to NZ$24 in decile 10 schools.[12] The second component provides funding on behalf of individual students in the form of an individual entitlement that can be used in any school they choose. The latter component was designed to provide more choice for students with severe disabilities by making it possible for them to attend a regular school rather than a special school for disabled children.

These new funding arrangements have raised some serious concerns. First, advocates for students with special needs worry that the government's interest in minimizing its financial exposure may result in a tight cap on the share of total funding for special education available for students with severe disabilities, thereby denying some of those students access to the funding and the services to which they are entitled.

Second, the block granting of the rest of the money provides undesirable incentives for individual schools and could easily lead to gross inequities across schools. The larger per pupil funding for low-decile schools appropriately recognizes that, within the population as a whole, students with special needs are disproportionately represented among families with lower socioeconomic status. However, the funding strategy does not account for the fact that, within a given decile of school, some schools are

11. Brown (1996: 143–45).
12. Ministry of Education (1998c).

likely to end up with much larger proportions of needy children than others. Given the small size of schools, this outcome could simply occur by chance. Alternatively, it could reflect the responses of the schools to the incentives of the funding program. A school can improve its financial situation by admitting as few children with special needs as possible. Despite the smaller number, it will continue to receive the same size block grant. While not legally allowed to turn away such children, schools undoubtedly do so in a variety of ways. During an interview with the child's parents the principal might simply point out that the school is less well equipped than another nearby school to meet their child's needs. There is a real danger that schools that gain a reputation as being open to such children will end up with more children than they have funding for and that others will end up with few such children.

Capital Funding

When operational authority was shifted from the former Department of Education to the new boards of trustees of each school, the government retained ownership of the school buildings and land. By maintaining control of the facilities, the government avoided placing the burden of capital spending on the schools, a lumpy expenditure burden that would have been difficult to fund equitably through block grants to the schools. Under the new arrangement, the schools took over responsibility for routine maintenance of the buildings out of their operations grant, and the government maintained responsibility for major renovations, modernization, and new facilities. In contrast to Crown-owned schools, Roman Catholic and other integrated schools own their own facilities, are responsible for their own capital costs, and are allowed to charge a compulsory fee to cover them. The government has on occasion paid for new facilities at integrated schools. For example, it recently purchased modular classrooms for Roman Catholic schools with the understanding that they could be moved elsewhere in the future as required by enrollment patterns.

Of course, not all Crown-owned schools had the same quality of facilities at the time of the transfer of authority. In the normal course of the government's capital program in the pre–Tomorrow's Schools period, some schools would have recently benefited from modernization of their facilities while others could have expected upgrades in subsequent years. Recognizing its responsibility to put schools on a level playing field, the ministry surveyed all schools in 1989–90 and promised to provide the needed upgrades over a period of years. In addition, the ministry took responsibility for all new capital projects with more than a ten-year life. Currently, it also provides financial assistance program for small capital projects on a sliding scale, with a larger government share for low-decile than for high-decile schools.

Government Funding of Private Schools

Because many schools that had been private were integrated into the public school system in 1975, only 3.5 percent of New Zealand school-children currently attend private schools. Since 1975, the remaining private schools have received some public subsidies. The subsidies have varied over time, with the Labour government reducing them significantly in the late 1980s. When the National Party returned to power in 1991, it restored the cuts and promised to increase the subsidies. In 1995, the National government changed the subsidies from a proportion of salaries to a proportion of the average costs of educating a pupil in a state school and increased funding on the grounds that independent schools "make a dynamic contribution to meeting the substantial growth in student numbers and meeting the more diverse needs of a modern education system."[13] In 1998, this subsidy represented 25 percent of comparable state school costs for years one through ten and 40 percent for years eleven and twelve. In 1999, the subsidy for years one through ten was increased again to 30 percent.

The minister of education in 1995 when the subsidies were increased was Lockwood Smith, and his motives were clear. The increased funding was designed to increase choice and to pave the way for a voucher system in education. Smith's 1995 budget briefing papers to the prime minister stated that the changed funding arrangements for private schools would "help establish the concept of a portable entitlement to schooling."[14] As a prototype for that system, the National government also introduced a small voucher program in 1996 with initial funding for three years. The targeted individual entitlement (TIE) scheme provides government funding

13. Birch (1995: 9).
14. This information was obtained under the Official Information Act by United member of Parliament Margaret Austin and reported in Laxon (1996).

for up to 160 new students a year from low-income families to attend private schools; by 1998 about 600 students were participating in the program. Under this program, eligible students apply to private schools, and the schools select which students they want. Although most students enter the TIE program as new entrants and primary school students, secondary schools have also been known to use the program to enroll star rugby players.[15]

Is Public Funding Adequate?

In any decentralized system in which the funding agency is separated from the spending agency, disputes will inevitably arise about the adequacy of resources. On the one hand, spending units typically complain that they have insufficient money to do what the funder expects of them. On the other, the funder has incentives to keep spending from growing too fast and to dismiss claims of inadequacy by shifting the blame to the spenders: if they were only more efficient, the funds they have would be sufficient. Such tensions are clearly evident in the Tomorrow's Schools reforms. Although the government increased its total spending on education during the early 1990s, it did not increase spending on primary and secondary schools, and determining the cost of an adequate education has proven too daunting a task for the ministry. In addition, the operations grant has become less generous over time, and schools have been forced to turn increasingly to local revenue sources.

How Much Is New Zealand Spending on Education?

Standard budget and accounting documents do not make it easy to distinguish, in a consistent way, spending on primary and secondary education from total educational spending. Even the definition of total spending on education is open to some ambiguity. Hence we are forced to rely on estimates by the Ministry of Education for the 1988–94 period (published in 1997).

Table 6-2 shows that the total amount the government spent on all levels of education (adjusted for inflation) increased significantly through

15. Michael Gaffney, interview with authors, Otago Children's Issues Centre, April 22, 1998.

Table 6-2. *Aggregate Spending on Education, 1988–94*

Year	Total spending in 1994 prices[a] (NZ$ millions)	Percent of total government spending	Percent of GDP
1988	3,848	12.5	5.0
1989	4,188	13.5	5.3
1990	4,402	13.9	5.3
1991	4,565	14.5	6.0
1992	4,581	15.3	6.1
1993	4,563	15.3	6.0
1994	4,654	15.8	5.8

Source: Ministry of Education (1997b: table 2.1).

a. Total spending includes spending on education, the national library, and the Education Review Office; it is deflated by the consumer price index.

1992, leveled off between 1992 and 1993 as the economy stagnated, and then rose again in 1994. As a percent of total government expenditure, which declined during the period, education's share rose from 14.5 in 1991 to 15.8 in 1994. During that same period spending on education hovered at about 6 percent of gross domestic product (GDP) except in 1994, when it fell to 5.8 percent as the economy expanded. The 6 percent of GDP in 1993 compares to a 5.1 percent share in the United States and a 4.7 percent share in the United Kingdom in that same year.

Although support for total educational spending remained relatively strong during the early 1990s, the share of that spending devoted to primary and secondary schools was declining. From its 69 percent share in 1984 it fell to 56 percent in 1994 as the proportion of preschool education and tertiary education increased.[16] An analysis of central government funding of primary and secondary schools for the 1990–94 period shows the following: operations grant funding per pupil increased about 5–10 percent in nominal dollars, while per student expenditure on teachers' salaries decreased except in secondary schools. Combining these trends by type of school, we conclude that per pupil funding remained relatively constant in nominal dollars in primary schools during the 1990–94 period; that it may have increased slightly in secondary schools; and that it

16. Ministry of Education (1997b: 5). Information on the share devoted to elementary and secondary schools was not reported for the years between 1984 and 1994.

Table 6-3. *Expenditure per Pupil and Relative to Gross Domestic Product per Capita, Selected Countries, 1995*

Country	Primary		Secondary	
	U.S. dollars	Relative to GDP (percent)	U.S. dollars	Relative to GDP (percent)
Australia	3,121	16	4,899	25
Ireland	2,144	12	3,395	20
New Zealand	2,638	16	4,140	24
United Kingdom	3,328	19	4,246	24
United States	5,371	20	6,812	26
OECD mean	3,546	19	4,606	27

Source: OECD (1998: tables B4.1, B4.3).

decreased in schools that offer all grades.[17] Hence it appears that per pupil spending in the compulsory sector declined in inflation-adjusted terms during the early 1990s.

With respect to the level of spending, the most natural comparison is across countries. We warn the reader that for a variety of reasons such cross-national spending comparisons can be misleading.[18] Nonetheless, we present one such comparison in table 6-3. The table reports per pupil spending (converted to U.S. dollars) on primary and secondary education in both public and private institutions for illustrative English-speaking countries. The table shows that New Zealand spends less on primary and secondary education than all the other countries with the exception of Ireland. Relative to its gross domestic product, however, New Zealand spends about the same amount on primary schools as Australia and on secondary schools the same as the United Kingdom. With these aggregate trends and levels as background, we turn now to the more specific question of whether government funding for the schools is adequate.

What Would an Adequate Education Cost?

Local flexibility with respect to the setting of school goals complicates the task of determining what an adequate education might cost. What

17. Ministry of Education (1997b: 30).
18. See Barro (1995).

one school principal judges to be adequate may differ from what another school principal thinks. As it transferred authority to the schools in 1989, the government initially made little serious effort to determine how much it would cost a typical school to achieve even the national educational guidelines. The Ministry of Education simply took the amount it had been spending on school operations before the reforms and, based on an analysis of spending patterns in a representative sample of schools, developed a distribution formula that would not force significant reductions in the operations spending of any school. With respect to teachers, the government based teacher entitlements for each school on specified teacher-pupil ratios by year of student.

While this approach to determining school funding and resourcing was not unreasonable, especially in light of the dramatic changes in authority resulting from the 1989 reforms, it is a far cry from a systematic and analytical approach to determining the cost of an adequate education. Several years into the reform, the ministry decided to explore the possibility of developing a more rational basis for the funding and resourcing of the schools. To that end, it commissioned the University of Otago Consulting Group to study the "technical feasibility of developing a mechanism for resourcing schools based on the services provided by schools and the cost to well-performing schools of delivering those services."[19] The ministry had hoped that a close analysis of schools' spending patterns would shed light on how much money was needed for each of the major activities performed by schools. However, in its September 1997 final report, the Otago group basically said that it was neither technically nor conceptually feasible to use actual spending patterns to determine what level of funding was adequate.

Despite the extensive financial data available at the school level, the consultants ran into technical difficulties because data were not available on how staff time was allocated among specific activities and because there was no single best way to allocate overhead costs to those activities. Requiring schools to generate the needed data would impose heavy compliance costs on the schools. The consultants further emphasized that even if it were possible to determine how much schools were currently spending on each of the major activities, that information would provide little insight into the adequacy of the funding. Only with additional informa-

19. University of Otago Consulting Group (1997: i).

tion about whether schools were effectively and efficiently delivering the services would one be able to judge the adequacy of their funding. But as was pointed out in the report itself and highlighted in a subsequent critique of the report, such judgments are impossible to make in the absence of a clear concept of effectiveness. Does it mean managerial effectiveness, effectiveness in producing outcomes, or what? Since even the best researchers do not have a good understanding of how educational inputs translate into educational outputs (a relationship referred to by economists as the educational production function), it is virtually impossible to determine what amount of funding would be required to ensure educational adequacy for individual schools.[20] Moreover, as one ministry official explained to us, discussions about the adequacy of overall funding can sometimes be too politically explosive to address and hence are taken off the table. Such was the case, for example, with respect to the new technology guidelines, which, if adequately funded, would have required the ministry to spend about NZ$700 million for new computers, an amount about equal to its total budget for the operations grant.[21]

Adequacy of Operations Funding over Time

Even if operations funding had been adequate in 1989, some schools were convinced that by the mid-1990s it was woefully inadequate. Wellington East Girls College is one such school. Bruce Campbell, the former treasurer of this decile 6 institution, documented a 22.7 percent decline in the purchasing power of the school's operations grant between 1989 and 1997. As part of his careful analysis, Campbell adjusted the school's 1989 grant for the decline in students in Wellington East and for inflation during that period, and he appropriately adjusted for shifts in ministry policy.

In an unanswered September 1997 letter to the minister of education, Campbell used these figures to take issue with the minister's claim on national radio that school operating grants had not decreased since they had been introduced. Campbell argued that schools have had to shoulder a variety of administrative costs that, according to the Picot task force

20. See critique of the report in ESRA (1997).
21. Tim McMahon, Ministry of Education, interview with authors, Wellington, March 4, 1998.

report, should have been included in the new operations grant in 1989 but were not.[22] He was referring here to increased administrative costs, realistic amounts for maintenance, and funding for computers. He also alluded to additional burdens that the schools bear that were not initially anticipated.

In a subsequent letter to the Labour Party spokesman on education and in discussions with us, Campbell described some of these burdens. They included items such as increased telephone charges related to the reclassification of schools as businesses, the payment of new sewer charges, the burdens imposed by the Health and Safety Act, which made schools responsible for unsafe acts on the premises, a significant increase in paperwork required by ERO inspections, and multiple wage increases for caretakers, cleaners, nonteaching support staff, and administrative staff negotiated by the government. In U.S. terminology, many of these burdens would be labeled *unfunded mandates*. "Is it any wonder that schools are struggling?" Campbell asked in his letter to the Labour spokesman.

Does Campbell's analysis for one school carry over to funding for all schools? There is good reason to believe that it does. In a decentralized system—one in which the funder differs from the spender—the government funder has an incentive to limit the rate of growth of funding because it bears the political costs of higher taxes while garnering few of the political gains from higher spending. At the same time, the government has an interest in presenting figures in a way to make itself look generous and in introducing new initiatives for which it can gain political credit. In New Zealand, these incentives, which even in good economic times might combine to squeeze the schools, were exacerbated by a slowdown in the national economy in the early 1990s.

OPERATIONS GRANT FOR ALL SCHOOLS, 1990–98. Figure 6-1 portrays growth in the aggregate funding for school operations per pupil during the period 1990–98.[23] Because the government changed the definition of what is included in funding for operations during this period, the growth

22. According to Campbell, the original task force report assumed that current administrative spending, which averaged NZ$133 per pupil, would be transferred to the schools to cover these costs. Since Wellington East Girls College was one of the test schools at the time of the transfer, it could easily confirm that no provision was made in the initial grant for those costs.

23. The figures exclude funding for private schools, special schools, and the correspondence school.

Figure 6-1. *Aggregate Operations Funding per Pupil, 1990–98*

NZ dollars

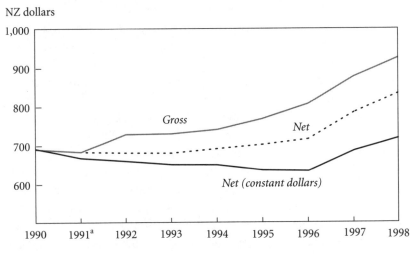

Source: Ministry of Education.
a. Deflator is annual consumer price index. 1991 figures converted to a twelve-month year.

in total funding for operations overstates the growth in what was originally defined as the operations grant. During the 1990–98 period the government transferred a number of programs, such as paying for relief
teachers and Maori language programs, from the salaries grant into the
operations grant. Thus the funding for these programs represents no additional funding for the schools at the same time that the transfer allowed
the government to assert that funding for operations was growing. Sub-
tracting out these programs generates net funding, which better represents the pattern of operations funding, consistently defined.

As can be seen, funding for operations as adjusted in this way remained
relatively constant in current dollars between 1990 and 1996. The growth in
1997 and 1998 represents both an increase in basic funding, primarily in the
form of the per pupil funding rate, and an increased commitment by the
government to the TFEA program, special education, and targeted rural
funding. By increasing funding for these latter programs the government
could take credit for specific programs at the same time that it could claim
that it was increasing overall funding for operations. The rub, of course, is
that not all schools benefit significantly from these latter programs.

The constant-dollar funding line of figure 6-1 tells the relevant story from the perspective of the schools. Funding declined by 8.4 percent between 1990 and 1996—from NZ$689 per pupil to NZ$631 per pupil.[24] After 1996, funding increased but did not rise to its original level until 1998, when it reached NZ$716. The ministry used the 1998 figure to emphasize its commitment to ensuring adequate operations funding for the schools, but three points are worth noting. First, because part of the recent increase in nominal spending is targeted to needy schools, the gains do not help the typical or average school. Second, during this period it is quite likely that other changes related to the broader economic reforms pushed up the prices of goods that schools purchase at a faster pace than the general inflation rate. Third, the schools have more to do in 1998 than they did in 1990. Hence it seems fair to conclude that the operations funding provided by the government to the typical school was less generous in 1998 than it was in 1990.

That interpretation is confirmed by the views of a national representative sample of primary school principals and trustees. In 1990, only 20 percent of the principals and a similar percent of trustees found their government funding inadequate. By 1996, the percent of trustees who believed their funding was inadequate had risen to more than 60 percent and of principals to more than 70 percent. These figures, it should be noted, understate the concerns of urban principals in that rural schools and very small schools were typically more satisfied with their funding that were urban schools.[25]

RISE IN LOCAL FUNDING.   Whatever the absolute definition of adequacy may be, the observation that schools are increasingly relying on locally generated funds provides further support for the conclusion that funding from the government has become less adequate over time. Our discussions with school officials suggest that these funds are not being used for frills but rather are needed to supplement the basic budget.

Table 6-4 indicates the increasing reliance on local funds between 1992 and 1996 by a sample of urban schools. The table reports the growth sepa-

24. The figure is based on the annualized deflator used by the Ministry of Education. The use of other versions of the consumer price index deflator would indicate even greater declines in inflation-adjusted funding. For example, based on the March anuual consumer price index, the decline in real funding between 1991 and 1996 would have been 12 percent, with larger drops in the early 1990s than those indicated in the figure.
25. Wylie (1997: 24–25).

Table 6-4. *Growth in Local Funding, by Type of Urban School, 1992 and 1996* [a]

Type of school	Local funds per pupil (NZ dollars)		Percent change
	1992	1996	
Secondary			
Gross	422	636	50.7
Net	256	386	50.8
Net revenue as share of operating grant (percent)	25.5	42.1	65.1
Primary (contributing)			
Gross	153	239	56.2
Net	89	155	74.2
Net revenue as share of operating grant (percent)	11.5	23.7	106.1

Source: 1992 data provided by University of Otago Consulting Group (1997); 1996 data from the Ministry of Education.

a. The sample in each case is all the relevant schools in the three urban areas that were also in the Otago study. Secondary schools are schools offering years nine through thirteen; the sample includes sixty-seven schools. Primary schools are schools that are contributing primaries (that is, they do not include middle school grades); the sample includes forty-two schools.

rately for secondary schools, which typically have greater access to nongovernmental funds, and for primary schools. The table shows that local funds increased by 51 percent (in constant dollars) in secondary schools and by 74 percent in primary schools. Because these rates of growth exceed the growth in operating grants, local funds have grown relative to the government's funding of operating grants. By 1996, local funds were about 42 percent the size of operating grants in secondary schools and about 24 percent in primary schools.

Conclusions

We focus in this section on the adequacy of the operations grant because that is the only pot of money over which all schools have discretion. Had bulk funding for teachers' salaries been fully implemented, adequacy issues would have arisen in that context as well. Because the government has been paying teachers at centrally bargained rates, however, the only adequacy issue that arises with respect to the large teachers' component of school budgets is whether the government has been making sound policy decisions with respect to the teacher-pupil ratios that determine each school's allotment of teachers' slots. Delving at this point into the large literature and debates about the precise relationship between teacher-pupil ratios—or its mirror image, class sizes—and student achievement would take us too far afield.[26] Suffice it to say that allocating funds or resources to the typical school based on professional or political judgments about appropriate class size is an eminently reasonable way for a central authority to fund a large part of the budgets of schools in a decentralized system.

Three caveats, however, are needed. The first and most crucial is that the schools be given the flexibility to allocate the allotted teachers among classes as they choose and not be constrained to the class size underlying the calculation of the allotted teachers. New Zealand schools had that type of flexibility. Second, in a fully decentralized system it would be desirable for schools to make their own decisions about how much to spend on teachers versus the other components of the budget. For all practical purposes, except for those that opted for bulk funding, the New Zealand schools did not have that flexibility. Third, because small class sizes seem to be especially productive for minority and disadvantaged students, the adequacy of teachers' resources could well require that schools serving such students be allocated more teachers' slots than other schools, something that does not happen in New Zealand.[27]

Is Public Funding Equitable?

A central issue in all school funding schemes is whether funds are fairly distributed across schools. Of course, the first and crucial question is what is meant by the term *fair*. In countries such as the United States, where funding is determined largely by local school districts, a major thrust of

---

26. The U.S. literature on the effects of class size is large and growing. See, for example, Hanushek (1997), who finds small or no systematic effects of class size, Ferguson and Ladd (1996), who find that smaller class sizes increased student achievement in Alabama schools, and evaluations of the Tennessee class-size experiment such as that by Krueger (1997), in which smaller class sizes in the early grades appear to generate larger achievement gains for African Americans than for white students.

27. Although low-decile schools receive larger operations funding and are free to use some of that for teachers, the operations grants are not large enough for this option to have much impact on the number of teachers they hire and hence on their class sizes.

finance reform for many years has been to ensure that schools in poor districts can spend as much money per pupil as schools in wealthy districts. However, even equality of funding would not be deemed fair if some schools face more costly educational challenges than other schools. Equitable treatment of schools facing above-average educational challenges would require that they have access to greater funding per pupil than other schools. Based on the reasonable working assumption that money can matter, additional funding for such schools would compensate them for the educational challenges they face.

Compared to the U.S. system of funding, government funding in New Zealand appears to be much more fair. Not only does New Zealand start with a basic presumption of equality of treatment, but in a number of ways it directs additional funding to the neediest schools. Working against equity, however, is the pattern of local fund-raising, whereby high-decile schools typically are able to raise more money from local sources than can low-decile schools. Our focus in this section is on the pattern of funding from all sources of revenue across schools grouped by decile. Because low-decile schools by definition are those that face greater educational challenges, a fair system of funding would ensure that such schools have greater funding than high-decile schools.

Tables 6-5 and 6-6 report average levels of per pupil funding based on 1996 data for schools in illustrative deciles in our three urban areas, table 6-5 referring to primary schools and table 6-6 to secondary schools. Isolating the schools by type recognizes the fact that the spending needs of schools vary depending on the age of their students. For example, secondary schools require more scientific laboratory equipment and more job counseling services than primary schools.

Table 6-5 shows that decile 1 urban primary schools have access to more funding per pupil than schools in higher deciles and that this outcome occurs despite their lesser success in raising funds from local sources. Total funds per pupil available to urban decile 1 schools are NZ$2,782, which exceeds that for decile 4 schools by 9 percent, decile 7 schools by 17 percent, and decile 10 schools by 11 percent. If we ignore the locally generated funding to focus on central funding, we find that the government funding for decile 1 schools exceeds that for the decile 7 and decile 10 schools by 20 percent. Several factors contribute to the greater funding, including a larger salaries grant, which may reflect the slightly smaller enrollments in decile 1 schools, and a significantly greater operations grant, much of which is accounted for by TFEA and some by Maori language funding.

Table 6-5. *Per Pupil Funding, Urban Primary Schools, by Illustrative Decile, 1996*[a]

NZ dollars[b]

Revenue source	Decile			
	1	*4*	*7*	*10*
Salaries grant	1,744	1,683	1,575	1,603
Operations grant	906	698	631	610
Other grants	16	11	7	11
Investment income	42	29	39	33
Net local funds	79	106	124	228
Total	2,782	2,532	2,375	2,497
Summary statistics				
Number of schools	55	20	16	69
Average student roll	345	315	329	373

Source: Based on data for schools in the three urban areas. Averages calculated by the authors based on data provided by the Ministry of Education.

a. Includes all contributing primary schools; that is, those offering years one through six, with student rolls greater than 100 students. Student roll is number of students used for the funding of each school.

b. Unweighted averages.

Table 6-6 portrays a similar pattern for secondary schools. The NZ$5,233 available for decile 1 schools exceeds that for decile 4 schools by 11 percent, decile 7 schools by 22 percent, and decile 10 schools by 32 percent. The larger salaries grant per pupil reflects their smaller size; the larger operations grant reflects TFEA and elements of the funding formula such as funding for vandalism. Once again, the percentage differences would be even greater if we ignored local funding, which is significantly lower in decile 1 schools (which unlike higher-decile schools, including those in decile 4, do not have access to additional funding from foreign fee-paying students). Government funding per pupil for decile 1 schools is a full 45 percent greater than that for decile 10 schools.

Leaving aside locally raised revenue, which reduces the fairness of the funding system, the government funding system is remarkably successful in targeting more dollars to low-decile than to high-decile schools. The most explicit targeting occurs through TFEA. That program is praiseworthy and clearly makes the funding system more equitable than it would otherwise be.

A case can be made, however, that the additional funding is insufficient

Table 6-6. *Per Pupil Funding, Urban Secondary Schools, by Illustrative Decile, 1996*[a]

NZ dollars[b]

	Decile			
Revenue source	*1*	*4*	*7*	*10*
Salaries grant	3,521	2,988	2,859	2,662
Operations grant	1,400	1,062	909	771
Other grants	64	91	9	6
Investment income	85	59	50	49
Net local funds	163	424	458	469
Total	5,233	4,664	4,285	3,959
Summary statistics				
Number of schools	8	12	6	19
Average student roll	598	1,048	951	1,405

Source: Averages calculated by the authors based on data provided by the Ministry of Education.

a. Includes only those secondary schools offering years nine through thirteen in the three urban areas. These schools represent about three-fourths of all the secondary schools in the four illustrative deciles. Student roll is number of students used for the funding of each school.

b. Unweighted averages.

to compensate low-decile schools for the challenges they face. In the next chapter we document that, despite their additional funding, low-decile schools are unable to retain many students who are able to exercise choice. Moreover, student performance in such schools falls far short of that in high-decile schools. In an alternative policy environment, such as that of the United States, one might be tempted to argue that the problem for such schools is not insufficient funding but rather insufficient incentives or flexibility for the schools to use the funds productively.[28] But such arguments ring hollow in the New Zealand context, especially for schools in urban areas, given that schools have both the authority to make significant changes in how they deliver educational services and strong incentives to make the sort of changes that keep students in the school.[29] Thus we conclude that, despite their additional funding, low-decile schools may well still be underfunded relative to high-decile schools.

28. That is the basic argument made by Hanushek (1994).

29. We distinguish urban from rural schools here because money could well be less of a constraint in rural districts than it is in urban districts, which face more immediate competition for skilled staff from other schools.

Bulk Funding Controversy

Concerns about funding inadequacies and inequities obviously generate tensions in the governance system. Even greater tensions—ones that raise equity and adequacy concerns but also extend well beyond them—have arisen over the issue of the bulk funding of teachers' salaries. Because the controversy over bulk funding raises so many issues crucial to a decentralized system of school governance, we describe the controversy in some detail.

Background and History

Although both the Picot task force report and the Tomorrow's Schools legislation of 1989 called for bulk funding of teachers' salaries as a logical component of the transfer of authority to the schools, the Labour government chose not to implement this part of the reform immediately. Its reasons were that the details had not yet been fully worked out, that the new boards of trustees already had their hands full dealing with all the other changes, and that one important source of their political support, teachers' unions, were opposed.[30] Consequently, bulk funding of teachers' salaries was put on hold, and teachers' slots were funded as described above.

With the National Party back in power after 1991, the new minister of education, Lockwood Smith, put the bulk funding issue back on the agenda. Despite Smith's strong support for bulk funding, however, he too had to back off in the face of a revolt within his own caucus. National members of Parliament were being pressured by schools and trustees opposed to the plan, and Prime Minister James Bolger reportedly had reservations based on the strong opposition of the teachers' unions and concern that National's majority in Parliament might be jeopardized.[31]

Smith worked out a compromise that permitted a voluntary trial of bulk funding. Schools that opted for this method would receive funding for the number of teachers to which they were entitled based essentially on average teachers' salaries by school type. Under such a formula, the only schools that would benefit financially from a shift to bulk funding were those currently employing a disproportionate number of teachers

---

30. Butterworth and Butterworth (1998: 167–69).
31. Bell and Dawson (1991); Laxon (1994).

who, because of their inexperience, were paid below the national average. When applications for the trial closed in July 1992, fewer than 3 percent of the schools had opted in.[32] The number was small not only because many schools would lose money under the program but also because teachers at many schools adamantly opposed the change. The primary and secondary teachers' unions both strongly opposed bulk funding and had called for new teachers to blacklist the schools that opted into the program.

The National government further angered the teachers when in 1992, without consulting the unions, it amended the Education Act to require all schools boards to pay the salaries of senior teachers and principals from a bulk grant. The unions correctly viewed this as an additional step toward required bulk funding for all salaries. Nor were the unions happy in 1996 when the government sweetened the incentive for bulk funding by adding funds, allegedly in recognition of the added administration and other costs associated with bulk funding. With the added funds, approximately 80 percent of the schools would either gain financially or be neutral if they shifted to bulk funding. Despite this sweetener, by May 1998 only 13 percent of schools, representing 15 percent of teachers, had opted for the bulk funding option.[33]

In 1998, the government added an even greater financial incentive for schools to volunteer for bulk funding. Called the fully funded option, this change specified that the bulk funding amounts would no longer be based on average salary levels for teachers but rather on top salary levels. Under such a formula *all* schools would gain—at least in the short run—by opting for bulk funding. In addition, schools would be able to bank any money they did not spend in any one period, earn interest on it in the interim, and spend it later as they saw fit. This financial incentive turned out to be too generous for many schools to turn down, and by March 1999 the number of bulk funded schools had risen to 720, or about 27 percent of all schools.

As the debate on bulk funding unfolded, the positions of various groups became solidified. In favor of bulk funding was the National Party and the much smaller party on its right wing, the ACT, which represented the interests of business. New Zealand First, a party started in 1993 that became part of the ruling coalition with National in 1996, generally op-

32. Ballantyne (1997: 83).
33. Ministry of Education (1998c).

posed bulk funding, but it apparently did not have enough power within the coalition either to limit the trial or to stop its expansion. Although the Labour Party had initially supported bulk funding, its opposition hardened over time as the opposition of the teachers' union became more vocal. The tiny left-wing Alliance Party adamantly opposed bulk funding through its main spokesperson on education, Liz Gordon. Before her 1996 election as a member of Parliament, Gordon had been an academic researcher at the University of Christchurch, from which she had argued vigorously along with other academic writers against bulk funding.

In terms of interest groups, the Post Primary Teachers' Association, the union for secondary school teachers, was the most persistent and vocal opponent, but it was followed closely by the union of primary teachers, the New Zealand Educational Institute (NZEI). Most strongly in favor of bulk funding were the Business Roundtable and its interest group on education, the Education Forum. After an initial period of apparent support, which put them at odds with much of their membership, the New Zealand School Trustees Association took a neutral position and asserted that each board should make its own decision.

Much was at stake in the debate over bulk funding of teachers' salaries. At one level, the issue was simply how much flexibility the schools should have to move funds from one category to another. On a number of other levels, however, the debate raised some fundamental political, economic, and educational issues and took on great symbolic significance for many of the groups involved.

Managerial Flexibility and Efficiency

No one disputed the fact that bulk funding of teachers' salaries would give the schools more flexibility in how they managed themselves. Schools that were not bulk funded effectively had a floor for the teachers' portion of their budgets. Although schools could use their operations grants to hire more teachers if they so chose, they were not allowed to shift funds from teachers' salaries to other purposes. In addition, they were not permitted to bank teachers' slots allocated in one period to use in another. The bulk funding option would free them up on both dimensions and allow them to carry salary resources over from one period to the next. Some of the most innovative and aggressive schools—including, as described in chapter 4, Ponsonby Intermediate and Gladstone Primary in

Auckland—have made productive use of the additional flexibility offered by bulk funding. In these cases, however, it is difficult to sort out the beneficial effects of the increased flexibility from the beneficial effects of simply having the fiscal sweeteners that were available to the schools that chose the bulk funding option.

If flexibility and managerial efficiency were the only issue, it would be hard to argue against bulk funding. The best argument against it—that the state has a responsibility to ensure that all schools use some minimum number of teachers—would have sounded paternalistic and would not have been consistent with the new environment of self-governing schools. But flexibility was clearly not the only issue.

A Way to Reduce Funding?

To many people, bulk funding and level of school funding were closely intertwined. That was clearly the case in the short run: schools that were bulk funded received more funding than they otherwise would have received. But what worked in a positive direction when a few schools were involved could well work in the other direction when many or all schools were involved. Teachers and other school officials feared that once many schools were bulk funded the government would squeeze the schools by turning the spigot down on overall funding for teachers' salaries.

How might that happen? Under the non-bulk-funded system, the total amount of funding for salaries was determined by teacher entitlements for each school (based on enrollment and policy decisions about appropriate teacher-pupil ratios) and the level of teachers' salaries as determined by collective bargaining. Because the government guaranteed each school a specific quantity of teachers, the amount of funding each school received rose automatically with the negotiated rise in teachers' salaries. Under that arrangement, the only way outside of the bargaining process for the government to reduce funding for salaries was through an explicit policy decision to reduce teacher-pupil ratios.

Once most schools were bulk funded the situation was likely to change, given the very real possibility that the government might stop bargaining with teachers' unions over salaries, leaving that task to individual schools or organizations of schools. If and when that occurred, the government would be in a position to appropriate funds for teachers that did not automatically rise in lockstep with the rise in the salaries that teachers were able to negotiate, and consequently the government could use its funding powers to drive those salaries down.

Teachers and their unions believed they had good reasons for fearing that the ministry would use bulk funding to drive down teachers' wages. First, they had experienced firsthand what had happened to the operations grant for schools during the early 1990s. The decline in real terms of that pot of funding did not bode well for a comparable pot of funding for teachers' salaries. Second, they drew a similar lesson from the 1992 shift to bulk funding for the salaries of kindergarten teachers. With that change had come a reduction in overall funding for kindergartens, which in turn led to increases in teachers' workloads. Third, they had observed that after the government fully bulk funded the tertiary sector in 1990, the government grant per student had been progressively reduced each year.[34]

On the other side, however, proponents of bulk funding claimed that the unions were simply making self-interested arguments. They discounted the relevance of the decline in the operations grant by pointing out that it occurred during a time of severe fiscal stringency for the entire budget. They dismissed the analogy to the funding of kindergartens on the ground that the change reflected a fundamental restructuring of the whole early childhood sector, which was intended to make the government funding of kindergartens more consistent with that of other preschool programs. And finally, they argued that the evidence from the tertiary sector was not particularly relevant, given the differences between that sector and the sector on compulsory education. Government cutbacks in funding for universities and polytechnics, they argued, were appropriate on policy grounds given the view that students, as the primary beneficiaries of the education, should pay a larger share of the bill.[35]

Although reasonable people can disagree about the evidence, the fears of the teachers' unions cannot be entirely discounted. While future funding levels are always uncertain, the basic issue was one of trust. Could the teachers and the schools trust the central government—especially a conservative National government—to provide adequate funding for teachers' salaries over time? The teachers' answer was a resounding nay.

34. Snook (1997: 3).
35. Gary Hawke, interview with authors, Wellington, February 24, 1998.

A Way to Break the Teachers' Unions?

Teachers differ from many other public sector employees in New Zealand in that their salaries continue to be negotiated centrally, with a central government agency. Before the country's economic and public sector reforms of the mid-1980s, central salary setting was common, even for private sector employees. Eliminating central bargaining and reducing the power of the unions was viewed by the Labour government, and subsequently by the National government, as a crucial step in making both the private and the public sectors more efficient. With the passage of the Employment Contracts Act in 1991, national awards and compulsory unionism were abandoned in favor of individual employment contracts. The goal was to break the unions, and the act was successful: total union membership as a percent of the total employed work force declined from a high of 45 percent in 1989 to 23 percent in December 1994.[36] Teachers received differential treatment on the grounds that their employee organizations were associations, not formal unions. The only major change affecting them was that the negotiation of teachers' salaries was moved from the State Services Commission to the Ministry of Education.

Many of New Zealand's reformers believed that the retention by the teachers' unions of the right to bargain centrally and their opposition to bulk funding were serious impediments to the development of an efficient and productive educational system. They were particularly aggravated by the secondary school teachers' union, the Post Primary Teachers' Association (PPTA), which had a reputation of being militantly self-interested, not only with respect to the bulk funding issue but also on other bargaining issues. In general, the primary teachers' union, the NZEI, was viewed in a somewhat more positive light, although it too was seen as thwarting the reform process by opposing bulk funding.

Exactly what would happen to central bargaining and the power of the teachers' unions under bulk funding was unclear. There was little doubt, however, that the National government was hoping that the change would reduce their power. By shifting funding fully toward the individual schools, the government was trying to encourage more site-based bargaining, more use of individual contracts, and the introduction of a performance pay policy—all policies that it has been pushing in other ways as well. While

36. Kelsey (1997: 180–85).

the bargaining could end up at the school level, a more likely outcome is that bargaining over teachers' salaries would occur in regional organizations. Whatever the specific outcome, the power of the teachers' unions to bargain effectively on behalf of their members would inevitably be eroded.

The very real threat that bulk funding poses to the unions helps explain why they so adamantly opposed such a move, and since teachers are more likely to vote for Labour than for National candidates, this threat helps explain Labour's opposition to bulk funding. At the same time, the increasing stridency of union opposition to bulk funding—especially that of the PPTA—fanned the fires for proponents of bulk funding. To them, bulk funding was not only a logical component of the move to self-governing schools but a way to break the power of self-interested unions as well.

A Threat to Quality Education for All?

The two teachers' unions also raised a number of educational and professional concerns regarding bulk funding. Such a policy, they argued, is designed to free government from any responsibility to ensure an adequate supply of teachers.[37] The government has historically played a major role in influencing the supply of teachers through its funding for teachers' training programs, through the salaries it negotiates, and through its recruitment of overseas teachers.

The unions have also raised concerns about what bulk funding would do to internal relationships within the schools. While the Tomorrow's Schools reforms promoted the concept of school communities, bulk funding, they fear, would generate a more antagonistic relationship between employers (that is, school boards and principals) and teachers. What will become, they ask, of the concept of the principal as educational leader of the teachers when the principal takes on more of the responsibilities of an employer, including the determination of salaries? A related concern is the unions' fear that cost-conscious boards of trustees may substitute lower-paid, less-experienced teachers for more-experienced teachers, thereby reducing the quality of the education offered.

The validity and significance of these concerns are difficult to evaluate. The key point, however, is that they are not independent of a much larger

37. Post Primary Teachers' Association (1997).

concern on the part of the unions and other opponents that the move to bulk funding would spell the end of a national educational system and the introduction of a more local and privatized system. Thus the real elephant in the living room is the threat of privatization.

A Further Step toward Vouchers and Privatization?

The opponents of bulk funding were well aware that the ultimate goal of many educational reformers—notably the business community, as represented by the Business Roundtable, the right-wing ACT Party, and many people at the Treasury Department—was a voucher system in which money would be given directly to students to use in whatever public or private school they prefer. To these people, bulk funding of teachers' salaries served as a logical step toward their ultimate goal. Concomitantly, one of the biggest fears of the opponents of vouchers was that bulk funding of salaries would hasten the move to vouchers and eventually to a system in which the government gets out of the business of running schools.

Bulk funding of teachers' salaries could be a logical step toward vouchers in that it tightens the link between the number of students in a school and its funding. The closer that link is, the easier it is to question why pupil-driven funding should be conditioned in any way on the ownership of the school. Should the focus not be instead on the students themselves and the quality of the education they receive? If so, why not give the money directly to the students and their families and permit them even greater school choice? A voucher program need not necessarily lead to the full privatization of education, but some proponents imagine scenarios under which it could. To the extent that private schools were allowed to supplement the voucher with additional fees, private provision of education would most likely expand, and because private entrepreneurs would have incentive to purchase public schools, the argument goes, the state might gradually be able to withdraw from the business of owning schools.[38]

This is not the place to rehearse the arguments for and against vouchers, since that has been done elsewhere.[39] The point is that proponents

38. This vision is expresssed clearly by Ruth Richardson (the minister of finance at the time), who wrote in "Making a Difference" (quoted in Snook [1997: 6]): "A voucher system would transform the NZ education system into a competitive market." "Entrepreneurs could be expected to purchase state sector assets." And "the government [would] gradually divest itself of all the schools it owned."

39. Wylie (1998).

and opponents of vouchers hold strong views on the issue, views that are rooted in deeply held values about educational opportunity and in beliefs about the potential for competition among schools to lead to desirable outcomes. Thus whatever its other advantages or disadvantages may be, because bulk funding is viewed as a step toward privatization of education, it arouses passionate responses and takes on great symbolic significance.

Consequences of Not Implementing Bulk Funding

Leaving aside the arguments of the teachers' unions, some of which are clearly self-serving, we now step back to consider briefly how the failure to implement bulk funding interfered with the objectives of the reformers. To the extent that one of their objectives was to break the unions, the answer is relatively clear. As long as the government was paying salaries directly to the teachers, salaries had to be negotiated centrally by the government. Otherwise, the government would be in the untenable position of funding teachers at locally negotiated salary rates that could well be inflated by the knowledge that the government would be paying for them. As a result, the failure to move to bulk funding meant that salary negotiations had to be maintained at the center and, for that reason, directly interfered with the reformers' goal of reducing the power of the unions.

There are, however, other considerations that relate to educational quality. One has already been mentioned, namely the fact that the greater flexibility in budgeting that would accompany bulk funding could well lead to more productive allocations of funds at the school level. How different those allocations would be is impossible to determine from the existing data.[40] Moreover, while some schools would undoubtedly make better decisions, others could well make shortsighted or foolish decisions, so predicting the overall effects is unclear.

Another consideration has to do with the allocation of high-quality teachers across schools. Under the current system in which the govern-

40. The schools that have opted for bulk funding are clearly not a random sample of schools. Indeed, the ones must likely to opt for bulk funding during the period of this study were those paying below-average teachers' salaries. In light of this nonrandom difference between schools that have opted for bulk funding and those that have not, it is not possible to determine how bulk funding has affected the allocation of school budgets.

ment allocates teaching slots to schools and pays the salaries of whatever teachers the individual schools are able to attract, one concern is that higher-decile schools end up with higher-quality teachers and at no cost to themselves. The supply of good teachers for high-decile schools is likely to be larger than that for low-decile schools because most teachers would prefer to teach more advantaged, more motivated students. If the good teachers happen to be the more experienced teachers—the ones who command higher salaries under the current salary structure—high-decile schools can hire those teachers without having to use any of their budget for the higher salaries. Of course, to the extent that low-decile schools are able to attract such teachers, they too would benefit from not having to use any of their scarce resources to pay the higher salaries.

If bulk funding were implemented based on average salary levels—that is, by allotting to each school a budget that would allow the schools to hire the allotted number of teachers at an average salary that continued to be centrally negotiated, the situation would change. Any school that hired more-experienced teachers would have to pay those teachers more. How this scenario would play out is unclear. One possibility is that the demand for experienced teachers would decline at all schools as schools substituted cheaper, less-experienced teachers for more-expensive, more-experienced ones. Another is that high-decile schools would continue to opt for more-experienced teachers but would hire slightly fewer teachers overall and put up with larger class size, while low-decile schools would opt for more teachers and lower quality in an attempt to keep class size small.

The scenario becomes more complicated if the schools themselves determine salary levels. One possible advantage of this scenario is that schools could fine-tune their salary offers to reflect teacher characteristics that they value, given the characteristics of the students they serve. Thus teachers would be rewarded for their actual performance rather than for experience. However, the downside is that bulk funding is likely to disadvantage low-decile schools, which would most likely have to pay higher salaries than would high-decile schools to attract good teachers. Only if the amount of their salary grant were sufficiently large for them to pay the higher salaries without reducing the number of teachers they hired would the teaching in low-decile schools improve. In the more likely case in which the salaries grant to schools did not vary with the decile of the school, the quality of education offered by low-decile schools would probably decline relative to that of high-decile schools.

In sum we are not convinced that the failure to fully implement bulk funding of teachers' salaries has had a negative effect on the overall quality of education provided by New Zealand schools. In addition, had it been fully implemented, we might have observed even greater differences in the quality of education between the low-decile and high-decile schools.

Schools as Agents of the State: Conclusions

The 1989 shift of operating authority away from the old Department of Education to the schools has brought with it a need to define a new relationship between the government and the schools. In the previous chapter we describe the Ministry of Education's role in setting goals and its mechanisms for holding schools accountable. In this chapter we see that central funding for schools has not always been adequate and that transferring full budgetary authority over salaries to the schools raised huge symbolic issues that were not easily resolved. One clear bright spot is the targeted funding for educational achievement (TFEA) program, which directs additional funds to schools facing the greatest educational challenges. Despite this program, however, significant disparities remain in the capacity of schools to meet the educational needs of their students, although this capacity need not and should not be measured only in monetary terms.

Is a Pure Tight-Loose-Tight Governance Arrangement Desirable?

Although New Zealand is trying to move toward a tight-loose-tight governance structure—one in which outcome goals are clearly specified, schools have considerable flexibility to manage themselves, and schools are held accountable for outcomes—it has not yet attained it. The accountability process is complicated by the fact that the outcomes of national concern are neither very well specified nor fully measurable and that boards of trustees of local schools are authorized to set some of their own outcome goals. Thus one challenge for such a governance arrangement is to specify what schools should be held accountable for. A second is to determine to whom they should be accountable.

New Zealand's answer to this last question was clear at the time of the initial legislation. Self-governing schools would be accountable to the public and to the government through the independent Education Review Office (ERO), a new agency that was part of government but separate from the Ministry of Education. With the introduction of full parental choice in 1991, New Zealand implicitly introduced a second element of accountability: the success of a school in addressing the interests of the parents and children it could potentially serve.

Both of these accountability mechanisms—direct accountability through the ERO and indirect accountability through the educational marketplace—have strengths and weaknesses. One potential advantage of parental choice as a mechanism of accountability is that it forces schools to think about the full range of outcomes that parents care about. In practice, however, parents may have limited information about what schools are accomplishing, their choices may be severely restricted by economic or other factors, or their interests may differ from those that prompt the government to run a system of compulsory education in the first place. These considerations suggest that, however desirable or functional it may be, accountability through parental choice alone will not suffice.

The alternative of the ERO inspection system has a lot to commend it. Through that mechanism, the state can provide information to the public and to consumers of education that otherwise would not be available. In addition, it can provide guidance to boards of trustees and principals about limitations in the school's operations. With the initial shift to self-governing schools, it is hard to imagine how many of the new boards would have known what was expected of them in the absence of the ERO inspection process.

Having said this, however, it is important to observe that the New Zealand inspection system is not without its flaws. The absence of information on student performance, especially at the primary school level, as well as a number of other considerations forced the ERO to focus heavily on processes rather than on student outcomes. To be sure, some of these processes are related to outcomes, such as whether the curriculum is being delivered and whether boards of trustees have any way of knowing what the students are learning. Nonetheless, the reviews often became mechanistic, were heavily focused on management, and did not necessarily foster better educational outcomes.

The availability of more information on student performance in the form of standardized test scores would permit greater accountability for outcomes. That would potentially be beneficial in that it would give the ERO a tool for encouraging boards of trustees to raise their expectations about student performance and thereby help to level expectations and performance across schools. As New Zealanders are well aware, however, too much focus on test scores brings with it some real dangers, and these dangers would no doubt be exacerbated in the policy environment of full parental choice. Test scores not only give information to school officials that could be useful for them in determining areas of strength and weaknesses, they also give information—some of it potentially misleading—to parents who are making choices about schools. At a minimum, the focus should be on the extent to which students in a school increase their learning, a focus that would require attention to gains in test scores rather than to the absolute levels of such scores.

It is interesting to speculate about whether accountability through test scores alone (with appropriate attention to the importance of value-added measures) could ever replace New Zealand's reliance on the ERO as a mechanism for holding schools accountable. The answer depends in part on whether it makes sense to hold schools accountable exclusively for outcomes to the exclusion of internal school processes.

Given that public funds are involved, some of the internal processes of schools clearly need to be monitored, such as the handling of public funds. Such processes are not at issue here, since schools presumably would continue to be subject to a separate financial auditing procedure. Schools would also be monitored for compliance with safety regulations and civil rights law. Instead, we are talking about other processes related to teaching and learning. The New Zealand experience suggests that in a decentralized system it makes sense for the government to monitor the internal processes of individual schools. While such monitoring does not ensure good educational outcomes, it can help a school understand and correct its weaknesses and can foster a more solid foundation for teaching and learning within the school. When principals spoke nostalgically about the loss of the former inspectors, they were telling us that they felt the loss of such support.

Our point is that if a pure tight-loose-tight governance structure requires that all relevant outcomes be clearly specified and measurable and that schools be held accountable only for outcomes, then it is probably neither a fully desirable nor a fully feasible governance structure for a system of compulsory education. Stated differently, the concepts of outcomes and managerial processes are not as distinct in practice as the tight-loose-tight governance structure would require.

Presumably, the government has some interest in ensuring good processes as well as good outcomes and in strengthening the linkage between the two. To that end, we believe that the New Zealand experience suggests that some form of an educational review office would be a desirable component of a decentralized educational system elsewhere. Ideally such a review agency would pay attention both to educational processes and to student outcomes, and it would take heed both of those that are measured by government-mandated student tests and of those specified by the local school community through its board of trustees. As we will spell out in chapter 10, we think this conclusion is particularly applicable to charter schools in the United States.

The Issue of Trust

One unsettling characteristic of the state educational system in New Zealand is the high level of distrust that principals, teachers, and others at the local school level express toward the government in general and the Ministry of Education in particular. A certain amount of tension between central authorities and schools is, of course, inevitable and possibly even desirable in any school system, and such tension is nothing new in New Zealand. Widespread resentment of the high-handedness of the former Department of Education was an important reason that the Tomorrow's Schools reforms came about in the first place. Nevertheless, it would seem that the success of a tight-loose-tight system like Tomorrow's Schools, built as it is around a complex set of rights and obligations on the part of the government and local governing bodies, requires a higher than usual degree of mutual trust by the respective parties. It is a fair question to ask whether the various structures now in place serve to maximize such trust or to undermine it.

Much of the mistrust of the center on the part of local schools has to do with long-term political agendas. Many people in the schools view the whole reform process simply as a cost-cutting measure on the part of a government committed to containing government spending as a matter of general policy. They are particularly distressed by trends in the operations funding, which the ministry has manipulated to make it look like it has grown when for many schools it has not. The government's relentless push for bulk funding of teachers' salaries is also viewed widely as a first step toward privatization and vouchers. Having failed to convince a majority of boards of trustees of the intrinsic merit of the idea, the ministry has adopted a tactical approach that looks suspiciously like it is bribing schools to acquiesce in bulk funding. Such an approach does not inspire trust.

It would be tempting to chalk such differences up to partisan squabbles. The National government is conservative, even right-wing, and the two teachers' unions have traditionally been aligned with Labour. While such differences have exacerbated the trust problem, though, its roots go back to the early years of the reform period when Labour was still in power. Public trust in the system was undermined early on by David Lange's rejection out of hand of the Picot task force's call to set up an education policy council that would give parents and the wider community a voice in shaping the advice that went from the ministry to the minister. Likewise, the community forums on education and the parent advocacy councils, both of which were part of the original legislation and had the potential to act as restraints on the ministry's freedom of action, were for all practical purposes stillborn.

What structural or policy changes could be made to increase the level of trust among the various groups? Concerns about long-term funding levels might be addressed by adopting an operations funding formula that would increase funding over time, based on a reasonable measure of inflation.[41] Some such assurance would certainly help in addressing suspicions related to the push for bulk funding.

Another way of addressing the distrust issue would be to make the policy decisionmaking process within the ministry more open. Because of concerns about provider capture, teachers were largely shut out of any role, even a consultative one, in policymaking. Such exclusion created great resentment when the ministry imposed bulk funding for principals and senior teachers without any discussion with teachers. By contrast, Nicholas Pole took pains to bring teachers into discussions on the design of the targeted funding for educational achievement program, and the resulting support that they showed for the idea turned out to be important to the ministry.

The Issue of Financial Risk

Another important question regarding the relationship between the center and the schools has to do with who bears the financial risk. Under

---

41. The feasibility of developing such an index is discussed in University of Otago Consulting Group (1997).

the centralized system that existed before Tomorrow's Schools, the Department of Education controlled both operational and capital budgets and thus assumed risk in both areas. Under the new decentralized system, in contrast, much of the risk with respect to operations has shifted to local schools.

The Ministry of Education still holds school property in its name and assumes responsibility for the construction of new facilities when needed. Schools need not worry, therefore, about the cost of significant capital repairs or improvements. With operating budgets, however, the story is quite different. Since operations funding is by strict formula, schools bear the risks of unforeseen increases in operational expenses, such as changes in telephone rates. The new policies on funding for special education, which provide bulk funding based on estimates of how many children with special needs a school is likely to enroll, work to the disadvantage of schools that serve large numbers of such pupils. If bulk funding of teachers' salaries becomes the norm, local boards of trustees will be financially vulnerable because they may have to finance pay increases that are negotiated by the ministry but that the ministry is no longer obligated to finance.

What about risks related to downturns in the economy? One of the more sophisticated arguments sometimes made against the bulk funding of teachers' salaries across the board is that it will make it all too easy for the government to reduce spending on schools in the event of such downturns. All that would be required would be for the ministry to turn down a single spigot. One can argue, of course, that even under the current system the overall level of spending on education is a political issue and that the government is accountable to the electorate for providing sufficient funds.

A key policy issue for Tomorrow's Schools is whether, in decentralizing governance, New Zealand has also followed the correct path in decentralizing financial risk as well. There are clear trade-offs involved. In order to get the desired efficiency gains from a decentralized system, some of the risk has to be shifted to the schools. The question is how much risk can appropriately be shifted, given that the smaller the school the more difficulty it has coping with financial risk. The challenge is to devise a system in which the benefits of shifting risk are maintained while the costs of that risk to individual schools are kept at manageable levels. For smaller schools, that may require a pooling of risks through some form of insurance program or through the consolidation of several schools for the purposes of financial management.

Equity of Funding

Finally, it is very important in any decentralized system that, since schools have a good deal of operational autonomy, they also receive support from the center on an equitable basis. Such a principle becomes even more important in an environment of parental choice.

Providing schools facing a wide variety of educational challenges with adequate and equitable funding is difficult because knowledge about how much different schools need to provide a quality education is limited. In our view, the TFEA mechanism is a good start in addressing this issue in New Zealand. It is relatively transparent and objective, and it is appropriately based on a broader set of family background measures than simply income and race. However, while the TFEA approach of classifying schools is an important first step, it provides no clear analytical guidance about how much additional compensation is appropriate. That still remains a political determination.

Another serious issue concerns the appropriateness of relying on user fees and charges to subsidize functions at the core of the educational enterprise. In one sense, fees and charges are a natural extension of self-governing schools. But serious equity issues arise, especially when the basic funding level is not adequate.

7 | *Parental Choice and Enrollment Patterns*

SHORTLY AFTER 6:30 P.M. on a Wednesday night in June scores of parents, accompanied by their early adolescent offspring, began streaming into the school auditorium of Aotea College near Wellington. They were there for Aotea's annual Open Evening, the occasion when parents and prospective first-year students get a chance to look the school over and weigh its virtues and liabilities against those of other schools they might attend. The visitors were greeted at the door by Aotea students dressed in matching blue blazers with white trim on the lapels and cuffs. The guests took copies of the school prospectus, found seats, and settled back to enjoy the preprogram entertainment. A trio of students played George Frideric Handel's *Flute Sonata.* Two girls played guitars, and a male barbershop quartet offered its rendition of *Swing Low, Sweet Chariot.*

Aotea College is a decile 2 school, which means that it serves a predominantly low socioeconomic status clientele, almost half of whom are Pacific Islanders or Maori. The school has about 800 students, with ample room for more, and Principal Brent Lewis and his staff have crafted a program with something for everyone. Lewis began his remarks by urging his listeners to "check schools out" and not just rely on reputations. Lewis stressed the large number of courses from which Aotea students can choose—"a variety that few schools can match"—and emphasized that Aotea teachers and administrators are committed to discerning and meeting individual needs. "At Aotea, discipline is important," he said, "but so is encouragement of students to fulfill their potential." Lewis was followed on the program by Barbara Lewis, the deputy chairperson of the board of trustees, who spoke "from a personal viewpoint as a parent." She said that she, too, liked the broad range of courses and sports offered at Aotea as well as the "multicultural nature of our student body." Several students offered testimonies about the strengths of Aotea, including Ruth Osborne, who said that the school had "helped me meet my potential and grow as a person."

After dividing into groups for a tour of the school and meetings with teachers, parents and prospective students congregated in the staff room to enjoy light refreshments, ask questions, and compare notes. Some of the parents had attended another open house the night before at nearby Tawa College, and much of the discussion revolved around comparisons of the two high schools, which differ in fundamental ways. Tawa is a decile 9 school with a reputation for rigorous academics; only 15 percent of its students are Maori or Pacific Island. It has had an enrollment scheme since 1991 and thus has more control of its character and destiny than Aotea. Parents at the Aotea Open Evening understood these differences. "I didn't like the attitude at Tawa," said one woman with a daughter in tow. "There was a lot of emphasis on regulations, like how long the skirts had to be, and there was not much celebration of students. I like the fact that Aotea is smaller and how they emphasize that everyone has a place." She conceded, though, that her daughter had a positive impression of Tawa. "It's better academically," said the girl. "They talked more about test scores. I thought it was a pretty cool place."

The Open Evening was Aotea's version of an academic mating ritual that has become increasingly important to the success of New Zealand secondary schools since school zoning was abolished and parents and students were given the choice of which school to attend.

The Picot task force and the *Tomorrow's Schools* policy paper took a cautious approach to parental choice. Although affirming the right of parents to select their child's schools and agreeing that traditional zoning schemes had outlived their usefulness, they were primarily concerned with ensuring that students had a right to attend the nearest neighborhood school. Task force members did not envision a system in which large numbers of parents would opt to send their children elsewhere. In situations in which particular schools did end up with more applicants than seats in the classroom, places would be allocated by lottery.

The National Party government that took power in 1991, however, had a very different vision of parental choice—one that made it the norm rather than the exception. They saw choice not only as a parental right to be vigorously affirmed but also as a force for improving the quality of teaching and learning and for making educational professionals more accountable. The 1991 Education Amendments set the stage for implementing this vision by abolishing the geographic enrollment zones from which secondary schools had traditionally drawn their students and by giving parents the right to enroll their child in any school willing to admit him or her. The effect of the new legislation was to send the Tomorrow's Schools reforms off in a radically new direction. Instead of seeking to improve state education through community participation in governance and decentralized management, these objectives would be accomplished by establishing an educational marketplace.

The results of this change were immediate and dramatic on both the demand- and supply-side of this new marketplace. Many parents came to believe that they had a strong moral obligation to exercise choice on behalf of their children, and they did so in large numbers and in ways that permanently altered enrollment patterns, especially in urban areas. Schools thrust into a new competitive environment became aggressive marketers and adopted other policies that significantly altered the culture of state education in New Zealand.

Arguments for Parental Choice

Advocates of parental choice of schools typically justify it as a means of promoting diversity, as a parental right, or as a means of increasing efficiency and accountability.

The diversity argument holds that giving parents choice will broaden the mix of educational options open to students and parents. Schools with different educational approaches are desirable both because the natural learning styles of children vary and because parents differ in what they want for their children. Only when parents are empowered to choose schools, this reasoning goes, will established schools have appropriate incentives to respond to these differences or will new schools, or schools within schools, be established to satisfy the multitude of parental wishes and student needs. Both the Picot task force report and *Tomorrow's Schools* recognized the need for diversity of school offerings but were cautious in calling for more parental choice and viewed the possibility of setting up new schools as a last resort. Although the National government may have been motivated in part by this argument, its decision to expand parental choice appears to rest more firmly on the two other arguments for choice.

The first argument is that parents have a fundamental right to decide what is in the best educational interests of their children.[1] According to this view, geographic zoning for schools is undesirable because it interferes with the rights of parents to pick the school they believe will best serve those interests. In keeping with the general trend in many countries to deregulate large segments of society, many people assert that education is a critical area over which parents should have more control. As New Zealand moved away from a highly regulated and controlled economy in the mid-1980s, it is not surprising that many New Zealanders found it increasingly anachronistic for families' educational options to be limited to schools located within a government-defined geographic zone.

The other argument embraced by the National government has to do with the potential of parental choice to make the educational system more productive and accountable. This argument, which is strongly held by the Treasury Department, asserts that when schools have to compete for students—and for the funding that accompanies each one—they will work harder to use whatever resources they have in the most effective manner possible. This argument for choice became increasingly dominant in New Zealand after 1990.

Current Policy on Parental Choice

The current policy on parental choice of schools has been in effect since 1992. The 1991 amendments to the 1989 Education Act abolished centrally set home zones and, in theory, permitted students to attend whatever school they wished. An important corollary of the change, however, is that students are no longer guaranteed a place in their local school. The new policy applies to primary, intermediate, and secondary schools and differs slightly for the 303 integrated schools. The latter have a lot more

---

1. For a forceful statement of the view that parents have a right to choice, see Gilles (1998).

flexibility to choose students, provided that 95 percent of the students fit the special character of the school. For Roman Catholic schools, which account for more than three-quarters of integrated schools, this requirement typically means that someone in the family must identify himself or herself as Catholic.

All Crown-owned schools are obligated to accept all students who apply for admission unless that school is operating at capacity. The definition of a school's capacity is negotiated by the school and the Ministry of Education. Once central authorities are convinced that the school is full and thus at risk of overcrowding, the ministry authorizes the school to draw up an enrollment scheme. In the spirit of the Tomorrow's Schools reforms, the schools were given full authority to design their own enrollment plans provided only that they do not breach the provisions of the Race Relations Act of 1971 and the Human Rights Act of 1993. The only other requirements were that the schemes be available for public inspection and that schools publish advisory notices in local daily newspapers when they are about to initiate, amend, or abandon an enrollment scheme. Significantly, the Ministry of Education did not have to approve a school's plan, only its right to have one.[2] In practice, enrollment schemes tend to have much in common. Most start with a small geographic zone and then give preference to siblings of current students and to the children of staff members and former students. But many schools, especially the most popular ones, have rules that for all practical purposes allow the principal to admit whomever he or she chooses.

At the primary school level, the procedure for applying for a place at a school is generally informal, and parents can often apply right up to the date their child plans to enroll. At the intermediate and secondary levels, however, the procedure becomes much more formal, and parents typically apply for admission well in advance of the beginning of classes. Schools usually hold their open houses in June, and parents begin applying immediately afterward for the opening of the new school year in late January.

The government provides little or no support for transporting students to schools in urban areas. The standard policy is to limit subsidies to chil-

2. The statement is valid for the period of our study. In late 1998, the legislation was changed to give every child a right to attend his or her local school, to require that schools consult with other schools before establishing an enrollment scheme, and to require ministry approval of the content of enrollment schemes.

dren with special needs and to students who live far from the nearest public school and where no public transportation is available, which excludes most urban residents. Paradoxically, the students most likely to be eligible for transportation assistance in a densely populated area like Auckland are those who live in wealthy, low-density enclaves. There are also some subsidies for students attending Maori and integrated schools.

Effects of Parental Choice on Enrollment Patterns

The policy shift to full parental choice for the 1992 school year technically applied only to secondary schools because the parents of primary schoolchildren in principle had always had the option of choosing which school their child would attend. In practice, however, feeder patterns involving particular primary, intermediate, and secondary schools were well established, and few parents of primary school children chose anything but their local school. Thus the opening up of choice had substantial impact at both the primary and secondary levels. A climate was created in which parents at all levels felt the need to exercise choice. To be a "good" parent one had to make a conscious decision about which was the best school for one's child. Some parents became excessively anxious and even obsessed about whether they were making the right decision. "Choice is like a neurosis," commented Guy Allen, a field officer for the Post Primary Teachers' Association in Auckland. "Parents are motivated by fear. They feel that they have to look around to make sure they will not destroy their children's futures."

The impact of the new system on school enrollments was rapid and profound. Parents were given options that were not available to them before, and many wasted little time availing themselves of these new opportunities. Parents and students began voting with their feet and sorting themselves among schools in demonstrably different ways than under the regime of zoning. In this sense, choice can be said to have been an almost immediate success.

In the following sections, we document the magnitude and nature of the enrollment changes resulting from the advent of full parental choice in three urban areas: Auckland, Wellington, and Christchurch. We focus primarily on the period between 1991 and 1996, years in which New Zealand conducted its quinquennial censuses, so we can compare actual enrollment changes to the changes that would be predicted based on changes in the number of school-age children as reported in the censuses. The predicted roll changes are intended to approximate the changes in enrollments that would have occurred had students continued to attend their local schools. For primary and intermediate schools, we define the local area as the political ward in which each school is located. For secondary schools we use a broader area, the territorial local authority (TLA), which is more like a municipality, to reflect the fact that secondary schools have historically drawn from broader catchment areas. The comparison of actual with projected changes in school rolls permits us to separate the effects of parental choice on school enrollments from the effects of population growth and movement.

For much of the analysis, we group schools into the decile categories introduced in chapter 4. Recall that the decile of a school is intended to measure the magnitude of the educational challenges faced by the school by virtue of the mix of students it serves. Low-decile schools serve students who are disproportionately minority and belong to families with low incomes, little job security, and little parental education. High-decile schools serve students who are more likely to be Pakeha, or European, and more likely to come from families with higher income, greater job security, and greater parental education. The decile classifications used here were introduced in 1995 and were based on 1994 enrollment patterns. We use these classifications to compare the enrollment of schools in each decile in 1991 with the enrollment in those same schools in 1996.

Movement from Low-Decile to High-Decile Schools

The first and most dramatic point to emerge from the data is that students gravitated from low-decile schools and toward high-decile schools. That is, they moved toward schools that served the more economically and socially advantaged students and that had lower proportions of minority students. As a result, low-decile schools on average became smaller, while high-decile schools got bigger.

The Wellington area clearly illustrates this pattern. (See figure 7-1 for primary and intermediate schools and figure 7-2 for secondary schools.) The dark bars in figure 7-1 show that student rolls in primary and secondary schools fell in deciles 1–3, grew slightly in schools in decile 4, and grew quite significantly in schools in deciles 5–10. The fact that school rolls did not expand even more in deciles 9 and 10 reflects capacity constraints in those schools.

Figure 7-1. *Enrollment Changes in Primary and Intermediate Schools, Wellington, by 1995 Decile, 1991–96*

Percent change

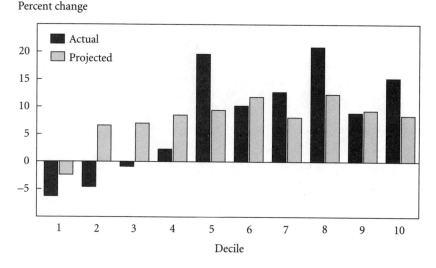

Decile

Source: Calculated by the authors based on enrollment data provided by the Ministry of Education and data on five- to fourteen-year-olds by ward (1995 definition) from Statistics New Zealand (1997).

The lighter bars in figure 7-1 document that these enrollment changes differed from those that would be predicted based on changes in the residential location of school-age children. In decile 1 schools, for example, only about a third of the 6.3 percent decline in school rolls can be attributed to a decline in five-to-fourteen-year-olds in the wards where those schools are located. For decile 2 schools, population trends suggest that enrollments would have increased by about 6.6 percent, whereas in fact student rolls actually declined by about 4.6 percent. In the higher deciles, the fact that school rolls typically increased much more than that predicted by the growth in school-aged children in the local wards confirms our conclusion that students gravitate to higher-decile schools.[3]

3. By way of comparison, we also looked at the 1986–91 enrollment changes. The comparison is not ideal since that was a period of declining rolls and the groupings of schools by their 1995 decile ranking is less meaningful. In that period, the predicted and actual changes are more similar and the patterns less clear. For example, in decile 1, the actual rolls fell slightly less than the projected rolls; in deciles 8 and 9 the actual and projected declines were almost identical.

Figure 7-2. *Enrollment Changes in Secondary Schools, Wellington, by 1995 Decile, 1991–96*

Percent change

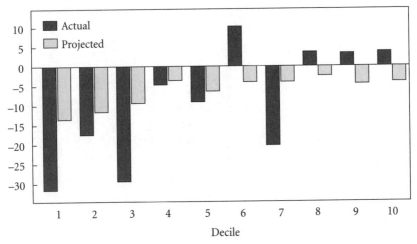

Decile

Source: Calculated by the authors based on enrollment data provided by the Ministry of Education and data on ten- to nineteen-year-olds by territorial local authority from Statistics New Zealand (1997).

Even more dramatic are the 1991–96 enrollment changes in Wellington's secondary schools. The dark bars in figure 7-2 show that rolls fell sharply in low-decile schools: by about 30 percent in deciles 1 and 3 and more than 17 percent in decile 2. Because each decile includes more than one school, the declines in average rolls mask even greater declines in individual institutions. A comparison of the dark and light bars for the three lowest deciles indicates that average declines are much greater than would have been predicted based on changes in the school-aged population, defined as ten-to-nineteen-year-olds, in the areas in which the schools are located.[4] As indicated by the dark bars, schools in deciles 8–10 experienced a small growth in rolls despite the declines in ten-to-nineteen-year-olds in the areas surrounding the school.

4. Census-based projections are less precise for secondary schools than for primary schools because they are based on territorial local authorities that, in many instances, are too encompassing. Projections based on ward data are similar but somewhat more dramatic. When projections are based on the smaller geographic unit of the ward, the patterns are similar but a bit more dramatic.

Figure 7-3. *Enrollment Changes in Secondary Schools, Auckland, by 1995 Decile, 1991–96*

Percent change

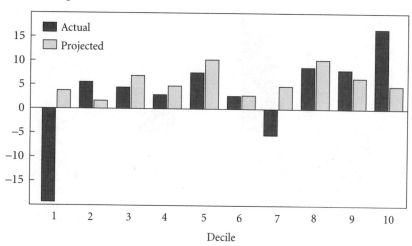

Decile

Source: Calculated by the authors based on enrollment data provided by the Ministry of Education and data on ten- to nineteen-year-olds by territorial local authority from Statistics New Zealand (1997).

The big drop in student rolls in decile 7 secondary schools illustrates a different point: the sensitivity of enrollment to specific events. It appears that much of that decline was a response to a number of suicides in one of the two secondary schools in that decile. Students in those schools apparently shifted either to decile 6 schools or to those in a higher decile.

The Auckland urban area experienced much greater growth than Wellington in 1991–96 enrollments. That overall growth resulted in a much more even increase of enrollments in primary and intermediate schools, with little clear evidence of flight of students from lower to higher deciles. Enrollment changes in secondary schools in Auckland, however, present a pattern similar to enrollment changes in Wellington (see figure 7-3). The dark bars depict a 19 percent decline in the number of students attending decile 1 schools despite a small increase in the number of ten-to-nineteen-year-olds in the area. Figures for decile 10 schools show a 16.6 percent increase in students even though the number of students living in the relevant areas increased by only 4.8 percent. This picture suggests that students in decile 1 schools may have shifted to decile 2 and decile 3 schools.

Figure 7-4. *Enrollment Changes in Secondary Schools, Christchurch, by 1995 Decile, 1991–96*

Percent change

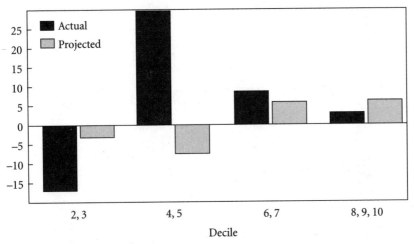

Source: Calculated by the authors based on enrollment data provided by the Ministry of Education and data on ten- to nineteen-year-olds by ward (1995 definition) from Statistics New Zealand (1997).

Similarly, some of the youth living near decile 7 or 8 schools may have shifted to schools in deciles 9 or 10.[5]

As with Auckland, the most revealing story in Christchurch, the smallest of the three urban areas, is found at the secondary school level (figure 7-4). Christchurch has no decile 1 secondary schools and only twenty-three secondary schools in total. To ensure a sufficient number of schools in each grouping, we grouped several deciles together. Moreover, because the Christchurch urban area has only one city (or TLA) and that city happens to be the largest TLA in the country in terms of geographic area, we used wards to approximate the relevant historical catchment zones.

Enrollment changes in Christchurch between 1991 and 1996 are striking. Students appear to have fled from low-decile schools (deciles 2 and 3) to those in a higher category, particularly deciles 4 and 5. The small rates

5. The results are similar when projections are based on wards rather than territorial local authorities.

Figure 7-5. *Change in Percent Minority, Primary and Intermediate Schools, Wellington, by 1995 Decile, 1991–96*

Percentage points

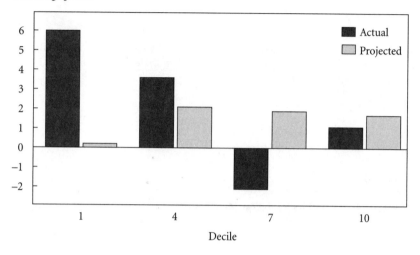

Decile

Source: Calculated by the authors based on enrollment data provided by the Ministry of Education and data on five- to fourteen-year-olds by ward (1995 definition) from Statistics New Zealand (1997).

of growth in the top deciles can be explained by capacity constraints and enrollment schemes in most of those schools.

Increased Ethnic Polarization

Flight from low-decile schools to higher-decile schools is clearly evident among Pakeha, or European, families, but it is not limited to them. Many minority families have eagerly embraced their opportunity to exercise choice. In practice, however, Pakeha families have been more aggressive in taking advantage of their new option, with the result that ethnic minorities have become increasingly concentrated in low-decile schools.

Figure 7-5 documents the patterns for Wellington primary and intermediate schools. The dark bars show the change in the fraction of Maori or Pacific Island pupils in four illustrative deciles of schools. In decile 1 schools, the share of minorities increased by 6 percentage points. This change raised the share of minorities in those schools from its 1991 level of 76.4 percent to 82.4 percent in 1996. The short light bar for decile 1

Table 7-1. *Enrollment Changes by Ethnic Group, Low-Decile Secondary Schools, by Urban Area, 1991–96*[a]

Percent except where indicated

Area and decile	Change in enrollments, 1991–96		Minorities in student body		Change in minorities, 1991–96 (percentage points)
	Pakeha	Minority	1991	1996	
Wellington					
Decile 1	−40.3	−28.7	75.2	78.4	3.2
Decile 2	−34.5	12.3	36.2	49.3	13.1
Decile 3	−33.3	−23.7	40.6	43.8	3.3
Auckland					
Decile 1	−39.9	−13.3	77.9	83.5	5.6
Decile 2	−12.2	25.2	47.3	56.1	8.8
Decile 3	8.7	−2.2	39.6	37.1	−2.5
Christchurch					
Deciles 2, 3	−22.2	5.6	18.7	23.8	5.1

a. Schools are grouped by their 1995 deciles. All changes are weighted by the enrollments of the schools in each decile.

schools shows that almost none of the greater concentration can be attributed to a change in the share of minority children in the relevant wards. Similarly, the minority share increased by more than was predicted in decile 4 schools. For higher-decile schools (7 and 10), the reverse is true: the minority share increased less than would have been predicted based on changes in the mix of school-aged children in the relevant wards.

Similar, and in some ways more striking, changes occurred at the secondary level. Table 7-1 focuses on the lowest three deciles in each of the three urban areas. In all three areas, the outward movement of Pakeha children from low-decile schools was dramatic. Only in Auckland, with its rapid growth of population, did the number of European children increase in any of the three lowest deciles. The pattern is more complex for minority students. The figures suggest that many minority students fled decile 1 schools by enrolling in decile 2 schools, leading to significant growth in minority enrollments in those schools. The impacts of these enrollment changes on the minority fractions of school populations are shown in the final column. The pattern is clear: low-decile schools, especially schools in decile 2, had much greater shares of minority students in 1996 than in 1991.

An alternative way of describing changes in the ethnic segregation of minorities makes use of a dissimilarity index. This measure, which is commonly used in describing neighborhood and school segregation in the United States, uses data from all schools and indicates the extent to which the distributions of two groups—in our case Pakeha and minorities—differ across schools. For example, if 15 percent of all students were minority and these students were distributed proportionately across schools so that 15 percent of the students in each school were minority, the dissimilarity index would register a minimum value of zero. The more dissimilar the distribution of the two groups across schools, the higher would be the index, until it reaches its maximum value of 100.[6] The index value itself (for example, 56) is often interpreted as the fraction of either minority or Pakeha students who would have to be moved among schools to even out the distribution of that group among schools.

Tables 7-2 and 7-3 schools show that the ethnic dissimilarity indexes increased in all three urban areas over the period 1991–97 and that this pattern holds true both for state schools as a group and for state and private schools combined. Although the increases in the indexes for primary and intermediate schools are of a relatively small order (1 to 1.5 percentage points), dissimilarity indexes predicted for schools based on ward data typically declined during this period. Thus the most accurate measure of the impact of parental choice on dissimilarity indexes for state schools would be the difference between actual and predicted differences. For the period 1991–96, these impacts would be +1.5 percentage points for Auckland, 4.4 for Wellington, and 1.8 for Christchurch.

At the secondary level, the effects are somewhat larger. For example, for state schools in Wellington, the index increased by 5 percentage points between 1991 and 1997, or by about 15 percent, at a time when the change predicted on the distribution of pupils among Wellington TLAs was moving in the other direction.

---

6. The formula for the dissimilarity index is $D = (100)(0.5)$(summation over all schools of the absolute value of $[X_i/X - Y_i/Y]$), where X_i is the number of students of one type (for example, minority) in the ith school and X is all students of that type; Y_i is the number of students of the other type (for example, Pakeha) in the ith school, and Y is all students of that type.

Table 7-2. *Dissimilarity Indexes (Minority versus Pakeha), Primary and Intermediate Schools and Wards, by Urban Area and Year*[a]

Area and year	State schools	State and private schools	By ward, 5–15-year-olds
Auckland			
1991	56.5	57.0	41.8
1996	57.8	58.4	41.6
1997	58.4	58.8	n.a.
Wellington			
1991	48.0	48.4	37.6
1996	49.0	49.9	34.2
1997	49.4	49.7	n.a.
Christchurch			
1991	39.3	39.7	19.8
1996	40.3	40.8	19.0
1997	41.1	41.9	n.a.

Source: Calculated by the authors from enrollment data from the Ministry of Education and population data from Statistics New Zealand (1997), Supermap 3.

a. Minority includes Maori and Pacific Islanders. Pakeha includes Europeans and Asians.

The end result is clear. Minorities are now more concentrated in low-decile schools, and overall segregation by ethnicity was somewhat higher in 1996 and 1997 than in 1991. Moreover, much of the change appears to be attributable to the exercise of school choice rather than to changes in the residential patterns of Pakeha and minority families.[7] Reasonable people may disagree about whether these changes are large or small and in particular whether they are large enough to affect students. While the changes appear relatively small for the overall system (except in Wellington), our interviews with school officials confirm that the impacts at the low end of the distribution of schools are large enough to have a significant impact on the educational environment in those schools.

7. The analysis does not account for the possibility that the introduction of parental choice could alter residential enrollment patterns. By breaking the link between residential location and schooling, parental choice may provide an incentive for some families to locate in lower-income residential areas to take advantage of lower housing prices than they would have done when enrollment patterns were linked to geographic zones of residence. Some theorists have argued that parental choice could well have the beneficial effect of reducing residential segregation by income. See, for example, Nechyba (1999).

Table 7-3. *Dissimilarity Indexes (Minority versus Pakeha), Secondary Schools and Political Jurisdictions, by Urban Area and Year*[a]

Area and year	State schools	State and private schools	10–19-year-olds by Territorial local authority	Ward
Auckland				
1991	46.1	49.1	20.0	41.4
1996	48.8	51.7	20.1	41.7
1997	50.1	53.2	n.a.	n.a.
Wellington				
1991	34.4	37.5	24.7	37.0
1996	37.5	40.6	23.9	33.7
1997	39.4	42.4	n.a.	n.a.
Christchurch				
1991	28.6	32.2	...	20.0
1996	31.8	34.8	...	19.9
1997	31.6	34.8	...	n.a.

Source: Calculated by the authors from enrollment data from the Ministry of Education and population data from Statistics New Zealand (1997), Supermap 3.

a. Minority includes Maori and Pacific Islanders. Pakeha includes Europeans and Asians.

Piecemeal Evidence on Polarization by Socioeconomic Status

The high correlation between ethnicity and socioeconomic status suggests that parental choice has also increased polarization of students by their socioeconomic status. Unfortunately, the absence of 1991 information on the family backgrounds of the students in each school means that we cannot examine this phenomenon directly. There is no doubt that very large concentrations of hard-to-educate children are now found in the lowest-decile schools, but the data do not permit us to document the magnitude of the changes in the concentrations over time.

Some piecemeal evidence on changes in the socioeconomic status of students across schools appears in the Smithfield Project.[8] As one part of their ambitious study, the researchers used information from a telephone survey to calculate two measures of the family background of more than 800 students who entered the first year of high school at eleven state schools in an anonymous urban area, referred to as Green City, in each of the years

8. See appendix B for description.

Table 7-4. *Dissimilarity Indexes by Socioeconomic Characteristics of Families, 1991–93*

Characteristics	1991	1992	1993
High status versus low status (based on occupation index)			
School	49.2	54.9	63.6
Zone	54.2	56.8	58.7
No parent employed versus at least one parent employed			
School	44.2	57.2	61.6
Zone	55.8	52.5	58.7

Source: Smithfield Project (1994: 29).

from 1990 to 1993. One measure was an occupational index that has been frequently used in New Zealand to characterize a family's socioeconomic status. The other measure was whether at least one parent was employed.

Based on data for six of the eleven schools (all the schools for which there were clear prior attendance zones), the Smithfield researchers reported dissimilarity indexes across schools and across the prior attendance zones of the six schools (see table 7-4). The indexes for "school" show the percentage of students in each category, such as high socioeconomic status, that would have to be moved among schools to achieve a uniform distribution of students by socioeconomic status across the six schools. The indexes for "zone" represent a measure of the dissimilarity of the distribution of the socioeconomic groups across the geographic areas defined by the prior attendance zones of each school.

For each socioeconomic measure, the dissimilarity indexes increased more during the period at the school level than at the zone level. These patterns imply that the group of new students that entered the six secondary schools in the sample became increasingly segregated by socioeconomic status compared to what would have been the case had zones alone determined enrollment patterns.[9]

9. Our focus here is on the patterns from 1991 on. The original Smithfield table also presents indexes for 1990. Interestingly, segregation across schools was somewhat higher than segregation by zone in that year, which suggests that even before the loosening up of enrollment policy, some schools were able to attract a more advantaged group of students than would be predicted by the zone alone. In addition, the indexes fell substantially between 1990 and 1991, a pattern that is hard to explain given that the 1991 changes were not very great.

The Smithfield researchers also note that the only year for which school dissimilarity indexes were lower than those for the historical zones was 1991. Because that was the only year in which the Labour government's balloting policy for oversubscribed schools was in place, the researchers attribute the difference to that policy. Based on these patterns, they argue that the lottery approach constitutes a more equitable enrollment policy than the National government's subsequent laissez-faire approach. While this is a plausible interpretation of the 1991 figures, the validity of this interpretation is hard to evaluate without identifying the six schools and determining which of them, if any, were oversubscribed and hence subject to the balloting requirement in 1991.

How Parents and Students Make Choices

Although we have no complete and systematic data of our own on how parents and students choose schools in New Zealand, we are able to shed light on this important issue by drawing on a variety of sources, including research by others, our own data, and anecdotal evidence obtained during school visits.

Single-Dimensional Preferences of Parents

The first, and perhaps most important, observation is that families with various characteristics rank school quality relatively similarly. If asked to categorize schools in a given geographic area by quality, most families in New Zealand would come up with similar groupings, and the rankings, it turns out, would be closely related to the socioeconomic and racial mix of the students in the school.

There are some notable exceptions to this generalization, the most obvious one being that some Maori parents prefer schools that put more emphasis on Maori language and culture. Moreover, among schools with a similar general ranking, parents and their children may well have differing preferences. For example, some parents might prefer a rigid and disciplined environment, while others might prefer a more relaxed atmosphere for their children. Nonetheless, the basic generalization of single-dimensional preferences seems to have substantial truth to it, and this general agreement on what makes for a good school has significant implications for how the market for schools operates in practice.

Table 7-5. *Unconstrained Preferences of Parents for Schools, by Socioeconomic Status*[a]

Percent except where indicated

Socioeconomic status	High-circuit schools	Middle-circuit schools	Low-circuit schools	Total number
High	69	25	5	111
Middle	66	30	4	113
Low	68	25	7	60
Average/total	68	27	5	284

Source: Lauder and Hughes (1999: table 4-1).

a. Socioeconomic status measured by occupation index; see appendix B. Chi-square = 1.55, $df = 4$, $p = 0.818$.

Evidence for this characterization of parental preferences emerges most clearly from the Smithfield Project. The researchers first classified each of the secondary schools in Green City into what they referred to as high, middle, or low "circuit" schools, with the classifications based primarily on the socioeconomic mix of the students in each school. In 1993, the researchers undertook a telephone survey to solicit the preferences of parents of year-eight students in Green City regarding the secondary schools their children might attend two years later. Among the questions they asked was where parents would like their child to go to secondary school assuming money and distance were no object. These unconstrained preferences, with parents grouped by socioeconomic background (as measured by the occupational index described in appendix B), are shown in table 7-5.

The table shows that the proportion of parents preferring high-circuit schools for their child is almost identical (about 68 percent) across socioeconomic groups and that the overall patterns of preferences are remarkably similar in all three groups. However, despite the fact that low socioeconomic status parents rank schools similarly to high socioeconomic status parents when they are asked to ignore constraints like money and distance, the Smithfield researchers go on to demonstrate significant differences among the groups when parents are asked which schools are feasible alternatives for their child. This distinction between unconstrained and constrained choices raises important additional issues, which we discuss in the next chapter.

Further suggestive evidence comes from a study by the New Zealand Council for Educational Research of the secondary school preferences expressed by parents of children aged five through eight. The researchers found that most of the parents were already thinking about secondary schools for their children and that the most important factor affecting their preferences was the school's reputation. Reputation, proximity to home, previous family attendance, and school type significantly dominated other considerations, such as those related to curriculum and school activities. More detailed analysis of the parents of eight-year-olds in the Wellington area who mentioned particular schools indicated a clear preference for high-decile, low-Maori schools.[10]

Student Mix as a Proxy for School Quality

The next question logically deals with the basis by which parents and students make their judgments about what constitutes a quality school. While we clearly do not know the answer for all parents, a good deal of anecdotal, and some empirical, evidence suggests that parents typically rely on the ethnic and socioeconomic mix of a school's student body as a shorthand measure of school quality. Such a criterion poses obvious problems for schools serving a high proportion of minority students. "People see little brown faces coming in our gate and immediately think that it's not a very good school," said Margaret Ngatai, principal of Rowley Primary School in Christchurch.

In some cases, no doubt, the decision to flee a school with a high proportion of minorities may reflect the racial prejudices of white parents. However, in many others cases—as is evident from the flight from low-decile schools by minority as well as by white children—the change in schools may simply reflect a quest for school quality. Within the new competitive environment, parents of all races appear to be making a judgment that schools that successfully attract and retain higher proportions of white and economically advantaged students must be of higher quality than other schools.

At the primary level, the absence of national tests in New Zealand means that parents have little or no direct information on which to base judg-

10. Wylie, Thompson, and Lythe (1999: tables 55, 56).

Table 7-6. *Urban Examination Results, Adjusted for Participation, by Illustrative Decile, 1996*

Percent

	Decile			
Examination and score	*1*	*4*	*7*	*10*
School certificate				
Pass rate	4.6	19.7	24.4	44.7
Bursary				
B or better grade	2.4	14.6	19.3	42.9
Bursary				
C or better grade	9.03	27.9	38.3	79.4

Source: Calculated by the authors based on benchmark goals data from the Ministry of Education.

ments about the relative student achievement in various schools. Their main sources of information about the academic quality of a school are the reports from the Education Review Office, views of other parents, and publicity from the school. For many parents, the mix of students at the school, and especially the ethnic mix, seems to dominate these other sources of imperfect information about school quality.

Parents of secondary school students have one additional source of information, namely the so-called league tables, which give details of how students at each school fared the previous year on national examinations taken by most secondary school students. These tables are published annually in the local newspapers. Table 7-6 documents the not surprising conclusion that scores on these tests are highly correlated with the mix of students in each school. The table is based on data for schools in the three urban areas, and it reports the pass rate for the school certificate examination and the percentages of students receiving a B or better grade or a C or better grade on bursary examinations. The reported pass rates and percents were adjusted to correct for the differing average proportions of eligible students who took each test in each decile.

Because the success of students rises so clearly with the decile of the school—and hence with the proportions of advantaged students and white students—it is not surprising that parents might use the mix of students as a shorthand for school quality. This behavior was evident when one of the authors visited a meeting of parents at a secondary school near Wellington on the day the league tables were published. The discussion came around to the relative academic quality of schools in the Porirua Valley, and one of the parents produced the league tables from that morning's paper. Significantly, the ensuing conversation focused not on what the league tables showed about the performance of each school's students on the various national tests but rather on the schools' decile rankings

Decile rankings are based on both socioeconomic background and ethnicity of the students. Once the decile rankings of schools were calculated and made public in 1995, parents had a compact summary measure on which to base their shorthand judgments about a school's quality. Before that, parents had much less information, especially on the socioeconomic backgrounds of a school's students. In contrast, the ethnic mix of the student body was often relatively obvious even to the most casual visitor to the school. This fact may have made the ethnic mix of a school play a particularly large role in school choice decisions before 1995. Even after the introduction of the deciles, however, ethnic mix appears to have continued to exert an independent influence on parental decisions. Evidence for this continuing influence appears in figure 7-6. All secondary schools in the three urban areas were grouped by their 1995 decile rankings, which were based on 1994 enrollment patterns. When the decile rankings were renormed for 1998 (on the basis of 1997 enrollment patterns), the decile ranking of some schools went up, a few went down, and many stayed the same. A rise in decile means that between 1994 and 1997 the school attracted a more advantaged group of students.

Figure 7-6 indicates that, for any given initial decile, the higher a school's initial proportion of minorities, the less likely it was to attract the sort of students who would raise its decile ranking. For example, consider the schools initially ranked at decile 5. The figure shows that, among this group of schools, the ones whose subsequent decile ranking rose were only about 24 percent minority in 1994, while the ones whose rankings did not change were about 37 percent minority. The fact that the line that indicates the initial percent minority in the schools whose deciles rose is below the other line for all deciles suggests that, within any initial decile of schools, parents seem to be distinguishing among schools on the basis of the ethnic mix of the students. As would be expected, the impact of ethnic mix appears to be larger in low-decile schools than in high-decile schools, where the initial proportions of minorities are small.

Figure 7-6. *Changes between 1994 and 1997 in Decile Rankings by Percent Minority, Three Urban Areas, by 1995 Decile*[a]

Percent minority

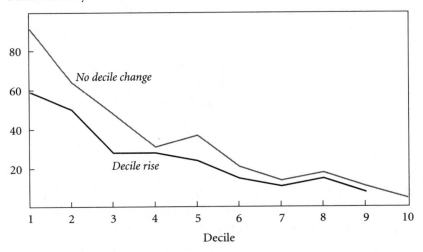

Decile

Source: Calculated by the authors based on data from the Ministry of Education.
a. Decile changes refer to deciles calculated based on 1994 and 1997 enrollment information.

Additional Statistical Evidence

The importance of the initial ethnic mix of students in a school is further supported by multivariate regression analyses of enrollment changes.[11] This statistical technique is useful in that it allows us to separate the effects of a school's mix of students from those of other determinants of

11. The following discussion is based on Ladd and Fiske (1999). For all equations, the unit of observation is an urban school. The equation explaining the variation in the 1991–96 annual rate of enrollment growth for 485 primary schools includes the predicted growth in enrollments, 1991 enrollment (in logarthmic form), indicator variables for Auckland and Christchurch, and a variable indicating whether the school had increased the number of grades during the period. The equation for 123 secondary schools is similar except for the exclusion of the last variable. Regression equations were also estimated to explain the variation in enrollment growth rates during the 1994–97 period. These equations are similar but they exclude the predicted change in enrollments and include information on the socioeconomic mix of the students and an indicator variable accounting for enrollment schemes. For secondary schools the equations also include average test scores.

enrollment changes. Regression equations, based on data for all public schools in the three urban areas, indicate that the greater the proportion of minority students in a school in 1991, the greater the decline in that school's enrollment (or the smaller the growth) in the following five-year period, after controlling for other determinants, including census-based predicted growth in enrollments.[12]

Unfortunately, the absence of 1991 data on the socioeconomic characteristics of the students in each school kept us from determining whether the negative impact of a higher proportion of minority students on a school's ability to attract students implied that parents were trying to avoid minorities or, alternatively, that they were seeking schools with a more economically advantaged group of students. To explore that issue, we analyzed enrollment changes between 1994 and 1997 and added to the equations information on the 1994 socioeconomic characteristics of the students in each school (as measured by the nonminority part of the decile ranking). For secondary schools, we also added 1994 test results. The inclusion of these additional variables did not alter the basic conclusion: schools with high initial proportions of minority students were at a competitive disadvantage relative to other schools in their ability to attract students. For secondary schools the equations suggest that a school in which the share of minorities in 1994 was double that of the typical school (which had a minority share of 26 percent) experienced an average annual growth rate during the following three years that was more than 2 percentage points lower that that of the typical school.[13]

Separate analyses of the rates of enrollment growth of the two ethnic groups, Pakeha and minority students, provide a more complete picture of the effects of a school's initial mix of students. Consider, for example, enrollment changes in secondary schools during the 1994–97 period. For Pakeha students, the results are mixed. In the regressions that include a composite measure of a school's initial socioeconomic mix of students, the equation suggests that students are fleeing from schools with high proportions of minorities rather than seeking schools with more

---

12. This conclusion emerges both for primary and for secondary schools. For primary schools the estimated coefficient (t-statistic) on the minority share variable is –0.23 (3.98); for secondary schools the coefficient (t-statistic) is –.084 (6.96). One standard deviation in the minority share is .29 for primary schools and .25 for secondary schools. See Ladd and Fiske (1999: tables 3, 5, and A1).

13. Ladd and Fiske (1999: tables 3, 6).

advantaged students or higher test scores. However, in regressions that replace the composite measure with its single most-relevant component— the one related to the educational level of parents—we find some evidence that Pakeha students appear to be seeking schools with higher proportions of students from educated families rather than fleeing from schools with high proportions of minorities.[14] This finding does not alter the basic conclusion that schools with large initial proportions of minorities are at a competitive disadvantage, but it does suggest the possibility of a more benign interpretation of the behavior of Pakeha students.

The regression findings for minority students are less auspicious. The equations show that not only are their rates of enrollment growth lower in schools that start out with initially high proportions of minorities but also that they are lower in schools that have higher proportions of advantaged students. Thus like their Pakeha counterparts, minority students appear to be trying to avoid schools with large minority populations. However, compared to Pakeha students, they apparently have more limited access to schools with higher proportions of students from advantaged families, presumably in large part because of the enrollment schemes that we describe further in chapter 8.

Is This Behavior Rational?

How rational is it for parents to use student mix as a proxy for school quality and, consequently, to try to move their children into schools that have higher decile rankings? Recall that the Ministry of Education introduced those rankings not as a measure of school quality but rather as a measure of the relative educational challenges facing schools so it could direct more funding toward schools facing the greatest challenges. Moreover, the fact that student test results are highly correlated with the decile ranking of schools need not mean that high-decile schools contribute more to the learning of students than low-decile schools. It simply reflects the well-known fact that students from more-advantaged backgrounds on average perform better in school than less-advantaged peers. Indeed, it could well be that a high-decile school contributes less learning in a value-

---

14. Ladd and Fiske (1999: table 7). The composite measure is the simple average of the decile rankings of the school for each of the five socioeconomic variables used in the overall decile ranking.

added sense to students than a low-decile school. Presumably, rational parents should be comparing schools based on the additional learning added by each school rather than on either the mix of children within each school or average pass rates.

The question, then, is whether it makes sense for parents to behave as if high-decile schools generated higher value added than low-decile schools. For a number of reasons, such behavior is probably quite rational and sensible, although we hasten to add that what is rational for individuals may not be rational for society as a whole.

The first reason such behavior may be rational is based on the concept of peer effects, which asserts that a student's learning depends in part on the characteristics of her fellow students. For example, if a child is in a classroom with students who are unmotivated and low achieving, that child may pick up some of the bad habits of her fellow students and become less motivated than she otherwise would be. Analogously, a child in a classroom of high-achieving and highly motivated students may become more motivated than otherwise. Because the spillover effects are positive in this case, the move from a lower- to a higher-decile school should increase the student's learning. However, such spillovers need not always be positive. In some cases, a low-performing and unmotivated student in a high-achievement environment may become discouraged, lose confidence, and choose to apply herself less effectively than if the other students were more similar to her. An alternative mechanism with the same outcome would occur if such a student were less successful than more confident and able students in commanding some of the teacher's limited time for individual guidance.

Because the theoretical predications can go in either direction, we cannot say with certainly that a student will learn more when she has more advantaged peers. However, existing empirical work from the United States, work that is admittedly imperfect, tends to support the concept of positive peer group effects in many situations and thus to confirm parents' intuition that their children will learn more if they are in high-decile schools.[15] A study based on international data for five countries, including New Zealand, provides additional evidence of positive peer effects but primarily for students of low ability.[16] Two studies focusing exclusively on

16. See Jencks and Mayer (1990).
16. Toma (forthcoming).

New Zealand also find positive effects from school mix, although these effects are quite small in one case. Both studies use the statistical technique of hierarchical linear modeling to isolate the effect of school mix on a student's performance on school certificate examinations. One study concludes that the effects of school mix "make only a small contribution, over and above the effects of the same variables at the individual level."[17] The Smithfield project finds that about 20 percent of the variance in individual scores is attributable to differences between schools and that about a third of this variance is explained by school-level variables, which include school-mix variables such as average socioeconomic status, ability, and proportion of the students who are minorities.[18]

A second and closely related reason that such behavior may be rational emerges from the work of Martin Thrupp in New Zealand. Based on a detailed and careful investigation of processes at four schools in Wellington, he describes and documents how schools serving high concentrations of disadvantaged pupils are forced to behave in ways, none of them conducive to high learning, that differ significantly from schools serving middle-class students. For example, compared to middle-class schools, low-decile schools have to spend a lot more time and effort establishing basic student routines, such as getting students to show up for class with the materials they need and to do their homework. Such schools also devote more attention to pastoral and disciplinary activities and, in light of students' poor absolute performance, to motivating and attracting staff. Thrupp's main conclusion is that students in low-decile schools may not do as well as other students largely because such schools cannot offer the middle-class types of school processes that are necessary for educational success.[19]

A third reason that parents' instincts about school quality may be valid is that high-decile schools are likely to be more successful than low-decile

17. Harker and Nash (1996: 158).
18. Lauder and Hughes (1999: 126–27). They also include a measure of enrollment stability as a school-level variable. From the results they report, it is not possible to separate the contribution of school-mix variables from that of the stability measure. Because they have included no other school-level variables related, for example, to school processes or resources, it could be that the included variables serve in part as proxies for these other variables. In addition to examining the effects of school mix on school certificate results, the researchers also explore the effects of school-mix variables on various tests that they administered themselves and that are less directly related to the curriculum. They find slightly larger school mix effects on those test results.
19. Thrupp (1997b).

Table 7-7. *Secondary School Teachers Recognized as among the Best by the New Zealand Qualifications Authority, by School Decile*

Percent

	Decile				
Teachers	1, 2	3, 4	5, 6	7, 8	9, 10
NZQA[a]	7.1	12.5	26.8	27.4	27.0
Total (full-time equivalent)[b]	12.7	23.7	25.0	19.5	19.1
Row 1 ÷ row 2	0.56	0.53	1.07	1.41	1.41

a. Teachers selected by the NZQA to be moderators for their programs in 1998. Distribution is based on 384 teachers.

b. All teachers in 1996, based on data provided by the Ministry of Education.

schools in attracting the most capable teachers. Currently, New Zealand teachers with a given amount of experience receive the same basic pay regardless of where they teach. Because it is often easier, and for some more satisfying, to teach students who are motivated and ready to learn, it would not be surprising to find that high-quality teachers gravitate to high-decile schools, in which the teaching environment is less harsh than in low-decile schools.

In the absence of direct evidence on how teachers' quality varies by decile, the indirect evidence in table 7-7 supports the point. Every year the New Zealand Qualifications Authority (NZQA) chooses a large number of teachers throughout the country to moderate its various seminars for teachers on the qualifications frameworks. Because the NZQA tries to pick teachers who possess the professional expertise, knowledge, and experience that will make them credible to their peers, it recruits teachers who are regarded as among the best teachers of their subjects. Of interest in table 7-7 is the high concentration of these good teachers in high-decile schools. However, since high-decile schools tend to be larger and have more teachers from which to choose, we also compare the distribution of the NZQA moderators with the distribution of teachers across schools. The table confirms the conclusion that the teachers recognized by the NZQA are disproportionately represented in high-decile schools.

A fourth and final reason for parents to link high-decile schools with high-quality education has to do with the resources provided by parents. High-decile schools are typically able to raise more local funds—from parents and other sources—than are low-decile schools. While these funds do not fully offset the greater funding that low-decile schools receive from the government, they represent but the tip of a larger iceberg of parental resources. The greater the educational and financial resources of parents in a school, the more they can contribute to the quality of that school. Such schools have ready access to the volunteer services of lawyers and accountants, to architects who can help with the design of new buildings, and to parents who can organize and assist with school trips and cultural activities and otherwise enrich the classroom environment.

For all these reasons, the desire by families to move their children up the decile rankings of schools seems quite rational. One problem is that not all families are equally able to exercise choice in that manner.

Greater Use of Choice by Families with High Socioeconomic Status

In an ideal choice environment, all families would have equal ability to exercise their choice among schools. For that to occur, all families would have to be able to afford their schools of choice, to have adequate information about the various schools, and to feel comfortable making school choices in unfamiliar neighborhoods. They would also have to have as good a chance as any other family of having their child accepted by the school.[20] These conditions do not hold in New Zealand, however, so those who are relatively more privileged than others in any neighborhood are more likely than other families to exercise choice.

Some evidence for this conclusion comes from the Smithfield project. With their large student-level data base for Green City, the Smithfield researchers were able to explore in some detail which families sent their secondary-school-age children out of what would have been the local zone for each school. The researchers measured a family's socioeconomic status using the occupation index used throughout the project. Their initial finding—that higher socioeconomic status families were less likely than lower socioeconomic status families to send their children out of the zone—may at first seem surprising, but only until one realizes that the existence of successful schools in high socioeconomic status neighborhoods gives little incentive to families living there to move their children.

The Smithfield researchers went on to document that the families who are more affluent or educated *relative to their neighbors* in their residential

20. Fiske (1991).

neighborhood are the most likely to exercise choice by sending their children to a school other than the local school. Their approach was to calculate a relative socioeconomic index for each student as the socioeconomic status for the student's family minus the average socioeconomic index of families in the students' neighborhood.[21] Then for the students in the first year of secondary school in the eleven schools in their Green City sample, they calculated the average relative index for students attending local schools, adjacent schools, or distant schools (defined as more than one school away from the local school) for each of the years 1990–95. For Maori and Pacific Islanders, they found that students who attended their local schools were from the relatively less-advantaged families in their respective neighborhoods and that students who attended adjacent schools were relatively advantaged. The patterns for distant schools were more mixed. Pakeha students attending the local schools were slightly advantaged relative to the averages for their neighborhoods but not relative to the students who attended adjacent or distant schools. The researchers concluded that "for all three ethnic groups, it was the relatively advantaged who were able to attend nonlocal schools."[22]

The Smithfield telephone surveys of two urban areas shed additional light on the reasons for these patterns. Views about the ideal school for one's child did not differ much across families ranked by socioeconomic status. However, in practice low socioeconomic status families were much less likely to consider a high-circuit school a feasible choice for them, and not surprisingly, they were less likely to apply to such a school than were high socioeconomic status families. For example, only 25 percent of low socioeconomic status parents applied for a high-circuit school, in contrast to 63 percent of high socioeconomic status parents.[23]

The Smithfield researchers characterize the declining interest in high-circuit schools by low socioeconomic status families as they get closer to

21. Lauder and Hughes (1999: 92–95). Unfortunately, neither in the original Smithfield report to the Ministry of Education nor in their book do the authors clarify how they define a neighborhood, other than it is smaller than a school zone. In addition, the authors are not clear about how they calculated the average socioeconomic index for each neighborhood. Because they calculated it year by year, they apparently used the data from their sample of students rather than from an alternative source, such as the census. It would have been useful to have information on how many of their sample students resided in each neighborhood.

22. Lauder and Hughes (1999: 95).

23. Lauder and Hughes (1999: table 4-4).

the actual decision as a "a cooling out." Consistent with their backgrounds as sociologists, the researchers attribute it to a variety of social class and ethnic factors. Although social class may be part of the story, some straightforward economic considerations would also seem highly relevant, such as the costs in time and money of traveling from some low-income neighborhoods to higher-decile schools.

Economic and Other Constraints on Low-Income Families

The New Zealand system of parental choice is decidedly not user-friendly to low-income families, especially those in urban areas. First, the government provides little or no transportation subsidy in urban areas, presumably on the grounds that students have access to public transportation. But daily public transportation can be costly for a family with little income, and it is far less convenient and flexible than the automobiles frequently available to high-income families. In her survey of primary school parents, Cathy Wylie found that among parents who had selected their child's next school, 21 percent mentioned money as an obstacle, 13 percent mentioned transportation, and 20 percent a school enrollment scheme. Maori and Pacific Islanders were more likely to mention transportation as an obstacle than were Pakeha households.[24]

Second, student fees in the higher-decile schools are not inconsequential. The NZ$450 fee for a Wellington College student, for example, would take a big chunk out of the budget of any low-income family. Although that fee is at the high end of the range, many schools charge substantial sums. While such fees are not technically compulsory, and indeed are waived for some students, their existence puts the low-income family in the difficult and embarrassing position of having to ask for special treatment. Moreover, the higher-decile schools are also likely to impose charges on students that do not show up in the official fees, such as the cost of school trips and athletic equipment; these are expenses that schools serving poorer constituencies cannot expect to recoup from parents.

Finally, disadvantaged families are constrained by the enrollment schemes that are most common in high-decile schools. Based on their small sample of secondary schools, the Smithfield researchers report that even after they control for student achievement, the probability that a

24. Wylie (1997: 158).

student will be accepted by a high-circuit school is higher for high socio-economic status students than for low socioeconomic status students.[25]

Choice and the Culture of Competition

It is clear from the foregoing that the exercise of parental choice has substantially altered enrollment patterns and that it is rational for parents to try to move their children up the decile rankings of schools. In addition, economic considerations, as well as considerations of social status, adversely affected the ability of some families to exercise choice.

As is evident from our description of parents and prospective students taking part in the Open Evening at Aotea College, the exercise of parental choice is not a one-way activity. The primary and secondary schools that families select or shun are not passive participants in a process largely beyond their control. To the contrary, as the leaders of Aotea College demonstrated, primary and secondary schools can do much to shape the way they are perceived by potential students and parents and thus to improve their competitive position. Just as parents have seized upon their new right to select the schools their children attend, so individual schools have taken advantage of their self-governing status to become more aggressive in marketing themselves.

The cumulative effect of parents exercising choice and schools struggling to increase their status and drawing power has been to establish a competitive environment that has drastically altered the culture of New Zealand schools. To this new culture of competition, we now direct our attention.

25. Lauder and Hughes (1999: 52, fn. 3). According to their covariance analysis, the probability of being accepted after adjusting for achievement was .89 for high socioeconomic status students, .85 for middle socioeconomic status students, and .79 for low socioeconomic status students. Separate analyses by ethnic group show that minority groups had a low probability of acceptance whatever their socioeconomic status and that the effects of such status were largest for Pakeha students.

8 | *Culture of Competition*

T HE HUTT RIVER VALLEY runs for twenty miles north of Wellington, and the communities that it has spawned range from prosperous hillside enclaves like Stokes Valley to flatland towns like Taita and Naenae that owe their existence to state housing projects. A commuter railroad links these communities with Wellington, carrying thousands of workers into the capital city each day and offering easy mobility to students who choose to enroll in schools at some distance from their homes.

For many years Upper Hutt College was the dominant secondary school in the upper valley, with enrollments that hovered around 1,300 students. It served students from the affluent areas of Silverstream and Pinehaven to the north and was known for turning out students who scored well on school-leaving examinations. By contrast, Heretaunga College, located only a mile away, was the poor country cousin. It drew heavily from areas of state housing to the south, and with rolls that rarely topped 900 students, seemed to lack distinction of any kind.

In the early 1990s, as the Tomorrow's Schools reforms began to make themselves felt, the two schools became locked in a battle for students. Brian Robb, who had become principal of Heretaunga in 1988, set out to change the lackluster image of the school where as a young teacher he had taught social studies. He conducted focus groups to determine what the community wanted from its secondary schools and began promoting

Heretaunga as a school that cared not only about test scores but about students' overall welfare. He mounted a computer literacy program for entering students and joined the local Rotary Club. He adopted a more stylish school uniform, wrote articles promoting the school for the local newspaper, and began building relationships with the principals of primary and intermediate schools in the area. Perhaps most important, he conspicuously suspended some disruptive students in order to send a message to the community about the school's values.

Meanwhile, Upper Hutt College was having its troubles. Its principal had alienated many students and parents by what many regarded as his overzealous interest in the rugby team, and he was widely viewed as having stayed in office beyond, as New Zealanders would say, his "use by" date. The school community was shocked by a series of student suicides. Although its examination results remained impressive, Upper Hutt came to be seen as an uncaring place and found itself shunned by many potential students and parents. Soon the traditional fortunes of the two schools had reversed. Enrollment at Heretaunga soared from 864 students in 1992 to 1,030 in 1998, while the rolls at its competitor plunged to a low of 769 in 1996. That was the year that the Upper Hutt board of trustees brought in Peter Lee as principal and charged him with reversing the decline.

Lee took his assignment seriously. He signaled his concern for the quality of teaching in the school by visiting classes and moved to increase the quality of the educational experience for minority students by building a *marae*, or meeting place, for Maoris. He took out newspaper advertisements promoting the impressive examination results of Upper Hutt students. Above all, Lee recruited vigorously and aggressively. He traveled abroad to recruit fee-paying students from Asia and Brazil; back home he took aim at students for whom the natural choice of secondary school was Taita College to the south. In his last year in office, Lee's predecessor had initiated a controversial policy of sending a bus each day into Stokes Valley to make it convenient for students to opt for Upper Hutt rather than the much closer Taita. Lee added a second bus. He also enlisted a board member who worked in the office of Avalon Intermediate School, a Taita feeder school, to surreptitiously obtain a list of the names and addresses of graduating students and then sent out letters inviting them to come to Upper Hutt. His marketing and recruiting efforts paid off, and by 1998 enrollment at Upper Hutt, not counting foreign students, had crept back up to 829.

The ongoing battle for students between Upper Hutt College and Heretaunga College is a good example of the way the market environment fostered by Tomorrow's Schools has altered the landscape and culture of primary and secondary education in New Zealand in situations in which schools are in a position to compete against each other on a fairly equal footing. Students and parents in the upper valley showed no reluctance to exercise their new right to select among competing secondary schools, and the resulting reversal of fortunes of the two institutions can be seen as a textbook example of an educational marketplace at work. The boards and professional leaders of both schools understood the importance of marketing in the new environment and acted accordingly.

The need to compete for students has brought a new level of energy to both institutions. As Lee put it, "One of the advantages of Tomorrow's Schools is that it sharpens your focus. It makes you more conscious about the need to deliver quality education." But Lee is also frank to admit that the culture of competition has led him to act in ways that he dislikes, both personally and professionally. He now admits that he went too far in obtaining of the names of students at Avalon Intermediate School and says he has assured the principal of Taita College that he will not do it again. As for sending buses into Taita's natural catchment area, he commented, "I was appointed to turn around a school. If I have to raid Stokes Valley, I'll do it. It's the market working. I don't particularly like the system, but it's the one I'm in, so I'll work it."

New Market Environment

Schools in New Zealand have always understood the need to cultivate positive relationships with the communities they serve, but the removal of zoning and the introduction of full parental choice in 1991 added new urgency to this task. Boards of trustees understood that to maintain ample enrollments in the new educational marketplace they must not only provide quality educational programs but also find ways to publicize them and to convince potential students and their parents that their offerings were preferable to those of the school down the road. For the first time, marketing became an important part of the job description of principals.

As with markets in the commercial sector, competition for students among New Zealand schools takes place within certain natural geographical areas. At the primary level, where the pupils are less mobile, these areas tend to be relatively small, although there are notable exceptions. Thorndon School, strategically located near the government offices and the downtown business area of Wellington, sponsors an after-school program that allows parents who commute into the capital to drop their children off in the morning and pick them up at the end of their own workday. "They enjoy the drive time with their children," commented Bill Sutton, the principal.

Markets at the secondary level are much larger geographically and tend to be defined by transportation patterns, such as the railway line that runs along the Hutt Valley. Another railway line extending north to Porirua and beyond makes it easy for students in bedroom communities like Whitby to commute into the city to desirable schools like Wellington College and Wellington Girls College. The trains that transport these daily legions of adolescents are known locally as Acne Express. The availability of an elaborate system of freeways in Auckland made possible the substantial migrations of students that occurred in that city after Tomorrow's Schools went into effect. Indeed, parental choice is seen by some as a significant contributor to Auckland's huge traffic congestion problem.

Certain marketing practices have now become standard. Virtually every primary and secondary school in New Zealand now sponsors open evenings for potential students and parents, and they all have promotional brochures. These range from simple flyers to elaborate viewbooks on glossy paper with four-color printing, comparable to those sent out by American colleges and universities.

Like Upper Hutt College, secondary schools frequently purchase newspaper advertisements, typically at reduced rates, to publicize their general programs or to publicize how their students did on national examinations. Some schools have even hired advertising agencies. Several years ago the board of trustees of Kaikorai Valley College in Dunedin bought television spots to promote itself as a safe environment. "We were the first to advertise on TV, so the national media picked up the story and gave us a lot more publicity," recalled Don Lawson, the principal. Every year Kaikorai Valley also drops school brochures in 12,000 letter boxes, far more than would be required to reach only potential students. "We want people in the community talking about us," said Lawson.

Leaders of schools with serious enrollment problems sometimes go to extraordinary lengths to market their institutions. When he took over a school that was experiencing enrollment declines and whose potential students had been targeted by Peter Lee of Upper Hutt College, Murray Trembath, the principal of Taita College, began spending an hour and a half every evening knocking on the door of every potential student. "I introduced myself as the principal of Taita and said that I understood that they had a child ready for secondary school and asked if I could talk with them," he said. "Some said no, that they had already decided on a school, but others agreed to talk. I asked them why they were leaning to Upper Hutt and then tried to get them to come to our open house. Every one who came ended up enrolling."

Perhaps the most ambitious marketing gambit at the primary level in the Wellington area can be found at the Russell School in Porirua East, which pays the round-trip taxi fares of 120 students a day so they can attend the school. The program costs the school NZ$40,000 a year, but it reaps many times that amount in added income. "My critics won't believe me, but we got into the taxi business by accident," said David Stanley, the principal. "We had quite a few students from refugee families who were only allowed to stay in their housing for one year. So we began to bring them back by taxi, and once the taxis were in place we began to say okay to others as well."

Schools have also become conscious of subtle ways in which they are projecting images that may hinder enrollment. Kaikorai Valley College removed an old fence and a run-down bike shed from the front of its property. "We wanted people to be aware that something was going on in the school," said Lawson. Images can be especially important when it comes to the ethnic mix of the student body. In his talks with parents who answered his door knocks, Murray Trembath discovered that many white parents thought of Taita as having a much higher proportion of Maori students than it actually did. One reason, he determined, was that the school's *marae* was easily visible to passing motorists—an image problem that was eased through some creative landscaping. Trembath also gave serious consideration to changing the name of his school to one that would not bring to mind a state housing project. "I was keen to get a name like Eastern Hutt High School or Hillview, but the idea went nowhere," he said. "I mentioned it at the fortieth renunion, and everyone wanted the old name—even though they were not sending their kids here."

While some principals undoubtedly view this emphasis on marketing as inappropriate and a distraction from the main mission of educating children, others have embraced it enthusiastically and see it in positive terms. Iain Taylor, the entrepreneurial principal of Ponsonby Intermediate School, has urged his fellow principals in print to understand the difference between marketing and mere self-promotion. To him marketing is a process of aligning the educational product of the schools with the needs of children and families. Marketing, he wrote in the *New Zealand Journal of Educational Administration,* "is not just about such glossy things as the front-of-house image, impressive brochures or expensive advertising. Marketing is a philosophy—it is about building an awareness in the specific audience you are trying to capture and letting them know that you have a service to offer, that you understand their needs, and what's more, can satisfy those needs." Carrying out such a program, he said, "demands that we continually strive to achieve and improve service and performance quality."[1]

Bigger Is Better

In addition to putting an increased premium on the need for schools to promote themselves, the introduction of an educational marketplace in New Zealand has brought with it a new set of rules that drive judgments about how large schools should aspire to become and the sort of students they should seek to attract. The first and most basic new rule is that bigger is better. Growth in enrollment up to the point of a school's capacity and, better still, having more applicants than places, are the new symbols of success in the marketplace.

As in other countries, size and status have traditionally gone hand in hand in New Zealand's state educational system. Principals have always received salary increases as they moved from smaller to larger schools, which made more administrative demands. Faculty and administration staffing lines increased as enrollment grew, and larger schools were more visible and thus had greater prestige among the general public. Since the Tomorrow's Schools program went into effect, enrollment in the more desirable higher-decile schools grew, while the rolls of lower-decile institutions shrank.

Although Tomorrow's Schools by no means introduced the notion that bigger is better, it pushed the concept to center stage. For one thing, by disrupting the relatively stable enrollment patterns of the past, parental

1. Taylor (1997: 6, 8).

choice created a situation in which it was now possible for schools to become as large as they wished. Ambitious administrators were no longer constrained by geography, established feeder patterns, or traditional public images of their school. Through effective planning and marketing they could recruit any student within commuting range in order to bolster their rolls. The professional and other rewards that flowed from being bigger became very real possibilities for the first time in hundreds of schools. So did the pitfalls of becoming smaller.

New financial incentives also contributed to the preoccupation with growth. Whereas previous staffing formulas were built around ranges of enrollment, with schools getting an additional teacher when enrollment reached designated plateaus, the new formulas are much more sensitive to small increases in student rolls. Moreover, self-governance offered opportunities for schools to become larger through the addition of more grades. Kaikorai Valley College amalgamated with an intermediate school, and some primary schools have opted to add grades and retain students for their intermediate school years. Principals of such schools have a strong incentive to encourage their boards to take such a step, since the new and larger institution would thrust him or her into a higher salary bracket.

Importance of Enrollment Schemes

The all-important corollary to the rule that bigger is better is the principle that success lies in controlling the mix of students. In the educational marketplace students are the coin of the realm. Parents are looking to enroll their child in the best possible school, while schools are seeking not only to fill all of their classroom seats but to do so with the best possible students. High-quality students are easy to teach and produce league tables of test scores that enhance the school's image, attracting other high-quality students. The strategic goal of every school in the educational marketplace is thus to increase in size to the point at which it qualifies for an enrollment scheme. Enrollment schemes are formal plans that guide schools with a surplus of applicants in determining which students they will accept and which they will reject.

It is difficult to overemphasize the importance of enrollment schemes in New Zealand schools. Once a school reaches the point at which it has such a mechanism, it is no longer subject to the whims of the marketplace. It can choose among applicants and shape the nature of its student body. It can take the smartest students and those from the most economically and socially advantaged families and refuse applicants who are not so able academically or who are likely to bring learning or behavioral problems. The only restrictions are that the terms of enrollment plans must be published and that schools cannot contravene civil rights provisions. By contrast, schools without enrollment schemes are obligated by law to take any student who shows up at the door. Once the schools in high demand have creamed the most desirable students, undersubscribed schools then compete for students whose own options are now restricted to such institutions.

Under the system of enrollment schemes, success breeds success. Schools with control over their student intake are not only in a position to ensure academically able student bodies but also have the ability to tailor their academic offerings to such students. They gain the right to tell the market what they are offering—such as a classic core curriculum—and then concentrate on honing these offerings. A narrow curriculum can also be used as a subtle way to divert applications from students they would just as soon not have. The principal of a school that does not offer woodworking or typing courses can with a clear conscience tell students wanting these courses that their needs would be better served elsewhere.

Schools without enrollment schemes, on the other hand, have no such luxury. The previous chapter showed how, at its open house for prospective students and parents, Aotea College stressed the breadth of its curricular offerings, but Brent Lewis, the principal, is quick to admit that this strategy has its risks. "We have to be all over the place, so we fund classes that are uneconomical and lose any sense of a strategic focus," he said. "This is a classic model for failure in New Zealand."

Establishing an Enrollment Scheme

Under the procedures set up by Tomorrow's Schools the minister of education must give formal permission to a school to enact an enrollment scheme. This typically follows a process of negotiation over what constitutes the school's capacity. Schools argue for the lowest possible definition in order to get the enrollment scheme as soon as possible, while the ministry tries to push the number as high as possible, primarily because it must provide spaces for the excess students elsewhere. The resulting figure is usually something of a compromise. At Heretaunga College, for example, the ministry wanted to set the roll at 1,100, but the school negotiated the number down to 980. In many cases the ministry rejects requests for enrollment schemes. Papanui High School in Christchurch, which has 1,073 students, believes that its capacity should be 1,000 students, but the ministry says that it is 1,200. "We have been turned down three times," said Marge Scott, the principal.

Although the ministry must give its approval for a school to enact an enrollment scheme, it has no authority over the content of the plan. Most schools begin by defining a geographic catchment area surrounding the school and then offering either automatic admission or preference to students who reside within that area. Most also give priority to children with siblings already attending the school, and many give preference to children of staff members and former students. In some schools these priority spots require that students apply by a specific deadline.

Even seemingly innocuous priorities lend themselves to manipulation. Early deadlines tend to favor the wealthy, who are better informed about such matters. Geographic boundaries are often gerrymandered to embrace predominantly middle-class residential areas. Wellington College's local recruiting area, which predates Tomorrow's Schools, is a map of the city's affluent neighborhoods. Its students find it convenient to frequent the McDonald's restaurant on nearby Adelaide Road, whose less-advantaged residents are outside the school's local zone. The catchment area of Hutt Valley High School outside Wellington does not include any of the contiguous light industrial area of Petone, but it does extend to the affluent coastal community of Eastbourne, several miles away.

Schools pursue quite different policies in filling spaces that are still available once their core criteria are exhausted. Some schools, such as Boulcott Primary School in Wellington, accept out-of-zone students on a first-come, first-served basis. Others, including Hutt Valley High School, use a lottery to fill those spaces. Some schools essentially leave such decisions up to the principal. The Tawa Intermediate School in that same urban area, for example, authorizes its principal to admit students based, among other things, on "the need of the student to attend Tawa Intermediate" and on "the preference of the child and his/her parents for the educational philosophy espoused by the school." Its policy guidelines define "need" as embracing "the personal or social needs of the child, the family circumstances of the child, subject needs, cultural or sporting needs." The policy

Figure 8-1. *Students in Crown-Owned Primary Schools with Enrollment Schemes, by Urban Area, 1993, 1995, 1997*[a]

Percent of students

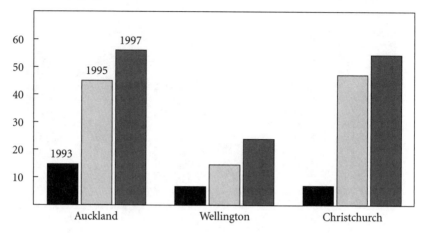

Source: Calculations by the authors based on data provided by the Ministry of Education.

a. In Auckland, the number of schools with enrollment schemes by year are 3 in 1993, 87 in 1995, and 112 in 1997; in Wellington, 7, 13, and 21; and in Christchurch, 4, 28, and 33.

of the Roseneath Primary School in Wellington is even more vague. After allowing for students living in its zone, siblings, and the children of staff members, its policy states that students will be admitted on the basis of "any other factor the Board or its delegated authority considers relevant." Some schools may request an interview with the applicant and parents or that supporting material be provided as part of the application. Two schools in Dunedin adopted a first-come, first-served policy that led to parents queuing up all night outside the school in the middle of winter.

Pervasiveness of Enrollment Schemes

As of 1997, the proportion of students in primary schools with enrollment schemes exceeded 50 percent in both the Auckland and Christchurch areas and was 24 percent in the Wellington area. Figure 8-1 portrays the rapid growth in these schemes in the three urban areas between 1993 and 1997. In all of these areas, the proportion of students increased in these years as the number of primary schools with such schemes increased from

Figure 8-2. *Students in Crown-Owned Secondary Schools with Enrollment Schemes, by Urban Area, 1993, 1995, 1997*[a]

Percent of students

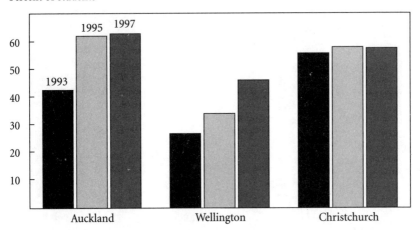

Source: Calculations by the authors based on data provided by the Ministry of Education.

a. In Auckland, the number of schools with enrollment schemes by year are 15 in 1993, 20 in 1995, and 23 in 1997; in Wellington, 4, 5, and 7; and in Christchurch, 7, 7, and 7.

23 to 112 in Auckland, from 4 to 33 in Christchurch, and from 7 to 21 in Wellington.

Because a larger proportion of secondary schools than of primary schools had enacted enrollment schemes by 1993, the growth of such schemes is not as dramatic as for the primary schools (see figure 8-2). Importantly, however, by 1997 the proportion of students in schools subject to enrollment schemes exceeded 50 percent in Auckland and Christchurch and was close to 50 percent in Wellington.

As one might expect, the prevalence of enrollment schemes is greater in high-decile than in low-decile schools. The pattern across groupings of deciles is shown in figure 8-3. Most striking is the fact that all of the schools in Christchurch in deciles 7–10 have enrollment schemes. This fact goes a long way toward explaining the pattern of enrollment growth in Christchurch secondary schools. Enrollments in the low deciles declined, in the middle deciles grew significantly, and in the high deciles hardly grew at all. In fast-growing Auckland even some low-decile schools have enrollment schemes. In that area, some students have had difficulty find-

Figure 8-3. *Students in Crown-Owned Secondary Schools with Enrollment Schemes, by Urban Area and Decile Group, 1997*[a]

Percent of students

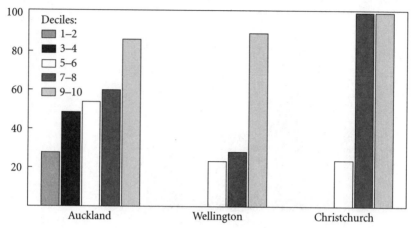

Source: Calculations by the authors based on data provided by the Ministry of Education.

a. In Wellington and Christchurch, there are no deciles 1 to 4 Crown-owned schools with enrollment schemes.

ing any school that would accept them, and in extreme cases the ministry has had to intervene to direct a school to take a student. In Wellington, the enrollment schemes are most prevalent in decile 9 and decile 10 schools. Thus for all practical purposes, most students who do not live near those schools will not have access to them. Indeed, as noted with respect to Wellington College, even some students who do live nearby may not have access if the local zone gerrymanders them out.

Figure 8-4 illustrates the prevalence of enrollment schemes by gender mix of the school. Once again, Christchurch stands out in that all the single-sex schools in that urban area have enrollment schemes. Historically, single-sex schools have been viewed as the most prestigious. They are now able to maintain their prestigious position by choosing their students. How they do so, however, varies significantly by school, which in turn has differential effects on nearby schools. For example, Neil Lancaster, the principal of Mairehau High School in Christchurch, told us that his school is surrounded by two schools with enrollment schemes that operate quite differently. Shirley Boys High School emphasizes academic ability and selects students by personal interview, while Avonside

Figure 8-4. *Students in Crown-Owned Secondary Schools with Enrollment Schemes, by Urban Area and Gender Mix, 1997*[a]

Percent of students

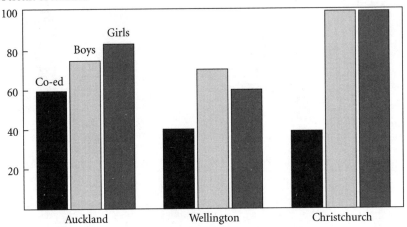

Source: Calculations by the authors based on data provided by the Ministry of Education.
a. In Auckland, the number of schools with enrollment schemes are eighteen co-ed, two boys, and three girls; in Wellington, five, one, and one; and in Christchurch, three, two, and two.

Girls High School selects by random ballot. The effect on Mairehau is significant: it gets a much more random group of girls than it does of boys, with the result that the girls at Mairehau perform significantly better than do the boys.

From Parental Choice to School Choice

The cumulative effect of this abundance of enrollment schemes is profound, for they have produced a fundamental change in the nature of New Zealand's state educational system as it applies to urban areas and to the most desirable schools. Oversubscribed schools have an enormous competitive advantage in the educational marketplace. As John Tapp, assistant principal at Porirua College, put it, "Parental choice has become a myth. Schools with enrollment schemes make it clear that they will accept only certain kinds of student, so they end up doing the choosing, not parents." What began as a system of parental choice has become, for all practical purposes, a system of school choice.

Many parents, to be sure, successfully place their children in the schools that they believe will best meet their academic, social, and other needs.

But many other families lack any leverage over desirable schools because their child does not fit into the school's profile of a desirable student. Such parents have thus been effectively frozen out of the selection process. They are free to exercise choice, but only among undersubscribed schools. The original school reform plan, the 1989 policy paper, *Tomorrow's Schools*, sought to head off such a situation by providing for supervised balloting in situations in which schools had more applicants than they could accept, but this policy was in effect for only one year. The 1991 decision by the new National government to move to an unfettered educational marketplace by abolishing enrollment zones and to expand parental choice with no constraints on schools thus had a pivotal impact on the course of New Zealand education.

The shift from parental to school choice is another reflection of the erosion of the democratic-populist philosophical current that was part of the original Tomorrow's Schools plan. The original conception, built into the Picot task force report, was that parents would exercise influence over schools through participation in their governance. The National government that assumed power in 1991 took a different approach to parental influence, preferring to use the exit mechanism of the marketplace and to lodge parental influence in their power to withdraw their child from schools with which they were dissatisfied. Parents still have this right, but as schools have regained control of the process through the use of enrollment schemes, the balance of power has tilted sharply in the schools' favor.

Successful and Unsuccessful Schools

The introduction of competition in New Zealand schools brings with it a specific definition of success. A successful school within the market is one that is attracting a growing number of students or that is filled to capacity and has been empowered to set up an enrollment scheme. An unsuccessful school is one that finds it difficult to attract students. Success in the marketplace need not be perfectly correlated with how well the school is delivering its educational program.

Successful Schools

Successful schools are obvious to all. They have students lining up to attend, have enrollment schemes, and have made effective use of their power to control the mix of students they accept. In New Zealand, they include most of the older secondary schools founded on the English grammar school model, which have traditionally been at the top of the educational pecking order and which have retained their position under the new rules—schools such as Auckland Grammar, Wellington College, and Kings College in Christchurch. But the ranks of successful schools also include institutions such as Heretaunga College in the Upper Hutt Valley that have figured out how to operate in the new educational marketplace.

Although successful schools tend to be concentrated among upper-decile schools, a few low-decile schools are relative winners as well. Otahuhu College in South Auckland, for example, was founded in 1931 and still has the grand feeling of the stately stone structures built in that era. Otahuhu educated numerous generations of blue-collar workers, but with the disappearance of jobs in meat packing plants and on the railway over the last quarter of a century, the demographics of the neighborhood and the school's constituency have changed. Since 1985 the proportion of Pakeha, or European, students at Otahuhu has fallen from 40 percent to 8 percent, while that of Pacific Islanders has increased from 27 percent to 58 percent.

Even though it is now a decile 1 school and loses students to higher-decile schools to the north, Otahuhu is oversubscribed and has an enrollment scheme that defines its capacity at 1,310. "The school retains its old image of providing a solid education to working-class whites, and we don't do anything to diminish this image," said Bill Gavin, who has been principal for thirteen years. Otahuhu has received two favorable reports from the Education Review Office, and it has become the school of choice for many families in the low-income areas of Otara and Mangere who are disappointed with the quality of troubled local high schools like Hillary and Tangaroa Colleges. "We attract many of the more ambitious families in these areas," said Gavin. "A key reason for our success is that we have a stable roll."

Unsuccessful Schools

Unsuccessful schools fall into a broad spectrum, ranging from schools such as Upper Hutt College, which have been edged out by some of their neighbors in the educational marketplace yet remain fully functional institutions, to schools whose very viability as educational institutions has been threatened. Of course, any urban school system in a developed country has struggling schools, and New Zealand had its share well before the Tomorrow's Schools reforms. But the educational marketplace has contributed to the emergence of a class of schools that have gone into a downward trajectory over which they have little control and from which it is difficult to escape. Just as success breeds success, so failure breeds failure. Needless to say, most of the downward spiraling schools serve predominantly low-income communities like Mangere and Otara in South Auckland and Porirua near Wellington.

A 1966 report commissioned by the Ministry of Education describes the downward spiraling process. The report focused on the eight decile 1 schools, all with high proportions of Pacific Island students, that were part of a ministry-sponsored school improvement project called AIMHI. The study was carried out by Kay Hawk and Jan Hill, educational researchers from Massey University. The authors concluded that all eight of the AIMHI schools had been disproportionately disadvantaged by the way in which the educational marketplace exacerbated existing problems related to demographics and poverty, and that five of the eight "have fallen into a spiral of decline that has become self-fulfilling as their rolls drop dramatically with dezoning."[2]

One of the downward spiraling schools is Porirua College, the only one of the AIMHI schools not located in Auckland. The college is located in Porirua City, a suburb of Wellington that is the site of the largest state-owned housing project in New Zealand. The city has been losing population because of loss of jobs and because the government's decision in the mid-1980s to reduce the rent subsidy in state housing forced many residents to move elsewhere. Before geographical zoning was abandoned, Porirua College had 1,100 students, about half white and half minority. With the introduction of parental choice, substantial numbers of families, especially white ones, began enrolling their children elsewhere. More than 40 percent of secondary-age students in Porirua now leave the city every day to attend school, and enrollment at Porirua College hovers just over 400. Between 1990 and 1992 the school lost eleven of its thirty-five staff positions.

Hawk and Hill describe a general pattern to the downward spiraling phenomenon at Porirua College and elsewhere. Rolls decline, which leads to a reduction in staff, which affects the quality of the academic program,

2. Hawk and Hill (1996, Executive Summary, no page number).

which triggers unfavorable reviews and negative publicity, which makes it even more difficult to attract skilled staff. While all this is happening the school is becoming smaller and thus losing the benefits from economies of scale available to larger schools. The researchers conceded that by definition there will always be schools in this "lowest" position in any society but added, "Once a Decile 1 secondary school's roll begins to drop, given current educational policy and resourcing, the impact of reduced staffing alone will make it almost impossible to reverse the trend, regardless of the quality of leadership and governance."[3]

Healthy and Unhealthy Competition

From a policy perspective, it is fitting to raise the question of whether it is desirable to set up a system under which you know from the outset that some schools will be successful and others unsuccessful—or more to the point, that some students will end up in successful schools and others will end up in unsuccessful ones.

The answer to this question depends in part on the relationship between the market test of success and other measures of success, such as the quality of education provided. Concern about having students in unsuccessful schools would conceivably be lessened if one were confident that, despite the school's lack of success in attracting students, its efforts to do so induced it to provide a higher-quality education than it otherwise would have provided. Concern would also be eased if one were confident that the school was basically healthy and had a good chance of rebounding and being more successful in the future.

Such was the case in the Upper Hutt Valley, where the two secondary schools described at the beginning of this chapter compete on fairly equal terms. In this case, the educational marketplace has worked fairly well, with Heretaunga College, the successful school, and Upper Hutt College, the unsuccessful one, and competition in the area healthy. Parents and students have gained control over their education, while the schools have been prodded to think carefully about their instructional offerings and climates and, one may presume, to become better schools in the process. Who knows what the relative situation of the two schools will be five or ten years down the road? While Upper Hutt College is currently strug-

3. Hawk and Hill (1996, Executive Summary, no page number).

gling, it remains a viable school and certainly has the human and cultural capital to make a comeback and possibly even regain its relative hegemony in the area sometime in the future.

However, the playing field of student choice is not typically so level. Many schools lack the ability to compete effectively because of factors outside their control, such as being located in a low-income area and serving disadvantaged minority students. In such cases, even the best management and instructional programs may not be sufficient to overcome a school's basic disadvantage. Because parents make schooling decisions partly based on a school's mix of students, a school may lose students to nearby areas regardless of how hard it tries to offer sound educational programs.

This line of reasoning suggests that the correlation between students' disadvantage and school success in the market might be used as a rough measure of the health of competition within an urban area. Where competition is healthy, we would expect to find both successful and unsuccessful schools within each socioeconomic stratum of schools and consequently no overrepresentation of disadvantaged students in the unsuccessful schools. In contrast, where competition is less healthy in that it reflects the movement of students toward schools with the "better" mix of students, we would expect to find disadvantaged students overrepresented in the unsuccessful schools.

Quantifying the Successes and the Failures

For the purposes of the following analysis, we classified the schools in our three metropolitan areas, as of 1997, into three categories: successful, unclear, and unsuccessful, using the same definitions for all three metropolitan areas. Successful schools comprise all schools with enrollment schemes as of 1997, those whose student rolls grew at least 5 percent between 1991 and 1997, and the few schools that were open in 1997 but not in 1991. The unclear category comprises schools without enrollment schemes that experienced changes in enrollments either positive or negative of less than 5 percent or that experienced overall declines of 5–20 percent but a growth in enrollments during 1994–97. Unsuccessful schools are those without enrollment schemes whose enrollments fell by 5 percent or more during the period and whose enrollment in 1997 was less than in 1994. Many of the secondary schools in this latter category experienced declines greater than 20 percent.

Two comments are worth making about the concept of success and the enrollment growth cutoff points we used. First, the 5 percent growth rate required for success is based on the Wellington area's average growth during the 1991–97 period. Thus in the Wellington area a school without an enrollment scheme must grow faster than the overall average growth of the area to be viewed as successful. Second, this low cutoff makes it quite easy—and perhaps excessively so—for a school to be classified as successful in either of the other two areas and especially in fast-growing Auckland. Although we could have modified the growth rate cutoff by area, we chose not to hide the fact that when an area is growing, a larger portion of the schools in a market system will be successful by any market definition of success. Similarly, in a slow-growing area, a larger portion will be viewed as unsuccessful. Some readers, however, may find it reasonable to classify the schools in the unclear category for Auckland or Christchurch as unsuccessful schools.

Table 8-1 shows for each of the three metropolitan areas the number of secondary schools, the distribution of schools and students across the categories of successful, unclear, and unsuccessful, and the characteristics of the schools in each of these categories. Note that the number of successful schools in each urban area is greater than the number of unsuccessful schools. However, if one considers schools in the unclear category as unsuccessful, the picture changes somewhat.

For example, the number of unsuccessful secondary schools in Auckland is either eleven or twenty-four, depending on whether one combines the unclear category with the unsuccessful category; and such schools include either 10 percent or 23 percent of the total students. But it is also true that 77 percent of all Auckland students attend successful schools, and moreover, a majority of minority students attend successful schools. However minority students are clearly overrepresented in Auckland's unsuccessful schools, and further, these schools have much higher proportions of Maori and Pacific Islanders than Auckland's successful schools do.

Schools in Wellington show a similar pattern, but a much higher proportion of students attend unsuccessful schools. This greater proportion is not surprising given the slower growth of the student population in Wellington. In addition, only 30 percent of Maori students and 21 percent of Pacific Island students are in successful schools, while about half of these students attend unsuccessful schools. Christchurch, with its medium rate of student growth, falls between the other two areas. As indicated by

Table 8-1. *Successful and Unsuccessful Secondary Schools, by Urban Area, 1997*[a]
Percent unless otherwise indicated

Area	All schools	Successful schools	Unclear schools	Unsuccessful schools
Auckland				
Number of schools	85	61	13	11
Distribution of students[b]				
All	100 (69,578)	77.1	12.7	10.2
Maori	100 (7,117)	60.4	16.8	22.8
Pacific Island	100 (11,127)	58.2	19.6	22.3
Characteristics of schools				
Maori[c]	10.2	8.0	13.6	22.8
Pacific Island[c]	16.0	12.1	24.6	34.9
Decile rank number	6.3	7.1	4.4	2.4
Wellington				
Number of schools	39	15	11	13
Distribution of students[b]				
All	100 (24,685)	45.6	29.0	25.4
Maori	100 (3,090)	29.4	25.6	45.0
Pacific Island	100 (2,442)	20.6	21.0	58.4
Characteristics of schools				
Maori[c]	12.5	8.1	11.1	22.2
Pacific Island[c]	9.9	4.5	7.2	22.7
Decile rank number	7.0	8.4	7.6	3.9
Christchurch				
Number of schools	30	20	6	4
Distribution of students[b]				
All	100 (22,831)	70.4	16.6	13.0
Maori	100 (1,502)	50.5	16.4	33.1
Pacific Island	100 (601)	43.4	21.5	35.1
Characteristics of schools				
Maori[c]	6.6	4.7	6.5	16.8
Pacific Island[c]	2.6	1.6	3.4	7.1
Decile rank number	7.5	8.3	7.3	3.3

Source: Calculated by the authors from data provided by the Ministry of Education.

a. Successful schools include schools with enrollment schemes as of 1997, those whose enrollment increased by 5 percent or more between 1991 and 1997, and those established between 1991 and 1997. Unsuccessful schools are those without enrollment schemes whose enrollment decreased by 5 percent or more between 1991 and 1997, provided enrollment did not increase between 1994 and 1997. Unclear schools are all other schools that were open in 1997.

b. Number in parentheses.

c. Percent of student body.

Table 8-2. *Student Performance by School Success and Urban Area, 1997*[a]

Percent unless otherwise indicated

Area	Successful schools	Unclear schools	Unsuccessful schools
Auckland			
1997 grades, all tests			
As and Bs	35.5	24.6	13.6
Ds and Es	36.0	47.5	63.7
1992–97 change (percentage points)			
As and Bs	2.3	–0.1	–0.8
Ds and Es	–2.7	–0.4	3.0
Wellington			
1997 grades, all tests			
As and Bs	37.2	35.2	16.8
Ds and Es	29.6	33.7	56.2
1992–97 change (percentage points)			
As and Bs	0.5	3.9	–4.1
Ds and Es	–3.1	–5.9	4.4
Christchurch			
1997 grades, all tests			
As and Bs	38.4	25.0	12.2
Ds and Es	30.4	42.9	60.6
1992–97 change (percentage points)			
As and Bs	–1.0	–6.8	–4.6
Ds and Es	1.6	6.7	4.0

Source: Calculated by the authors from data provided by the New Zealand Qualifications Authority.

a. Data are for all school certificate tests taken by the students in each school. Entries are weighted averages for each type of school.

school decile rankings in all three areas, the challenges of educating students are far greater in unsuccessful than in successful schools.

Table 8-2, which provides information on the academic performance of secondary school students by type of school, shows that students in unsuccessful schools perform less well on the school certificate exam. The table summarizes test score results based on the whole array of subject tests included in the school certificate. Although these are national tests, not all students take them, and some students may delay taking them in order to increase their chance of passing them. Thus the average results in the table are at best rough measures of student performance. Nonetheless, clear patterns emerge: students in unsuccessful schools are substantially less likely to earn grades of A or B and more likely to earn grades of D or E than students in more successful schools.

In addition, the table shows the changes in test performance over the period 1992 (the earliest year with tests that are comparable to those in 1997) to 1997. During this period, average performance in unsuccessful schools deteriorated (with the proportion of students receiving As and Bs going down and the proportion receiving Ds and Es going up); the reverse is true in successful schools. We emphasize that, because of changes in the mix of students within the schools and possibly in who takes the tests, these changes provide no evidence about the quality of a school's educational offerings or about changes in the quality of those offerings over time. Instead, the point is simply that the disparity in average achievement between successful and unsuccessful schools increased over time.

Table 8-3 replicates table 8-1 for primary and intermediate schools. While the patterns are similar to those for the secondary schools, the differences between successful and unsuccessful schools in the types of student they serve is somewhat less pronounced, especially in the Wellington area, where the picture of the effects of market competition is most benign in that minority and low-income students are no more overrepresented in unsuccessful schools than in unclear schools.

The evidence makes it quite clear that, especially in secondary schools, the competitive system generates a situation in which high-income, nonminority, high-performing students are significantly overrepresented in successful schools. The other side of this coin is that low-income, minority, low-performing students are overrepresented in unsuccessful schools.

Winners and Losers among Students and Families

By implication, the existence of successes and failures among schools means that the market model has also produced winners and losers among the students and families served by these schools. There is no doubt that many middle- and high-income Pakeha, or European, families are better off under Tomorrow's Schools than they were under the previous system.

Table 8-3. *Successful and Unsuccessful Primary and Intermediate Schools, by Urban Area, 1997*[a]

Percent unless otherwise indicated

Area	All schools	Successful schools	Unclear schools	Unsuccessful schools
Auckland				
Number of schools	334	284	24	26
Distribution of students[b]				
All	100 (119,428)	88.4	6.8	4.8
Maori	100 (19,949)	83.7	7.9	8.4
Pacific Island	100 (24,315)	83.3	8.5	8.1
Characteristics of schools				
Maori[c]	16.7	15.8	19.5	29.4
Pacific Island[c]	20.4	19.2	25.6	34.7
Decile rank number	5.3	5.5	3.6	2.8
Wellington				
Number of schools[b]	185	111	35	39
Distribution of students				
All	100 (42,979)	62.3	19.6	18.1
Maori	100 (7,644)	52.8	26.5	20.8
Pacific Islander	100 (4,696)	47.6	23.9	28.5
Characteristics of schools				
Maori[c]	17.8	15.1	24.0	20.4
Pacific Island[c]	10.9	8.3	13.3	17.2
Decile rank number	6.5	6.9	5.3	5.8
Christchurch				
Number of schools	116	82	21	13
Distribution of students[b]				
All	100 (31,473)	75.1	17.0	7.9
Maori	100 (3,147)	56.7	25.6	17.7
Pacific Islander	100 (1,147)	51.1	28.1	20.8
Characteristics of schools				
Maori[c]	10.0	7.5	15.0	22.5
Pacific Island[c]	3.6	2.5	6.0	9.7
Decile rank number	6.3	7.1	4.6	2.9

Source: See table 8-1.

a. See table 8-1.

b. Numbers in parentheses.

c. Percent of student body.

To be more precise, such parents *believe* they are better off by being empowered to choose the school their child will attend and by carrying through on that right. One can question, of course, whether these Pakeha students are in fact better off: they are now being educated in a more homogeneous environment in preparation to take their places in a multicultural world. But that is another issue.

Individual winners also include the many low-income and minority students who now attend higher-quality schools than they would have under the old system. Parents who exercise the option of not using a local school tend to be relatively well-off compared to their neighbors, even in low-income neighborhoods. Bill Gavin confirmed this general pattern for Otahuhu College, the successful decile 1 school in South Auckland. Otahuhu holds an enrollment week every July during which virtually any student who signs up is admitted. "The parents who lose out are ones who live in the school's old enrollment area who don't take advantage of the July enrollment," he said. "The more ambitious parents are the winners." Donald Lawson, principal of Kaikorai Valley College in Dunedin, painted a similar picture: "The losers are disorganized, low-income families."

Other losers among students and families include those who have no reasonable choice of school by virtue of where they live. In significant sections of Christchurch and Auckland all secondary schools have enrollment schemes, and many students must travel substantial distances—and past numerous other schools—to find a place with a vacancy. George Hawkins, a member of Parliament from Auckland, provoked a furor when he cited the situation of a Maori constituent who quite literally could find no local school with a place available, even when accompanied by his father. "So for two years this kid, Johnny, did not go to school at all," said Hawkins. "That is a disgrace."

Other losers are those effectively excluded from choice by the cost of exercising it. These costs include transportation to and from school, which for most students is not subsidized, and user fees, which almost all New Zealand schools ask families to contribute.

Some students and families end up as losers even when they appear to be winners, because higher-decile schools do not always welcome parents who take advantage of their right to exercise choice. The mother of a student at Tamaki College told of her effort to enroll him in a higher-decile school. "People assume that any child at a school like Tamaki is at the bottom," she said. "This is the school that gets dumped with all the dredges.

My son is bright, and we thought he would be better off at this other school, which has better facilities. But they didn't care whether he failed or passed. He didn't get the attention he needed, and when he decided not to work they didn't follow up at all. So he's back at Tamaki." Parents and administrators at schools such as Tamaki say that it is not uncommon for higher-decile schools to encourage students who are not fitting in to stay until shortly after March 1, the date when the ministry certifies the size of a school's enrollment and determines which school receives the per pupil allotment that goes with each student. The lower-decile school to which the student returns then has the obligation to teach him or her, but the revenue to do so stays with the former school.

Characteristics of Overburdened Schools

Another consequence of the culture of competition has been a sifting and sorting process by which low-decile schools are repositories for a disproportionate share of the country's most difficult-to-teach students.

Table 8-4 summarizes the characteristics of the students in decile 1 and decile 2 schools in New Zealand's three urban areas in 1997. The students in these schools tend to be disproportionately minority and to have parents with low income and limited education who work in unskilled jobs or receive income support payments and who live in overcrowded housing. The easiest characteristics to interpret are those related to educational background of parents and ethnic mix of students. In decile 1 schools more than 50 percent of parents have no secondary school qualification (comparable to a high school dropout in the United States); 85 percent of primary and intermediate students and more than 90 percent of secondary students are ethnic minorities, defined as Maoris and Pacific Islanders. These proportions compare to about 15 percent with no educational qualification and about 5.5 percent minority in decile 10 schools.

By concentrating on selected measurable characteristics of school populations that are correlated with student performance, the table fails to highlight many other harder-to-measure characteristics that also contribute significantly to the ability of students to learn. Among these other characteristics, health and nutrition are particularly important.

Overburdened primary schools include the likes of Cannon's Creek School in Porirua, near Wellington. Cannon's Creek is a decile 1A school,

Table 8-4. *Characteristics of Students in Low-Decile Urban Schools, 1997*
Percent unless otherwise indicated

School decile	Low income	Persons per bedroom	With no education qualifications	With income support	In unskilled occupation	Minority
			Primary and intermediate schools			
1	22.4	1.51	51.6	38.0	30.6	84.6
2	20.9	1.44	42.9	31.0	25.3	56.3
			Secondary schools			
1	20.0	1.54	54.2	36.5	32.6	90.9
2	18.2	1.46	44.5	29.5	25.3	67.8

Source: Figures in first five columns estimated by the authors based on decile rankings for each school for each category, using median values of decile rankings. Last column is based on actual percentage of minority students (Maori and Pacific Island) in each school.

which means that the student population ranks among the bottom 2 percent in New Zealand by economic and social indicators. An estimated one-third of children in Cannon's Creek have iron deficiency, and many do not have a regular place to sleep. "When I first told people that I was working in Porirua, they would ask me if I had to get shots and a passport to get to work," said Ashley Blair, the principal. Problems such as glue ear, for example, are endemic, and Blair spends much of his workday looking for ways to improve the health and nutrition of students as a means of keeping them fit to learn. Several years ago he went so far as to hold classes for parents on how to make a nutritious lunch for their children to bring to school. "We found that many parents did not know how to do it," he recalled.

Tamaki College in South Auckland has set up the Puna Waiora Health Center in a renovated classroom building. The center, whose name means Healing Spring, houses three full-time staff members—a guidance counselor, a social worker, and a nurse—and is financed jointly by the school, the Ministry of Education, and social welfare agencies. A family physician visits the school on Wednesdays. The center was set up by John Grant, then the Tamaki principal, as a way of locating needed social services where students had ready access to them. Staff members say that health problems such as iron deficiency and high cholesterol levels are rampant among students, and a high proportion of students arrive at school without breakfast. The center runs regular programs aimed at anger management and raising student self-esteem, and the three staff workers work together to identify and deal with problems such as violence or sexual abuse in the home, in some cases making referrals to the judicial system.

In one sense, none of this is new. Like all industrialized countries, New Zealand has its share of overburdened urban schools, and recent social changes have intensified the problems. Changes in the global economy have raised the level of skills demanded of new entrants to the work force and have led to a drying up of jobs for school dropouts. In light of these new realities, New Zealand in 1991 increased the age of compulsory schooling, from fifteen to sixteen years. This has meant that many academically unenthusiastic students who in the past would have left school may now remain in these urban schools.

However, the new competitive environment and the downward spiraling process have clearly exacerbated the challenges faced by the schools on the lowest rung of the educational ladder. Earlier, we describe how parental choice has increased the concentration of minorities and economically disadvantaged students in such schools.[4] We now turn to the trickle-down effect of student expulsions on low-decile schools.

Suspended Students

That low-decile schools end up with the hardest-to-educate students is documented vividly by the movements of students who have been formally suspended from school. By law, schools have the right to expel students for gross misconduct or continual disobedience. If the student

4. In chapter 7 we document the increased ethnic concentration in low-decile schools (see table 7-1 and figure 7-5). Unfortunately, we do not have sufficient data to document changes in the socioeconomic mix of students in low-decile schools. Our data on measurable family characteristics (approximated by mesh-block data from the 1991 and 1996 censuses applied to 1994 and 1997 enrollment data) do not permit a clear analysis of the changes in the socioeconomic characteristics of students in decile 1 schools. But the logic is still compelling: in a choice situation, students who remain in decile 1 schools are likely to be those who have no choice, those from the most dysfunctional families, or those with the most problems. Hence the challenges faced by low-decile schools as a result of choice are more serious than those that would occur in the absence of parental choice.

has not yet reached the school-leaving age of sixteen, the principal taking the disciplinary action must find a place for him or her in another school. In practice, principals in a given geographic area develop informal working relationships under which they agree to take unruly students off each other's hands. The 1996 data from the Ministry of Education on the origins and destinations of expelled students, however, show that these working relationships are far from equal. More often than not, the school receiving an expelled student has a lower decile ranking than the sending school. As Brent Lewis at Aotea College, a decile 2 school, said regarding nearby Tawa College, which is decile 9, "Every kid I get from Tawa is either learning disabled, a behavior problem, or there are problems in the family."

The Ministry of Education reported 982 cases in 1996 of students suspended from one school and subsequently enrolled in another. Of these, nearly half (47 percent) moved to a lower-decile school, while not quite one-third (31 percent) moved to a higher-decile school. The remaining 22 percent moved laterally. If we eliminate students expelled from schools in deciles 1 and 10, where movement is possible in only one direction, the pattern of suspended students moving down the decile scale is even clearer (see table 8-5). Of the 862 students expelled from schools in deciles 2–9, slightly more than half moved down, while only 30 percent moved up. In deciles 4–7, where the possibilities for mobility are greatest, the pattern is more striking still. Among the 488 students expelled, the number of those moving down the decile rankings is 55 percent, while the number moving up is 28 percent.

The data also show that schools in the lowest two deciles carry a disproportionate share of the burden of dealing with expelled students (table 8-6). Schools in the lowest two deciles were the only ones that took in more suspended students than they sent, while those in the other eight deciles sent out at least as many as they received. Schools in deciles 3–10 expelled 767 students and took in only 675, while those in deciles 1 and 2 expelled 215 students but took in 307.

A New Equilibrium?

One might argue that the polarization that resulted from the creation of winner and loser schools has led to a new equilibrium that could be

Table 8-5. *National Student Suspensions, by School Decile, 1996*

School decile	Number	Percent
2 to 9		
Student moved to lower-decile school	446	51
Student moved to same-decile school	155	18
Student moved to higher-decile school	261	31
Total	862	100
4 to 7		
Student moved to lower-decile school	268	55
Student moved to same-decile school	86	18
Student moved to higher-decile school	134	28
Total	488	100

Source: Tabulated by the authors from data provided by the Ministry of Education. Deciles 1 and 10 were eliminated from this tabulation since students suspended from decile 1 schools cannot move down and those from decile 10 schools cannot move up.

academically and ethically acceptable. True, schools like Porirua College are but shadows of their former selves in terms of enrollment, and they are serving a high proportion of difficult-to-teach students. But perhaps they are now in a position to develop the expertise to serve these students effectively. Perhaps the market has created a situation in which these schools offer more value-added academics to such students.

A major problem with such reasoning, however, is that the system has no way of rewarding value-added instruction. There are no financial or professional incentives for good teachers to take jobs in such schools, and the league tables by which the public judges schools do not give credit for value added.

Moreover, just as enrollment has become the currency of the realm for principals and boards of trustees, so the ministry in its own way is committed to the principle that bigger is better. It rewards growth and pays little attention to academic quality in a steady-state context. David Hodge, principal of Tamaki College, recalls a conversation with a ministry official in which he outlined the school's plans under the AIMHI project and pointed out that, while it would lead to better teaching, it would not necessarily lead to a larger enrollment. "He told me I was naïve if I did not understand that the point of the whole exercise was to increase enroll-

Table 8-6. *National Student Suspensions, Sending and Receiving Schools, by School Decile, 1996*

School decile	Suspended students received	Suspended students	Ratio of students received to students suspended
1	168	89	1.89
2	139	126	1.10
3	137	147	0.93
4	156	170	0.92
5	133	156	0.85
6	89	89	1.00
7	48	73	0.65
8	53	66	0.80
9	29	35	0.82
10	30	31	0.96

Source: Tabulated by the authors from data provided by the Ministry of Education.

ment," Hodge said. "The ministry's interest in helping schools has nothing to do with academics. It has to do with where you can increase your rolls and cut the cost of building facilities elsewhere. Serving kids well is not the issue. They don't care about this."

In any case, it is hard to rationalize the new equilibrium as being desirable in that it is one in which the schools at the bottom rung of the educational ladder have higher proportions of failing students than they did in the past. Table 8-7 documents this pattern for those decile 1 urban schools for which complete data are available for the period 1992–97 (the longest period of comparable test data). The table shows that, for these schools, students with scores of D or E on the math exam increased from 75.6 percent in 1992 to 87.5 percent in 1997, while those with scores of A or B decreased from 11.2 to 7.5 percent. In contrast, across all secondary schools in the three urban areas, students scoring D or E decreased from 43.3 percent to 37.1 percent, while those scoring A or B stayed about constant (not shown in table). Similar patterns also emerge, albeit somewhat less dramatically, for the aggregate of all subject tests.

We conclude that in the new equilibrium the discrepancy in student performance between schools at the bottom and the average urban school exceeds what it would have been in the absence of the new competitive environment.

Table 8-7. *School Certificate Results for Decile 1 Urban Schools, 1992 and 1997*[a]

Percent unless otherwise indicated

Test and year	Number of tests taken	As and Bs	Ds and Es
Mathematics			
1992	818	11.2	75.6
1997	624	7.5	87.5
All tests			
1992	5,268	8.2	74.2
1997	3,849	6.4	75.2

Source: Calculated by the authors based on data provided by the New Zealand Qualifications Authority.

a. The results are based on information for seven urban schools that were in decile 1 in 1997. The schools are De La Salle College, Hillary College, Mangere College, McCauley High School, Otahuu College, Porirua College, and Tamaki College. These are all the decile 1 secondary schools in the Auckland, Wellington, and Christchurch areas for which data are available for both years.

Other Consequences of Choice and Competition

The emphasis on market competition has altered the culture of the state educational system in other ways as well. The first and most important question is what it has done to the quality of academic programs.

Quality of School Offerings

For the secondary school level, it is hard to say much in a systematic way about how the reforms have affected the quality of education. We cannot draw any conclusions about quality from the results of the school certificate examinations because they are not required and are not taken by all students. Moreover, given that they are graded on a curve, they cannot be used as a yardstick to measure changes in the performance of the system over time.[5]

5. One careful study of the New Zealand experience appears to argue that the market system has reduced overall student performance because of the peer effect and that the way to improve overall performance would be to introduce a controlled-choice program that balances the mix of students in each school (Lauder and Hughes [1999: 136]). However, the existence of peer effects is not sufficient by itself to reach the conclusion

One can certainly find examples of schools and principals who have responded to the pressure of competition by trying hard to address such problems. One example is Susanne Jurgensen, who was named principal in 1997 of Porirua College, a decile 1 secondary school in the Wellington area. She introduced a number of programs aimed at improving the quality of education at the school, including an after-school homework center with a tutor to help students prepare for bursary exams. The school has embarked on a literacy action plan aimed at getting 99 percent of students reading at appropriate levels by 1999. The general consensus among educators familiar with Porirua College seems to be that the school is teaching its students effectively even though, given students' socioeconomic backgrounds, the school does not look good in league tables. However, documenting general patterns and evaluating their significance for educational quality is difficult.

The most systematic problem relating to academic quality facing low-decile schools that are losing students is the difficulty they face in attracting good teachers and administrators. This obstacle was identified by the Education Review Office (ERO) in its 1996 report on South Auckland schools and reaffirmed by the ERO in its 1998 comparison of rich and poor schools. The challenge such schools face in attracting good teachers is consistent with the data on teacher quality by school decile and was confirmed in interviews with teachers and administrators. In some cases, low-decile schools have been reluctant to fire teachers who are clearly not competent for fear that any new replacement teacher might be even worse. Whereas in the past teachers were given modest financial incentives to work in difficult situations, such incentives now work in the other direction. Bonuses for taking on extra administrative or other assignments, known as management units, tend to be available only in schools in which the rolls are increasing, which is to say in higher-decile institutions. In addition, the work is hard and a teacher often has to be willing to sacrifice career advancement to work in a school that the market has labeled failing. Given this reality, it is hard to believe that low-decile schools provide a higher-quality education than they provided in the past.

---

that the polarized system generated by market forces reduces overall student achievement. Although students who remain in low-decile schools may be worse off and achieve at lower levels, those who move to higher-decile schools will be better off and may achieve at higher levels than they otherwise would. The net effect is unclear.

Some of the same pressures apply to administrators. "A lot of people told me not to apply to be principal of a decile 1 school," said David Hodge of Tamaki College, an AIMHI school. "They said that everything is against you and that you will inevitably be labeled a failure." Robin Staples, the principal of Hillary College, suggested that the personnel situation in downward spiraling schools need not be as dismal as it is. "Teachers will come to schools like this if they are exciting places and the rewards are appropriate," he said. "But changing the rewards currently requires central decisionmaking, which is at odds with Tomorrow's Schools thinking."

Similar considerations apply to primary schools. "For teachers to teach in low-decile schools they must either be saints or be incompetent and have no alternatives," said Diane Forbes, a star teacher at Gladstone Primary School in Auckland. "These schools are not well supplied and the work is hard. If you are a good teacher, you have to be willing to sacrifice career advancement to work with these students. I would be interested in doing it for a while, but only if I had assurance of getting my old job back."

At the primary school level, more systematic information is available about educational quality, although it is in the form not of concrete measures but rather of professional judgment. The evidence is based on Wylie's national surveys of principals and teachers about the effect of the Tomorrow's Schools reforms. Such surveys were carried out in 1989, 1993, and 1996.

Table 8-8 reports principals' views about the impact of Tomorrow's Schools on their schools. More than half of the principals believed that the Tomorrow's Schools reforms had a positive impact on the quality of children's learning, the content of teaching, and teaching style. These responses are more positive than those in surveys of prior years. A similar picture emerges from surveys of teachers. Table 8-9 shows that 47 percent of the teachers believed that the reforms had a positive impact on the quality of children's learning, 67 percent on teaching content, and 59 percent on teaching style, and that these responses were significantly more positive than in prior surveys. It is worth noting that teachers separated their views about the impacts on teaching from their views about job satisfaction and their quality of life: 57 percent said that the reforms had a negative impact on their job satisfaction and 76 percent said the reforms had a negative impact on the quality of their life outside school.

These positive views about the impacts of Tomorrow's Schools on teaching and learning need to be interpreted with care. Do they represent the positive effects of competition or of the new curriculum frameworks introduced in the mid-1990s? Because the results are based on a national,

Table 8-8. *Principals' Views on the Impact of Tomorrow's Schools on Their Schools, 1997*[a]

Percent

Impact area	Positive change	No impact	Negative change
Quality of children's learning	52[b]	37	11
Teaching content	71[b]	19[c]	12
Teaching style	56[b]	34[c]	12
Relations between teachers and parents	48	32	20
Relations between principal and teacher	49[b]	36[c]	14
Relations between teachers	42	39	14
Relations with other local schools	32	36	30

Source: Adapted from Wylie (1997: table 75).

a. Sample size is 181 principals. Percentages do not add to 100 because of rounding errors. Positive change is the sum of major positive and minor positive change; no impact is the sum of no impact and hard to tell; negative change is the sum of minor negative and major negative change.

b. Signifies that one or both of the components that make up the category are statistically different from prior surveys in a positive direction.

c. Signifies that one or both of the components that make up the category are statistically different from prior surveys in a negative direction.

rather than an urban, sample of schools, many of the schools were not in a competitive situation. Principals who identified themselves as competing with other schools were more likely than other principals to report a negative impact on the content of teaching (22 percent versus 8 percent). Moreover, those who had lost students were more likely than those who had gained students to note a general negative impact on their students (16 percent versus 3 percent). Those who lost a lot of students were more likely to believe that the reforms had a major negative impact on the teaching content at their schools (25 percent versus 1 percent of the others, including those whose rolls had fallen slightly).[6] Thus competition by itself may well have led to lower educational quality, at least in some schools.

The fact that teachers had a more positive view of the effects of the reforms on teaching and learning in 1996 than in earlier surveys might be explained in terms of adjustment costs. During the early period of Tomorrow's Schools, the new administrative responsibilities placed on schools were burdensome and took time and attention away from teaching. By the mid-1990s, however, administrative structures were in place

6. Wylie (1997: 162).

Table 8-9. *Teachers' Views on the Impact of Tomorrow's Schools on Their Schools, 1996* [a]

Percent

Impact area	Positive change	No impact	Negative change
Quality of children's learning	47[b]	43[c]	10
Teaching content	67[b]	21[c]	12
Teaching style	59[b]	32	9
Relations with parents	36	55[c]	8
Relations with principal	28	54	17
Relations with fellow teachers	32	57	11
Relations with support staff	29	69[b]	2
Relations with other local teachers	20	69[b]	11
Job satisfaction	25	19	57
Quality of life outside school	5	20	76[b]

Source: Based on Wylie (1997: table 76).

a. Entries are percentages of the teachers who were teaching in 1989 and who answered the question. The number of respondents for each item is about 85 percent of the 361 teachers interviewed. Percentages do not add to 100 because of rounding errors. Positive change is the sum of major positive and minor positive change; no impact is the sum of no impact and hard to tell; negative change is the sum of minor negative and major negative change.

b. Signifies that one or both of the components that make up the category are statistically different from prior surveys in a positive direction.

c. Signifies that one or both of the components that make up the category are statistically different from prior surveys in a negative direction.

and the pace of change had slowed down, so teachers were able to refocus attention on teaching and learning. Wylie, however, suggests an alternative explanation for the improvements in teaching and learning, namely the introduction in 1993 of a new national curriculum, which brought with it new opportunities for professional development and new resources.

To summarize, by 1996 a majority of principals and teachers in primary schools believed that the Tomorrow's Schools reforms had had a positive impact on teaching and learning. However, one must be cautious in attributing whatever improvements did in fact emerge to parental choice and competition alone.

Decline of Professional Collegiality

State education in New Zealand has traditionally been characterized by a high degree of collegiality among professional educators. The former

Department of Education worked closely with the teachers' unions on matters of curriculum and other educational policy issues. Principals in various geographical areas met on a regular basis to discuss common problems. Principals in the Hutt Valley, for example, collaborated on drawing up the boundaries that defined their respective enrollment zones.

By introducing the concept of an educational marketplace, however, the Tomorrow's Schools reforms put serious strains on this tradition of collaboration. Principals began to view each other not as professional colleagues but as competitors, whose success constituted a threat to their own student rolls, and they began to have second thoughts about sharing good ideas that might be used against them. "Collegiality has disappeared," said Ashley Blair of Cannon's Creek School. "It used to be that those of us working in low-decile schools with lots of Pacific Islanders would get together to talk about health issues, but that doesn't happen any more." Some support for this conclusion appears in table 8-8: in the national sample, 30 percent of the principals of primary schools reported that the reforms had a negative impact on relations with other schools, the largest negative effect reported in the table.

The new competitive environment has also encouraged educators to believe that good ideas have economic value. Rather than automatically sharing insights with their colleagues, principals have begun looking for ways to exploit them for financial gain. Some entrepreneurial principals have taken the policy statements they drafted to meet the requirements of the Education Review Office and made them available to other schools for a fee. Others have marketed professional development plans. "The old system had mechanisms for identifying the best people and distributing their knowledge to other schools," said Brent Lewis, principal of Aotea College. "Professional development is still a priority, but there's no collaboration. It's a matter of co-opting rather than getting people to volunteer, and the attitude has become, 'You pay me, and I'll do the course.'"

Moral and Other Issues

Many principals report discomfort at some of the activities they find themselves undertaking in order to compete in an educational marketplace. These range from questionable recruiting techniques to the roles of principals implicit in the functioning of enrollment schemes. Some school heads, for example, frankly dislike being put in the position of deciding how to allocate desirable places in a state system of compulsory education. "There are lots of decent kids that you'd like to take but cannot," said Bruce Murray of Tawa College. "You're put in the position of playing God. I hate it." Roger Moses, principal of Wellington College, said that he wonders about the effect of his decisions on other schools. "What do you say to Polynesian parents from Porirua who want their child to come here?" he asked. "You know you are handing them the keys to the kingdom, but you also ask whether you would be taking him from another school that needs him."

Educators see at least two other specific problems that have arisen from the introduction of market competition. The first flows from the shift in thinking about how parents would exercise their influence over schools. Whereas the initial theory of Tomorrow's Schools held that such influence would flow from parental involvement in the governance of schools, the market mentality lodges parental influence primarily in their power to exit. While that power could well enhance the voice of those parents who keep their children in the school, by opening up other options, it also reduces the incentive for some parents to work to make the original school a better place.

The second has to do with institutional stability. One of the arguments for establishing residential zoning in the first place was to minimize the possibility of big—or at least unanticipated—fluctuations in school enrollment. Actually, the introduction of market competition makes it more difficult for managers of individual schools to plan from year to year, because they do not know how many students they will have. It is also difficult for the system as a whole to engage in long-range planning, especially in the area of capital expenses. "The Ministry of Education has to worry about future generations as well as the current one," said Jonathan Boston, a professor of public policy at Victoria University of Wellington.

Some administrators argue in principle against using commercial categories to think about the state educational system. "Salvation through management with local site management and salvation through market forces are not solutions that I accept," said Murray Trembath, principal of Taita College. "Education, by its nature, is about individuals learning to live with themselves and society. The market is essentially selfish and about profit and loss, balance sheets, and return on investments. Education is the social process by which society enables or empowers its members in order that it, society, may survive. Public education, in the interests of the society it serves, should be free, and free of the control of the marketplace."[7]

Choice and Diversity of Educational Offerings

One of the arguments frequently advanced in support of market competition in public education is that it will generate more diversity in the type of schools available. Because students and parents have different needs and wishes regarding schooling, the argument goes, a competitive environment will lead to the establishment of schools serving a variety of niche markets: schools that focus on the basics, schools that emphasize particular academic areas like the performing arts, schools that use athletics or art as a vehicle for teaching the standard curriculum. This argument relating to supply-side diversity is one that is heard frequently from proponents of charter schools in the United States.

The Picot task force expected that giving communities more influence over school governance would generate a more diverse range of educational offerings available to parents, if only through the creation of schools within schools.[8] The *Tomorrow's Schools* policy paper picked up on such thinking and also held out the possibility that, as a last resort, parents dissatisfied with the offerings of local schools would start their own school, with support from the ministry.

The Tomorrow's Schools reforms did introduce some supply-side diversity into the New Zealand school system. Earlier, we described the way in which Gladstone Primary School organized its curriculum around the psychologist Howard Gardner's theories of multiple intelligences and how Aranui High School broke new ground with its sports and other academies. There are also instances in which schools found themselves operating in radically changed student markets and reorganized their programs accordingly.

A good example of such a school is Mana College, north of Wellington, where John Russell became the principal in 1989 on the day that Tomorrow's Schools went into effect. According to Russell, Mana would

---

7. Transcribed notes by Murray Trembath of his remarks at a 1998 meeting of principals in the Wellington area.
8. Task Force (1988: xii).

have been about a decile 5 school at that time, with a student body fairly well balanced ethnically, drawing a substantial number of children from wealthy Pakeha families in nearby Whitby. When parental choice was introduced, however, Mana began to lose many of these Pakeha students to Tawa College and to two other schools further up the coast. The school's mix of students gradually changed, giving it a decile 2 rating in 1995. In 1993 Russell decided that he would try to replace the Pakeha students with upwardly mobile Maori families, many of whom were fleeing Porirua College, as its problems became more evident and its student body became increasingly dominated by Pacific Islanders. Mana began offering bilingual classes. It developed a unit that offered work experience to students and provided learning support for students in mainstream classes. As a result of these efforts, Mana increased the Maori proportion of its student body from 30 percent in 1991 to 51 percent in 1997, while still holding its European proportion at 30 percent. Enrollment, which fell from 621 in 1991 to 497 in 1996, was up to 525 in 1997. "We sent out the message to the community: you don't have to leave to get a good education," said Russell.

Although the introduction by the Ministry of Education of a range of new programs serving Maori students and families can be viewed as a major effort to introduce diversity to the system, broader national policies toward the Maori people and culture are as much at its root as educational policies originating in Tomorrow's Schools. Between 1991 and 1997, eleven new Maori primary schools and one composite school (serving all grades) were set up in the three urban areas. All the new schools were quite small. In 1997, the six Maori primary schools in Auckland enrolled a total of 454 students; the two in Wellington, 69 students; and the three in Christchurch, 141 students. The composite school in Auckland enrolled 215 students.

Other than Maori schools, only a few new schools have been established specifically to serve niche markets. One example is the School for Teen-age Parents, or Te Huarahi Tamariki. This school was set up by Susan Baragwanath, an educator with considerable international experience and the wife of a prominent New Zealand judge. Baragwanath, who was teaching at Porirua College, became concerned about female students who became pregnant. She set up an alternative institution for teenage parents of both sexes in an abandoned tavern down the hill from the college. The school, which has thirty-eight students, has been a success, but it is significant that it is still technically regarded and funded by the Ministry of Education as a single classroom of Porirua College. Baragwanath encountered enormous bureaucratic opposition to starting up such a school, and in the absence of her persistence and social connections it most likely would never have gotten off the ground.

Another example is the Hutt International Boys School (HIBS), a decile 10 school that came into being through the system of integrated schools, which are privately sponsored but publicly supported. The school was founded in 1991 by a group of wealthy parents in Wellington who sought a male counterpart to a nearby Anglican school for girls. In 1995 the school moved into six prefabricated buildings on property it purchased adjacent to the Trentham Race Track. It subsequently built a large gymnasium and other buildings. HIBS, which has a tuition of NZ$4,000 per year, draws students from up and down the Hutt Valley railway line and sends a bus over the hills to Whitby. HIBS, which promotes languages and an international focus in its curriculum as its special character, wasted little time applying for status within the state system as an integrated school, which was granted for the 1995 school year. Buino Vink, the acting principal, said that becoming part of the state system "was not part of the plan from the beginning." Such a move, he added, was necessary to maintain the school's growth. However, other educators in the area are skeptical about this claim, and relations between HIBS and other schools are frosty. The Ministry of Education has never had a formal policy on how to deal with schools created with the aim, tacit or otherwise, of becoming part of the state system. In the past, private schools had the right to integrate once certain legal issues were negotiated, but the law was changed in 1999 to give the minister of education absolute discretion to allow or forbid integration by any particular school.

These examples of schools going after niche markets are unusual. The Tomorrow's Schools reforms have led to relatively little supply-side diversity, and it is fair to say that while the reforms permit innovation, they do not promote it in a systematic manner. Several factors account for this situation. First, as Graeme Marshall of Hutt Valley High School put it, "New Zealand is a small country, in which people have generally been satisfied with their schools. There's not a lot of support for creating niches." Second, and probably more important, the incentive system of the competitive model does not encourage boards and principals of existing schools to look for niche markets. Since the name of the game is to maximize enrollment—at least up to the school's capacity—boards are much more likely to offer broad traditional programs aimed at attracting many students than to offer quality to a few. Third, to start up a school from scratch requires significant capital. It is not a coincidence that the best example of such a start-up is the Hutt International Boys School, a school for the children of wealthy families. Other groups interested in starting a new school are unlikely to have the necessary resources.

Conclusions

The New Zealand experience with choice and competition provides insight into how a market in education might work elsewhere. Despite the absence of aggregate test data that would provide information on student achievement, much can be learned from New Zealand's foray into the realm of full parental choice and competition.

First, the system clearly works better for some types of student than for others. Changes in enrollment patterns show that parents appear to be trying to move their children up the decile ranking of schools; further, it is quite rational for them to do so. Although some minority and low-income families clearly benefit from having choice, parental choice nonetheless increases the concentration of minority and disadvantaged students by more than can be explained by changes in residential patterns alone. In addition, disadvantaged students are significantly overrepresented in the schools that are least able to compete for students and hence, by the market definition of success, are failing schools. Because the playing field is not level, competition is not healthy, and it leads to a situation in which the benefits to the schools serving advantaged students are intensified and the problems of the schools serving disadvantaged students are exacerbated.

Second, full parental choice is not sustainable over time, especially in fast-growing areas like Auckland. Unless policymakers have no concern for the efficient use of existing resources and are willing to invest in new school facilities while others remain underutilized, a system of parental choice can quite quickly become a system in which schools do much of the choosing. While that outcome is not inevitable, it is certainly what occurred in New Zealand.

Third, despite the strong incentives imposed by competition for schools at the bottom to improve, the New Zealand experience documents that it is very difficult for them to do so on their own. The educational challenges they face are formidable. Not only are parental choice and competition not the solution for their problems, they exacerbate those problems. Belatedly the New Zealand Ministry of Education acknowledged the difficulties that the Tomorrow's Schools reforms caused for a significant proportion of schools and began taking steps to ease them. How the ministry confronted the need for damage control is the subject of the next chapter.

Policy Implications
of Tomorrow's Schools

III

9 | *Picking Up the Pieces*

IN OCTOBER 1995 one of New Zealand's major television networks, Television 1, broadcast a prime-time program entitled "The Forgotten Schools" that documented the shattering effect of the Tomorrow's Schools reforms on several secondary schools in South Auckland. The television reporters showed how enrollments and staff sizes at these schools had plummeted because of the large numbers of students opting for secondary schools elsewhere. They interviewed teachers and principals about their struggles to halt the downward spiraling, and they questioned students about what it was like to feel trapped in a school that had been shunned by many of their peers and where half of the students ended up with no formal academic credentials. Among those interviewed was Eliza Osterika, a student at Tangaroa College, who said that she dreamed of going into medicine but quickly added, "At our school, dreams seem so far away."[1]

"The Forgotten Schools" was a milestone in public perceptions about the Tomorrow's Schools reforms. For many New Zealanders it provided the first concrete evidence that the reforms had seriously compounded the difficulties of some schools. Aware of the impact that the program might have on public opinion, a nervous Ministry of Education chose the

1. Transcript of "The Forgotten Schools," October 19, 1995.

eve of the broadcast to announce the release of some previously promised funds to assist schools in South Auckland.

Although the problems highlighted by "The Forgotten Schools" may have been news to some viewers, they did not surprise educational policymakers in the Ministry of Education. For more than a year they had been accumulating disturbing evidence that the overarching vision of self-governing schools operating in a competitive environment had serious flaws. Most primary and secondary schools, it seemed, were handling their new operational autonomy quite well, but a significant minority were finding the burden much too heavy. Forcing schools to compete for students may have been salutary in areas in which the playing fields were relatively level, but it turned out that, to survive as viable institutions, a significant minority of schools needed more than incentives to compete and good management skills.

The idea began to develop in educational policymaking circles that some of the underlying concepts of Tomorrow's Schools were perhaps not universally applicable and that adjustments would have to be made. This point was made bluntly on "The Forgotten Schools" by John Graham, who, as one of New Zealand's all-time great rugby players and a former principal of the upscale Auckland Grammar School, is one of the country's most prominent citizens. Graham had served as commissioner of the failing Nga Tapuwae College in Auckland and had come to the conclusion that "the model for [secondary] education envisaged by Tomorrow's Schools is not the right model for South Auckland."[2]

Over time, other senior educational officials came to accept Graham's analysis. In several discussions with the authors, Howard Fancy, the secretary of education, variously estimated the number of schools for which the reforms were not working at 10–30 percent. In an interview for this book, Brian Donnelly, a former school principal who was then serving as associate minister of education with oversight of the Education Review Office, acknowledged, "Some schools will never work under this system, and for them we will have to have a different system. Some will have to be back under direct control of ministry, and South Auckland will get a design for schooling that will be unique."

This chapter describes how the Ministry of Education was forced to come to the rescue of schools that were battered by the Tomorrow's Schools

2. Transcript of "The Forgotten Schools," October 19, 1995.

formula of self-governing schools and a market environment. The ministry's actions in this regard were driven not only by its obligations to promote quality education for the full range of students but also by outside political pressures and internal budgetary concerns.

The process of picking up the pieces of the "forgotten schools" has proved to be particularly formidable for two reasons. The first has to do with the sheer magnitude and complexity of the task and the lack of consensus about how to accomplish it. Every developed country faces the problems of what to do with failing urban schools, and none has developed a sure-fire formula for turning such schools around. Many schools in South Auckland have been struggling for a long time. Tomorrow's Schools merely compounded their problems.

Second, to complicate the matter, the Tomorrow's Schools model provided no basis for ministry-inspired rescue missions aimed at troubled schools. Indeed, each of the three defining strands militated against such intrusion. The model of self-governing schools operating in a competitive environment presumed that individual schools would either find ways to compete effectively or disappear and be replaced by more viable institutions. Neither eventuality required the hand of a strong central authority. In embracing the concept of schools as agents of the state, designers of the new system could have created a Ministry of Education with a mandate to provide positive support to schools. Instead, they opted for one whose primary obligation was to offer policy advice to the minister.

When it became clear to ministry officials that they could no longer avoid becoming involved in the affairs of troubled schools, they sought to do so in as minimalist a manner as possible and to explain their actions using the rhetoric of Tomorrow's Schools. An initial strategy was to define the difficulties of these schools as essentially managerial and to provide support consistent with such analysis. Over time the level of ministry involvement with troubled schools escalated, and this evolution raised important philosophical issues about the relationship between the state and local schools.

Managing Risk

The highly regulated system that was replaced by Tomorrow's Schools had left little doubt about who was responsible for how schools fared. The former Department of Education controlled both the funding and spending side of school finance. It maintained operational control of primary schools through the regional boards of education and, to a somewhat lesser extent, of high schools through their governing boards. Tomorrow's Schools took a very different approach to the assignment of responsibility for success and failure. By devolving responsibility to local schools, the architects of the reforms sought to insulate the ministry and the government as a whole from both political and economic risk. The results on both counts have turned out to be mixed.

Political Imperatives

The whole point of the new self-governance and accountability mechanisms was that local schools must accept responsibility for their own success or failure. If particular schools failed, fingers should be pointed not to the center but to the schools themselves. "Minimizing downside risk and decentralizing blame for failure was an important motive behind the reforms," said Philip Capper, a consultant who worked with the ministry on several school consolidation situations. "The government figured that under the decentralization people would blame local boards of trustees, not the government, for the failure of schools." Schools that went into tailspins and became nonviable would simply close, and their demise would be chalked up to the proper functioning of an educational marketplace.

One problem with importing this economic model into the delivery of public education is that it ignored political realities. Media reports such as "The Forgotten Schools" made it impossible for the ministry to turn its back on the plight of schools in places like South Auckland and rural areas. "The reality of failing schools was obvious to all, and the wider culture refused to blame schools for their own failures," said Capper. "The government turned out to have been politically naïve."

The political problems were further complicated by a constant stream of studies by the Education Review Office. In August 1996, for example, the ERO issued the devastating and well-publicized study of forty-five schools in two districts of South Auckland. The document, entitled *Improving Schooling in Mangere and Otara* and based on ERO reviews, reported that only 20 percent of schools in the two districts, all of them primary schools, were providing "effective education" for their students and that 42 percent "are performing very poorly or are under-performing" as measured by standards of effective management. Other damaging reports would be forthcoming from both the ERO and other research groups, such as the Smithfield reports and the New Zealand Council for Educational Research. The political pressure applied by the ERO is particularly interesting because it is a state agency that chose to use its statutory independence to offer critiques not only of individual schools but of the system itself.

Political pressure on the government and the ministry to do something to address the problems of downward spiraling schools became more intense as the extent of their problems became increasingly evident. "At first the ministry shrugged it off," said Bill Gavin, the principal of Otahuhu College in South Auckland. "The attitude was 'If they sink, they sink.' But now there are too many sinking schools to ignore. You're talking about 10 percent of all schools and even some entire regions like the East Coast and Northland. The ministry can no longer see whole areas laid to waste."

Economic Imperatives

The Ministry of Education also had important economic incentives to rescue failing schools. Under the Tomorrow's Schools model the Ministry of Education maintained central ownership of the physical plant of state schools (except for integrated schools), leaving it to market forces to determine how much demand there would be for any particular facility. Such an arrangement put the ministry in the risky position of allowing others to define its obligations for capital investment.

Such risks are negligible in places in which the student population is relatively stable, and they were minimized in rural areas, where the ministry succeeded in reducing its financial obligation by consolidating schools. The situation was far more complicated, though, in situations in which the school population was growing or in which demand was concentrated on a few schools. In some cases "winner" schools were bursting at the seams while nearby "loser" schools had excess capacity.

Such situations presented the ministry with a conflict between two cherished political objectives: parental choice and lower state spending. Should the ministry find the funds to back up its commitment to the educational marketplace by adding capacity to popular schools? Or should it save money by forcing substantial numbers of students to occupy existing space in nonpreferred schools? During the early years of Tomorrow's Schools the ministry held to a policy of not adding physical capacity to popular schools, but by 1998 some exceptions were being made.

The most difficult situations arose when particular schools were sent into tailspins by the new competitive environment and lost so many students that their continued existence as institutions was called into question. The theory of market competition holds that such schools should be closed and replaced by competitors. However, New Zealand learned that attempts to close down state schools with strong links to their communities are likely to produce political backlash.

Only a very few downward-spiraling urban schools in New Zealand have been closed. Petone College, which lies in an industrial area adjacent to Wellington at the bottom of the Hutt Valley, had a strong reputation for its technical and vocational educational offerings. But its enrollment began to decline in the 1980s, when several major employers pulled out of the area. The decline was intensified when the school proved unable to compete effectively in the new educational marketplace against Hutt Valley High School, located just across the Hutt River. Petone enrollment dropped from 889 students in 1984 to 242 in 1997. Numerous efforts were made by community leaders to save the school, but in 1998 Minister of Education Wyatt Creech pulled the plug.

In the face of the political and economic realities described above, the Ministry of Education began to rethink its previous policies of nonintervention in the problems of autonomous schools. "The pendulum swung from bureaucratic involvement to a New Right hands-off attitude," said Neil Lancaster, principal of Mairehau High School in Christchurch. "Now it is swinging back to the center. They are accepting the idea that some intervention can be okay."

Schools Improvement Project

In 1989, when Tomorrow's Schools went into effect, the only possibility that the Ministry of Education had for intervening in the affairs of local schools was to dissolve a board of trustees or to initiate legal proceedings. Formal efforts by the ministry to intervene with troubled schools evolved over time and can be divided roughly into two periods, each of which had its own distinctive dynamics. The first period opened in 1991 with the announcement of the Education Development Initiative designed to consolidate schools in rural areas and to assist individual schools facing managerial and financial difficulties. By 1994 it was clear that more extensive intervention was needed in the case of failing schools, and the ministry undertook what came to be known as the Schools Improvement

Project intended to serve as a safety net for individual schools. This program in turn evolved into one aimed at addressing the needs of whole clusters of schools and at preventing failure before it occurred. Following is a brief summary of this evolution.

The Education Development Initiative

The first structural problem that the ministry perceived following the Tomorrow's Schools reforms was excess school capacity and a preponderance of small inefficient schools, primarily in rural areas—a problem that predated the 1989 reform efforts. In 1991, 341 of New Zealand's schools had enrollments of fifty pupils or fewer, and more than 85 percent had at least 10 percent more capacity than they needed. Because of local sensitivities, however, and a reluctance to have young children travel long distances to school, it was politically difficult to consolidate schools into a more efficient arrangement.[3] The situation was complicated by the fact that the new funding arrangements introduced as part of Tomorrow's Schools included base funding for small schools, a feature that provided a financial incentive for schools to remain small.

In its 1991 budget the government announced the establishment of the Education Development Initiative designed to rationalize the distribution of schools while respecting the new principles of self-governance. The strategy was to convince local communities of the curricular and other educational advantages of larger schools and to offer financial incentives to merge schools, such as capital investment in a new site and the funding of transitional costs.

A substantial number of the new initiatives, known as EDIs, involved the consolidating of two or more primary schools in rural areas facing declining populations, while others aimed at amalgamating intermediate and high schools. For example, in Invercargill at the southern tip of the South Island, where the population has declined, the boards of trustees of Lithgow Intermediate School and Hawthorndale Primary School accepted financial incentives to merge into a single school offering seven years of postprimary instruction. When trustees of a third primary school, Surrey Park, refused to accept the merger, the minister closed Surrey Park. In an effort to rationalize high schools in Invercargill, both Cargill High School

---

3. Butterfield and Butterfield (1998: 215).

and Kingswell High School were closed, and a new school was opened on the site of Cargill.

In some cases the EDIs involved quite large numbers of schools, such as one in Ashburton that encompassed twenty-seven schools. In Oamaru, where the capacity of eighteen primary, intermediate, and secondary schools was far too high for its declining population, the ministry succeeded in forcing a number of mergers after protracted squabbles. The overall effects of the consolidation efforts, however, were limited. During the decade from 1987 to 1997 the number of state primary and intermediate schools declined, but the number of state secondary, composite, and special schools increased. Overall, there was a net reduction of 44 schools, from 2,707 in 1987 to 2,663 in 1997.[4]

Schools Support Project

The ministry also began to realize that many boards of trustees and school staffs were having difficulty assuming the managerial and competitive burdens imposed on them by the Tomorrow's Schools reforms. The nature of the problems varied widely, from difficulties in implementing the national curriculum to personality and policy struggles within boards of trustees, or between boards of trustees and principals, or between schools and their communities. Quite a few schools found themselves in financial crises, sometimes because the board and the principal lacked the requisite management skills and in a few cases because of outright corruption.

In 1994 the ministry acknowledged that some schools had problems they could not resolve without help and announced a new Schools Support Project (SSP) designed to assist individual schools facing such difficulties.[5] The SSP, which was also known as the Supporting Schools in Self-Management Project, provides for a progression of interventions depending on the seriousness of the difficulties in question.

INFORMAL AND FORMAL ACTION PLANS. The first intervention step is an informal action plan, under which the ministry, usually acting through one of its six regional offices, assists struggling boards of trustees by pro-

4. Ministry of Education (1997a: 23).
5. The original name was Schools at Risk, but officials decided that *support* conveyed a more positive and appropriate message.

viding consultation services. In some cases these services are carried out by ministry staff members. In other situations the ministry sets up a local support network, which brings in representatives of educational groups, such as the Secondary School Principals Association and the New Zealand School Trustees Association as well as teachers' training colleges and Maori community groups. When informal plans are not sufficient, the ministry draws up a more elaborate formal action plan, which can also draw on the services of local support networks or other outside consultants. In 1997, fifty schools were involved in informal action plans and forty-eight in formal ones.

The most drastic option available to the ministry for schools that fail to fulfill their responsibilities under Tomorrow's Schools is direct intervention, formally known as statutory action. For a school in which serious mismanagement has taken place and in which informal and formal action has failed, the minister or the secretary of education may appoint a commissioner to take over the running of the school or to order the board to enlist the help of a financial manager. In some cases the board of trustees is dissolved and new elections are organized. About half a dozen such commissioners are appointed every year.

Ministry officials also began to recognize that in many cases the problems faced by schools were too complex to be solved either by informal or formal action plans or even by the draconian step of direct intervention and that far more substantive and long-term assistance from the ministry was demanded. They concluded that addressing long-term financial and managerial problems before they turned into major crises would be less costly, both financially and politically, than dealing with messy situations after the fact. Such thinking led to two additional sets of initiatives.

BUSINESS PLANS. The first new approach involved business plans, a logical extension of the fact that Tomorrow's Schools was at its core a set of managerial reforms. The report of the Picot task force that initiated the reforms was entitled *Administering for Excellence: Effective Administration in Education,* and over time, as the National government replaced the Labour government, the conviction grew among policymakers that most of the problems facing schools could be solved if only schools adopted sound management practices. Given this assumption, it seemed appropriate for the ministry to seek ways of putting schools on a solid managerial and financial footing.

In its 1996 budget the government authorized the Ministry of Education, upon agreement with the boards of trustees of schools facing serious problems, to undertake studies on the viability of such schools to develop a business plan that would become the basis for long-term financial and other assistance by the ministry to a local board of trustees. Business plans, also known as business cases, were to be prepared by outside consultants, and they could either stand alone or constitute part of a formal action plan or direct intervention. In either situation they would be accompanied by stringent monitoring.

The ministry currently processes from twelve to twenty business plans a year to deal with a wide range of difficulties. For example, a plan was drawn up for Timaru Girls High School, which in 1994 was ordered by a court to pay NZ$450,000 to settle a lawsuit brought by a former principal who charged that she had been unjustifiably dismissed. A subsequent ERO report said that the costs incurred by the legal proceedings were effectively "placing a mortgage on the future education of the students," and the plan laid out a procedure for managing the debt. Business plans were also drawn up for Northcote College, which had been the victim of a NZ$1.2 million fraud, and for Saint Stephen's School, a Maori boarding school that was facing problems of violence, inadequate curriculum delivery, and poor management and was struggling under the burden of an old debt related to an overseas sports tour. The Saint Stephen's business plan provided for suspension of the debt until the school was in a position to repay it.

Other business cases were far more sweeping and complex. Plans were completed for two downward spiraling schools in South Auckland, Hillary and Tangaroa Colleges, after a consulting firm advised the ministry that it would be less expensive and more politically sound to put additional resources into the schools than it would be to close them down. The plan for Hillary College provides for more than NZ$2 million over a three-year period for purposes such as the buyout of "underperforming" staff members, an antiviolence program, counseling services, a public relations campaign, and new equipment. The plan for Tangaroa College involves a commitment of NZ$1.7 million for purposes that include staff buyouts, professional development, retaining home economics as a subject, purchasing new equipment, and supporting a guidance clinic staff, a nurse, a truancy officer, and a part-time sports coordinator.

Perhaps the most ambitious business plans was the consolidation of three troubled South Auckland schools—Nga Tapuwae College, Mangere

Intermediate School, and Southern Cross Primary School—into a single operating unit known as the Southern Cross Campus that would offer the full range of instruction from first entrants through high school. Each of the three schools maintains its own identity, but they share the physical property, and the overarching structure allows them to broaden the pool of parents available to serve on boards of trustees and to make efficient use of resources such as specialized teachers and dental and medical services. Terry Bates, principal of the whole campus, said that there are pedagogical advantages as well. "We can offer students and parents long-term continuity in their education," he said. "We can get students thinking about a good job or further education from year one on." The protracted financial and staffing troubles experienced by Nga Tapuwae during the late 1980s were a major reason that the Tomorrow's Schools legislation gave power to the state to take over troubled schools.[6]

SCHOOLING IMPROVEMENT CLUSTER INITIATIVES. The next step in the evolution of the Schools Improvement Project was to shift the focus of ministry initiatives from bailing out individual schools to working with clusters of schools facing common problems. Such an approach represents a fundamental departure from the concept of autonomous schools, of course, but it was a reasonable response to the public pressure generated by ERO reports documenting the failures of schools in entire areas such as South Auckland. Six such cluster initiatives have been undertaken, and four of them are discussed below.

The first and best known of the cluster interventions is the project known as Achievement in Multicultural High Schools, or AIMHI. This project involves eight decile 1 schools with high proportions of Pacific Island and, to a lesser extent, Maori students; seven of the schools are in Auckland, one is in Wellington. Three of the participating schools had received favorable ERO reports, and one (Otahuhu) even had an enrollment scheme; three others had had commissioners appointed at one time or another. Central to the work of AIMHI was the December 1996 report by two Massey University researchers, Kay Hawk and Jan Hill, who were commissioned by the ministry to study ways in which these eight schools could increase their market share, raise the level of student performance, and achieve "sustainable self-managing" status. The report documented the

6. Nga Tapuwae is located in the electorate of former prime minister David Lange.

obstacles these schools face, including the effects of poverty, poor nutrition, language difficulties, and lack of parental experience with schooling.[7]

With the report as background, the Ministry of Education organized the principals of the eight schools into an advisory group that met monthly in an effort to develop coordinated responses to the problems they faced. The project was slow getting started, in part because the principals rebelled at the way ministry officials were dealing with them. The principals sought to speak with a collective voice in negotiating with central authorities, while the ministry, although theoretically committed to addressing common problems, insisted on negotiating contracts with schools on an individual basis. The ministry's position was fully consistent with the principle of self-governance and the notion that the individual school is the basic unit of a state educational system. The situation can also be viewed, however, as another example of the center doing what it believed necessary to protect itself from financial or other risks that might arise from having to deal with a group of schools offering a common front. "The most useful thing about AIMHI was that it allowed us to talk about our problems and work on them together," said Jim Peters, principal of Tangaroa College at the time. "But this is exactly what the ministry did not want us to do."

The control issue came to a head at a retreat at which the principals decided to organize into a forum that would negotiate with the ministry over AIMHI policies. The ministry eventually agreed to enter into a contract with the forum, but in the absence of funding, plans and projects at the eight schools were put on hold for half a year. Further delays were caused when the treasury kept changing the procedures for releasing funds to the schools. Despite the fact that the schools now had a collective contract, it was not at all clear that the ministry was comfortable with the arrangement. "They still haven't learned," said Bill Gavin, the principal of Otahuhu College. "They still treat us as individual schools, not as a group."

The eventual direction of AIMHI is still in flux. In their first collective effort, in 1998, the participating schools published a guidebook for Pacific Island parents and caregivers on how to work with their child's school to promote education. Individual schools also submitted action plans proposing support for a wide variety of activities. The Tamaki College submission, for example, proposed a major enhancement of on-site social

7. Hawk and Hill (1996).

services so as to coordinate educational, health, and welfare services to students and their families. Other items included provision for a full-time receptionist to welcome parents to the school, better communication between the school and parents, a student motivation program, language and employment programs, and the upgrading of information technology.

A second major Schools Improvement Project was mounted in Christchurch under the rubric Schools Making a Difference, or SMAD. The introduction of a competitive educational marketplace in Christchurch had led to a situation in which popular high-decile secondary schools were bursting at the seams while their lower-decile counterparts had empty seats and in some cases sharply declining enrollment (see figure 7-3). The city's school population was projected to rise in coming years, and officials at the Ministry of Education feared that they would be forced into adding physical capacity at the popular schools while about 2,000 seats were not being occupied at less popular schools. The decision was made to try to make the lower-decile schools more attractive and thus to make more efficient use of existing capital resources.

In late 1995 leaders of SMAD, which involved both primary and secondary schools, identified seven lower-decile schools with a history of static or declining enrollment. These seven were invited to a conference to discuss their common problems and to explore ways, as ministry officials put it, to "kick start" a process of making them more viable in the educational marketplace.[8] Principals were initially skeptical of the ministry's intentions, especially after the project was launched with a fancy reception, complete with wine and sausage rolls, that led some to conclude that they were being manipulated. Principals openly wondered whether, given its desire to save capital funds, the ministry was seriously committed to improving the quality of teaching and learning.

SMAD engaged a consultant, Philip Capper, to collect baseline data about the participating schools and to initiate what has become an annual survey of parental attitudes on the quality of service delivery. Each of the schools was given NZ$100,000 the first year to carry out an improvement plan of its own design, with the understanding that a similar amount would be forthcoming in each of the next two years if appropriate benchmarks were met. Programs had to become self-funding after the project

---

8. An eighth school, run by Seventh-Day Adventists, was invited but declined to participate.

was completed. Gradually, the rhetoric about the program shifted from talk about enrollment numbers to discussion of educational quality. The ministry sponsored a retreat at which principals spent an entire day pouring out their problems and brainstorming about possible solutions. "They decided to become proactive and not wait until failure was endemic before taking action," said Robin Bowden, a ministry official in Christchurch.

The seven schools participating in SMAD took quite different approaches. Aranui High School, a decile 1 school best known for its Sports Academy, used its funds, among other things, for computers, a behavior modification program, and staff training. Hillmorton High School set up a special support class for thirteen students who had been disruptive in other classes; employed a part-time staff member to phone parents at home if students were absent or assignments were not done; and purchased a new commercial reading program available to all students. "We set out to create an atmosphere of continuous improvement," said Ann Brockenshire, the deputy principal. Other SMAD initiatives included the purchase of new technology, staff development in areas like behavioral management, and leadership training for senior students.

In June 1997, the ministry announced an initiative known as Strengthening Education in Mangere and Otara, or SEMO. This project was a direct response to the August 1996 ERO report documenting conditions in forty-five schools in two low-income areas of South Auckland.[9] Under SEMO, which has a three-year budget of NZ$6.5 million, the ministry will work with each of the forty-five schools to negotiate a "school supply agreement," by which the ministry will provide additional funds for extra services, such as staff training. Brian Annan, a former head of the Auckland Primary Principals Association, was named to head a five-person team overseeing the project, which is still in its early stages. Annan proposed spending nearly half of the available funds on a Communities in Schools project, which would draw on community resources for tutoring, mentoring, homework supervision, and other purposes. Other proposed projects involve early childhood education, literacy, computer programs, and Maori and Pacific Island resource centers.

A fourth cluster project is an initiative for dealing with schools on the economically struggling East Coast, where 90 percent of residents are Maori. The ministry has entered into an agreement with the *runanga*, or

---

9. Education Review Office (1996).

Maori trust, to seek ways of improving schools. This project is potentially significant because it represents the first time that the ministry has accepted the proposition that solutions to educational problems may lie beyond the capabilities of the individual schools. In AIMHI, SMAD, and SEMO, while the ministry paid lip service to addressing schools in clusters, it still sought to deal with them on an individual basis. In the case of the East Coast project, the ministry tacitly acknowledged that such solutions must be sought not only at a level above the individual school but outside the school system itself. "This is the first time that the ministry has said that we can't do it by ourselves," said Mary Sinclair, project manager for the Schools Support Project.

Managerialism

The Ministry of Education is clearly struggling to find ways to make the Tomorrow's Schools structures work for all schools. It has put together a number of rescue packages for different situations, but these efforts were complicated by the absence of any coherent rationale for them in the Tomorrow's Schools model. At best, such interventions constituted the exceptions that proved the rule that a state system could be organized around autonomous schools in a market environment.

One theme that runs through these various interventions is an emphasis on effective management. In the absence of national tests of student achievement, the Education Review Office placed heavy reliance on managerial effectiveness in evaluating schools. A parallel emphasis on management also emerged in the Schools Improvement Project. In looking for ways to address the difficulties of troubled schools, ministry officials tended to dismiss arguments that these problems were rooted either in insufficient funding or in forces external to the school, such as the effects of poverty. Rather, they were inclined toward the view that the problems were the result of poor internal management.

Given this analysis of the problem, it followed that improving management was the way to solve it. If schools were run well using sound managerial principles, the reasoning went, then pedagogical, personnel, marketing, and financial problems could be successfully addressed. Such a minimalist and indirect approach made sense for a ministry that was reluctant to become involved with supposedly autonomous schools in the first place. This approach also made sense politically, because faith in good management was central to the value system of the Treasury Department, which had to approve funds for the Schools Improvement Project. The emphasis on managerialism is most readily apparent in the formal business plans discussed above, but it also affected both the style and substance of AIMHI and SMAD.

Important corollaries to the belief that most problems were at root managerial were that intervention from the center would be short term and that it would involve tight accountability provisions. In allocating resources to these projects, ministry officials ran a tight supervisory ship. Funds were allocated for short periods, typically six months, and release of additional promised funds was made contingent on meeting certain performance milestones. In the event that schools failed to meet these milestones, they were obligated to return the funds with 11 percent interest. While the spirit of Tomorrow's Schools was to give maximum discretion to boards of trustees and to educators closest to the actual delivery of teaching and learning, a wholly different philosophy pervaded the school improvement efforts. Schools that were not succeeding under the normal rules were not going to get long leashes under the Schools Improvement Project.

Several difficulties soon developed regarding the ministry's emphasis on management, including a challenge to the assumption that failing schools must be poorly managed. Shortly after the AIMHI project was launched, the ministry summoned principals of the eight participating schools to a three-day retreat at the White Herron Lodge in Auckland, led by a management consultant from Lion Nathan, a major corporation. Before the retreat the principals filled out questionnaires that explored their management styles. Questionnaires were also sent to five subordinates and to a substantial number of students in their schools. The answers were analyzed by the management consultant before the retreat.

Although his mandate was to offer the assembled principals some insights into how to improve their leadership, the management consultant concluded that all eight of the principals were already capable managers. "He said that he would invest in any company that we were running," recalled John Grant, then the principal of Tamaki College. "At that point the retreat took off in a whole new direction. We came to a collective agreement that we knew some of the answers, and we spent the next three days plotting against the ministry and trying to figure out how to get them to just give us the money so we could get on with the job." The turnabout at the Auckland retreat, subsequently known as "the coup," led to the revised structure of AIMHI described above.

While the ministry was seeking to improve the managerial capacity of school principals, many educators were beginning to have their doubts about the ministry's own capabilities in this area. Many argued, for example, that making the release of funds contingent on the meeting of short-term performance milestones was itself poor management. Principals pointed out that they needed to be able to hire good people for projects designed to take at least two or three years to complete. If funding was guaranteed for no more than six months, they would find it difficult to lure such people away from jobs with secure salaries. "Six-month deadlines are not milestones," said Terry Bates, the principal of the Southern Cross Campus. "They're 100-meter dashes."

School administrators accused ministry officials of showing little understanding of what constituted good management in an educational setting and having no feeling for the way schools operated. "The ministry always treated me in a nonprofessional way," said David Hodge, the principal of Tamaki College. "First they would want a six-page memo. Then they would say they did not need six pages, only one. They would call us up at 5 p.m. and want things by the next morning. They created an enormous amount of additional work for us because they themselves did not have a clear plan for what they were doing." In drawing up budgets and making policy decisions regarding projects such as AIMHI and SEMO, ministry officials rarely consulted the principals involved. In one case the ministry publicly floated the idea of merging four schools without mentioning the idea to the schools involved, much less asking for volunteers.

SMAD was initially beset by squabbling between the Ministry of Education and the Treasury Department over the disbursement of funds. Although monies were appropriated for the project in the 1997–98 government budget, treasury held up their release while it continued to ask basic questions about the project and, in effect, to second-guess the ministry. Among other things, treasury officials questioned whether schools that had reserve funds should be the recipients of additional monies from SMAD. This resulted in something of a catch-22 situation for the schools. "If we managed our affairs well and built up reserves, we were penalized for not needing help," said Neil Lancaster, the principal of Mairehau High School. "If we didn't have any reserves, then they said we were a basket case and not deserving of help." After several months, schools finally got the funds that had been promised to them.

To some educators the prevailing ethos was what John Grant termed "managerialism." "The assumption is that management is a skill in its own right and that you don't have to know all that much about what it is you are managing," he said. A liaison officer at the ministry's regional office in Auckland agreed with this assessment. "Management is all," he commented. "The idea is deeply ingrained that once school administrators can get their management act together, the sun will shine." Practitioners complained, though, that such thinking is unrealistic. "Some issues of education are independent of governance," said Robin Staples of Hillary College. "But the people in Wellington have no concept of this. Their method is simply to throw in money, set milestones, and then, if they meet them, give them some more money six months later."

Others saw the problems facing the Schools Improvement Project as rooted in the issue of control. A ministry that preached delegation and self-governance at the school level was reluctant to accept the same principle when applied to situations where its own money and reputation were on the line. The control issue even applied to relations within the government. "Treasury was not even giving the ministry the power to get on with its job," said Staples.

The ministry has continued to push a management model in other ways. A major goal has been popular acceptance of the notion of the principal as a chief executive officer. As it has evolved thus far, the Tomorrow's Schools model makes boards of trustees the employers of both principals and teachers, although in practice principals exercise considerable influence in the choosing of teachers. Under a principal-as-CEO model, the principal would become the employer of teachers, and trustees would be limited to determining whether or not the principal was performing satisfactorily. Principals would also have fixed-term contracts negotiated individually rather than collectively.

Proponents of the principal-as-CEO model find ample justification in scholarly research for this approach. Peter Bushnell, deputy secretary of the treasury, cited a central finding of the "effective schools" literature to the effect that having a strong principal is a key to having a successful school. He linked this to "general management literature" on how to manage staffs and reward administrators for performance. "All of our evidence shows that the quality of the school is a function of the ability of the principal," he said. Critics, however, say that such literature is being mis-interpreted. Philip Capper of the Center for Research on Work, Educa-tion, and Business, argues that the effective schools literature talks about the principal as an "instructional leader," which is not the same concept as an effective manager in a commercial setting. Moreover, he said, propo-nents of the principal as CEO have a "poverty-stricken" image of general managerial literature. "The best literature talks about collaborative orga-nizational structures and about CEOs who are servants of the larger orga-nization," he said. "It does not talk about accountability in the way we are hearing it applied to the schools."

Some principals of struggling schools suggest that in mounting school support projects the ministry is less concerned about improving the qual-ity of education in areas such as South Auckland than it is in avoiding the need to make new capital investments in popular schools. "They are pre-dicting a boom in numbers, and they don't want to have unused capacity," said David Hodge of Tamaki College. Hodge and others find it significant that the only low-performing schools to attract ministry attention are those like South Auckland in which enrollments are expected to increase dra-matically. "You don't see them looking to improve achievement in decile 1 schools elsewhere," he said. "The big issue is whether there is the political will to put the resources into these schools and make them work." It is also arguable that the SMAD project would not have come about in the ab-sence of pressure on facilities in the other schools of Christchurch.

Mary Sinclair, who runs the Schools Support Project for the ministry, argues that attitudes within the government are evolving. "The initial ex-pectation was that the SSP would not be a permanent program," she said. "Now treasury has come around and asked for a budget for the next three years." She added, however, that even under a multiyear plan schools would not be able to get funds for more than one year at a time. "And I'm not sure that doing so would be such a good idea. New Zealand schools are not very good at being accountable and strategic."

Conclusions

The process of picking up the pieces after the dramatic changes wrought by Tomorrow's Schools has only begun. Just as the reform package evolved over a period of years, so has the ministry's approach to dealing with those schools that, it turned out, were not well served by the reforms. After first putting their faith in school autonomy and competition to provide a rising tide for all ships, political and educational leaders slowly came to understand that, whatever their benefits, these theories had practical limitations. After trying to deal with these limitations at arm's length through the indirect mechanism of managerial improvement, the ministry has grudgingly accepted the notion that in a state education system in a democratic country the center cannot absolve itself of responsibility for failing schools. Senior officials, including Howard Fancy, the secretary of education, and Brian Donnelly, the former associate minister of education, acknowledge the need to move away from a monolithic system built on the twin pillars of self-governance and competition. They recognize that special provisions, presumably with more direct ties to the ministry, are required for struggling schools.

With the wisdom of hindsight, it is possible to understand how the particular combination of self-governing schools and a competitive environment built into Tomorrow's Schools was destined from the outset to be destructive to some schools. New Zealand policymakers learned this lesson the hard way and are now struggling to make appropriate adjustments. In the United States and other countries where similar ideas are still in an earlier stage of implementation, however, policymakers are in a position to learn lessons from New Zealand's experience and to construct safeguards that may spare them from some of the same troubles. In the concluding chapter we consider some of these lessons.

10 | Lessons for the United States and Other Countries

THE SEARCH FOR more effective ways to organize and manage state educational systems has become a global phenomenon. Sensitive to the critical importance of education to their nation's economic development and overall social stability, political and educational leaders in developed and developing countries alike have been experimenting with new ways to fund public education, motivate teachers and administrators, promote community and parental involvement in schools, and hold educators accountable for student performance. In recent years attention in many countries has focused on two distinct but interrelated sets of ideas.

The first set of ideas revolves around the concept of decentralization. Many reformers believe that the transferring of governance and management authority from a centralized state educational agency to local schools will energize schools by giving parents and local communities a greater role in setting school missions. Others favor such decentralization as part of a broader governance and management strategy involving the exchange of control for accountability. The pure form of this arrangement might be referred to as a tight-loose-tight governance structure, in which the central authority *tightly* specifies schools' missions and outcome standards, *loosely* allows schools to use whatever methods they choose to achieve those standards, and then *tightly* holds schools accountable for results.[1]

The second set of ideas is centered in parental choice and market competition. Proponents believe that the quality and efficiency of education are enhanced when parents are given the right to select the school their child will attend, thereby putting schools in a position of having to compete for students. Some see choice as a way of promoting more coherent school communities of persons with shared values and encouraging a proliferation of schools tailored to children with particular academic, social, or other needs. Others argue that if individual schools can no longer treat parents and students as captive customers, teachers and school administrators will be forced to become responsive to the needs of their students, and they will deliver education that is both higher quality and more cost-effective.[2]

Significant experimentation with such ideas has taken place in many countries, including England, Australia, New Zealand, and Chile, and they have attracted growing attention in the United States. For more than a decade U.S. school districts have sought to decentralize the running of schools through policies known as school-based or school-site management. Policymakers in Chicago experimented with a system under which substantial governing powers were shifted from the central board of education to parent-controlled councils in each local school.[3] In addition, a

1. The idea that individual schools should be the focus of reform efforts has received a lot of attention among countries in the Organization for Economic Cooperation and Development. See for example OECD (1995), which includes discussions of decentralization to the school level in countries such as Australia, Sweden, England, and New Zealand. In the United States, discussion centers on reform ideas such as school-site management, local school councils, and charter schools.

2. The literature on school choice is voluminous. Among the relevant books are Chubb and Moe (1990); Henig (1995); Peterson and Hassel (1998). Also see Whitty (1997) for a comparison of educational quasi-markets in three countries; OECD (1994) for discussion of choice in six countries; and Witte (1996) for an analysis of the effects of choice on performance. Brandl (1998) provides a discussion of the complementarity between the two potential effects of choice—competition and community—as a means of improving education.

3. The Chicago School Reform Act of 1988 set up elected local school councils and devolved significant authority and resources to the schools. For a discussion of the effects of this reform effort plus the debate about whether the recentralization of authority that occurred in 1995 represents a dramatic policy turnaround or the logical extension of decentralization, see Bryk (1999).

sizable movement has developed behind the concept of charter schools, which are exempted from traditional rules and regulations in return for agreeing to meet certain performance standards. At last count there were more than 1,200 charter schools in twenty-seven states, with the number rising steadily.

Parental choice and market competition have also attracted enormous attention. Whereas high-income parents have always had significant choice of school through their selection of residential location, the new programs are designed to break the link for all students between their school and place of residence. They do so by permitting children to enroll in other schools within the school district or, in some cases, across district lines. Two major cities (Cleveland and Milwaukee) as well as one state (Florida) have taken the concept of parental choice a major step further and adopted plans in which students from low-income families or those in underperforming schools are eligible to receive vouchers that can be used in any school of their choice, including private ones.

While the question of whether such reforms, or various packages of them, are desirable for the United States or other countries is a hotly contested issue, the debate thus far has tended to generate more heat than light. Judgments about the potential benefits of the two sets of ideas and the general relevance of economic models to educational systems tap into deeply held values, and much of the discussion has been carried on at the level of first principles. Debate is particularly contentious around voucher programs that channel public funds to private schools.

Discussion of these important policy issues has also been hampered by a lack of practical experience with them. Charter schools are still too new to permit definitive analysis of their impact, and while both publicly and privately funded voucher programs are being intensely studied, existing ones have to date been far too small to determine whether they could have the desirable overall effects promoted by their advocates.[4] To move the debate about this whole cluster of reform ideas forward it would be useful to have a large-scale experiment in which self-governing schools operate in a competitive environment involving extensive parental choice over a long period of time.

New Zealand provides just such a large-scale experiment. In 1989 this

4. A summary of these experiments (not including the Florida plan) can be found in Peterson (1999).

nation of 3.8 million persons adopted a school reform package, known as Tomorrow's Schools, that overnight transferred operating responsibility from the Department of Education to each school's newly elected governing board of trustees. Two years later, in 1991, with a new government in power, New Zealand enacted further reforms that introduced full parental choice of school and established a competitive environment in the state educational system.

Previous chapters describe the effects of this reform package under the rubric of its three main strands: self-governing schools, schools as agents of the state, and choice and competition. In this concluding chapter we explore lessons that New Zealand's experience may hold for other nations. We believe that New Zealand is particularly suitable for such lessons. Although it is a tiny country, it has the same population as that of the median American state. Since education in the United States is a state responsibility, the Ministry of Education in New Zealand is thus the functional equivalent of a typical state department of education. New Zealand also has close cultural links to the United States, and its schools contain a sizable minority of non-Caucasian students, mostly Maori and Pacific Islander, many of them concentrated in inner cities.

It is important, of course, to recognize the distinctive features of New Zealand's experience with self-governing schools operating in a competitive environment. The Tomorrow's Schools reform package inevitably reflects this nation's particular politics, history, and culture, and it cannot be said to provide a full-blown test of any of the reform ideas in their pure form. The reforms fell short in some important ways not only of the ideals that many reformers were advocating in New Zealand but of those advocated by many reformers in the United States.

Having said that, we suggest that New Zealand offers as reasonable and useful a laboratory to observe these ideas in practice as one could hope to find. While it is possible to argue in the abstract about the virtues of school autonomy or parental choice, these ideals are rarely, if ever, implemented in pure form. To become operational, they require particular social, political, cultural, and economic contexts that inevitably affect and shape them. The resulting deviations from ideal models, of course, are interesting in their own right, and they serve to highlight significant policy decisions for other countries or states. The factors that forced New Zealand policymakers to back away from some of the original theories of Tomorrow's Schools are likely to be present in other countries as well.

The absence of national test score data in New Zealand prevents us from addressing a question relevant to any reform package: To what extent has it generated gains in overall student achievement? Hence, we can offer no overall conclusions about whether the New Zealand reforms represent a net improvement or a net loss for the system as a whole. Instead, we use the New Zealand experience to draw conclusions and lessons related to specific issues and to highlight potential areas of concern that policymakers in other countries or states will need to address if they choose to proceed down a reform path similar to that taken by New Zealand. We highlight conclusions and lessons related to the following issues:

—*Oversubscribed schools.* The fact that there are limited seats in popular schools means that some mechanism must be devised for rationing places in such schools. Any such mechanism will inevitably place constraints on parental choice and will involve trade-offs among various policy objectives.

—*Low-performing schools.* Contrary to the hopes of some advocates of market-based solutions to the problems of schools serving large numbers of disadvantaged students, providing such schools with management flexibility and strong incentives to retain students is not sufficient to solve their problems. The overwhelming problems they face cannot be solved by governance and management changes alone.

—*Self-governance combined with competition.* While a carefully designed system of self-governance can work well for many schools, the problems for some schools are exacerbated when self-governance is combined with parental choice and market competition.

In addition to these findings and lessons, our examination of New Zealand's experience with self-governing schools operating in a competitive environment raises a number of broad concerns that are worthy of the attention of political and educational leaders seeking to implement these ideas in other countries. We highlight three concerns:

—*Polarization.* Such a system appears likely to exacerbate the polarization of enrollment patterns by racial and ethnic group and by socio-economic status. Is such polarization acceptable? Are there ways to minimize it?

—*Winners and losers.* The promotion of a competitive educational environment assumes that some schools will be successful and others unsuccessful. Is it desirable to reform a state educational system in such a way that you know from the outset that some schools—and more important, the students in them—will find themselves in a worse situation than before? If not, are there ways in which damage to students in unsuccessful schools can be negated or minimized without significantly reducing the benefits to students in successful schools?

—*Balancing interests.* The Tomorrow's Schools reforms created a situation in which the interests of a particular group of stakeholders—the parents of current students in a school—take precedence over the interests of other stakeholders and over the interests of the system as a whole. What safeguards are needed to balance the legitimate competing interests of the various stakeholders?

New Zealand Reform Package

The Tomorrow's Schools reforms are described in detail in chapter 3 and summarized in table 3-1. Significantly, the reforms departed from the original intentions of their architects in regard to two central elements: the role of school charters and the funding of teachers' salaries.

The initial idea was for each self-governing school to draft a charter—with community input and approval by the new Ministry of Education—that would define the school's mission and objectives. The school charter was envisioned as a contract of mutual obligations among the state, the school, and the local community. In effect, however, the charters became one-way documents defining the obligations of schools to the central authorities. The initial reform package also called for a number of community-based structures that would reconcile conflicts of interest between the trustees of different schools or between schools and central authorities. As the reforms played out, these structures did not materialize.

In addition, the Tomorrow's Schools reforms called for the government to give each school a single grant with two components, one for teachers' salaries and one for operating expenses. As described in chapter 6, however, teachers' unions adamantly opposed the lump-sum funding of teachers' salaries, as did many school trustees. Such opposition, reinforced by doubts on the part of some officials about whether schools could handle the responsibility, has meant that the government has continued to pay teachers in most schools directly. Thus each school receives a block grant for its operations expenses, which varies with the number of students it serves, and it is allocated a certain number of teaching and administrative slots based on its enrolllment and the grades it offers. Only in the past year has the government moved more aggressively to encourage schools to accept bulk funding of teachers' salaries.

Policy Lessons

Certain policy conclusions emerge from New Zealand's experience that are relevant to policymakers in other countries regardless of their political or ideological leanings. Although we do not claim that any of these conclusions or lessons are new to the literature on decentralization and school choice, the fact that they have emerged so clearly in practice when adopted for an entire public school system should give them added credibility and a claim on policymakers' attention. For advocates of greater school autonomy and parental choice, these policy conclusions raise issues that need to be understood and addressed if such reform efforts are to be pursued. For those who oppose such reforms, these policy conclusions may provide additional ammunition against them. We would argue, though, that none of the negatives is devastating. What matters is how these issues are addressed, not that they arise. Moreover, just because New Zealand implemented these ideas one way need not mean that other countries would have to follow the same course. There are clear policy decisions to be made.

Oversubscribed Schools

Any solution to the problem of oversubscribed schools will inevitably place constraints on parental choice and will involve trade-offs among various policy objectives.

Markets require a mechanism to deal with situations in which demand for a particular item exceeds its supply. The standard mechanism is price. When the demand for good wine exceeds the supply, the price will rise to clear the market. The rise in price will induce consumers to buy a bit less and the suppliers to supply a bit more, so that the quantity that consumers choose to buy ends up equal to what producers supply. Even in markets in which supply is fixed, price plays a crucial role in allocating the limited supply among the demanders. When the consumer item in question is not a loaf of bread or a jug of wine but places in a desirable public school, the balancing of supply and demand is considerably more complicated.

As parental choice and competition have played out in New Zealand, the demand for places in many popular schools has far exceeded the number of seats available. We argue in chapter 7 that this excess demand for some schools in New Zealand largely reflects parents' desires to move their children up the decile rankings of schools (where the decile rankings indicate the mix of students who are in the schools, with higher-decile rankings indicating greater socioeconomic advantage and a lower proportion of minority students). But whatever the cause, some schools will always be oversubscribed unless there is significant overcapacity in the system. The question then is how to allocate the scarce spaces in such schools. Under a literal application of the economic marketplace analogy, the answer would be simple: charge students and families for entry into the desirable schools. To a limited extent, this is what New Zealand is doing. Student fees and in many cases transportation costs are higher for the more desirable, high-decile schools, and some families are indeed priced out of the market. However, given that in a state system of compulsory education every child is supposedly ensured a quality education, it would be inappropriate to use pricing as the primary mechanism for allocating scarce places in elementary and secondary schools.

In the absence of an explicit pricing mechanism to ration a fixed number of spaces, an alternative approach would be to increase the supply of spaces in the most desirable schools to meet the demands of all comers. However, the New Zealand experience highlights the difficulty of doing so. The government has been understandably reluctant to invest in the expansion of popular schools when other schools are operating at excess capacity. Because the government owns all traditional public schools, it has a strong financial interest in making sure that they are used in a cost-effective manner. When spaces are available in existing schools, building new schools is not a cost-effective way to meet student demand. Moreover, the managers of popular schools in New Zealand have little incentive to expand. To the extent that the popularity of their schools reflects the fact that they have a select student body and are able to provide a coherent educational program for these students, their competitive position would be weakened if expansion resulted in a less select student mix. In addition, unlike the owners or managers of private sector firms, the manager of a public school—whether it be a trustee or the principal—has few personal incentives, financial or otherwise, to see the operation grow beyond a certain point.

One might ask, however, why the expansion of schools must be within the traditional public sector. If excess demand exists for a particular type of school, parents and educators conceivably could set up a new school and then request public funding for it. In the New Zealand context, that would require setting up a new private school that could then be integrated into the public school system, as was done by Hutt International Boys School in Wellington. In that case, the parents were relatively wealthy and able to pay the initial fees that covered both operating and capital costs. Even after the school was integrated into the public school system, parents continued to pay large mandatory fees for the capital costs of the school. Thus nongovernment ownership of a school does not solve the problem of paying for capital costs; in this particular case the burden was simply shifted to the families or the owners of the new school. If the government's policy were to encourage the development of new schools, which in New Zealand it has not been, some means would have to be found to pay for their capital costs. Unless some form of public funding is found, it is unlikely that new schools of this sort are likely to play a major role in addressing the issue of oversubscribed schools.

So how should scarce spaces in popular schools be allocated? New Zealand's decision to let oversubscribed schools have enrollment schemes over which the ministry exerts no control is consistent with that country's model of self-governing schools. This plan, however, has restricted the ability of many parents to exercise full choice. The percentages of students in schools with enrollment schemes has increased dramatically, with the result that by 1997 more than 50 percent of students in primary schools in Auckland and Christchurch had such plans. For secondary schools in 1997, the percentages of students in schools with enrollment schemes were 62 percent in Auckland, 57 percent in Christchurch, and 46 percent in Wellington.

Thus what started out at the beginning of the decade as a system of parental choice has rapidly become a system in which schools play a significant role in choosing their students. Although schools' choosing students could mean a better match between school offerings and student preference, in practice it is undesirable because of its distributional effects. By limiting the schools available to students who do not fit the enrollment criteria of popular schools, such choice has an adverse effect on disadvantaged students. In addition, while it makes it easier for some schools—those with enrollment schemes—to offer coherent and well-defined educational programs, it makes it more difficult for other schools to attract students.

Another downside of the New Zealand approach is that some parents may not gain access to a school for their child within a reasonable distance of where they live. This problem was especially acute in heavily populated Auckland, where students would sometimes travel past several schools before arriving at one that would accept them.

By 1999, the practical difficulties created by enrollment schemes had became so problematic that Parliament changed the law to require approval of school schemes by the secretary of education. Moreover, the ministry will now grant this approval only if the proposed scheme has been worked out in consultation with parents, the community, and other schools likely to be affected by it. Satisfactory enrollment schemes must now take into account students' desire to attend a "reasonably convenient" school, a provision that includes students who arrive during the school year. The ministry is now empowered to force a school board to abandon its enrollment scheme if overcrowding ceases to be a problem, and it can appoint a facilitator if there is a dispute between boards over a scheme, with the ministry having the final say. The secretary of education may also direct a board of trustees to enroll a particular student who has been denied a place in their school. Under the new arrangement, parents are still free to shop among schools, but they are assured that the school in its locale is available to their child. In effect, the government has now partially restored residential zoning as the basis of enrollment policy.

New Zealand's solution of leaving it up to oversubscribed schools to decide whom to admit is only one of several alternatives available to policymakers. For those who are committed to giving parents more control over which school their child will attend but who also believe that this right should extend equally to all parents, the key question becomes: How do you keep control of the process from shifting from parents to schools? Several options have been discussed in New Zealand and are worth mentioning.

REQUIRE THAT SCHOOLS ACCEPT EVERYONE WHO APPLIES. Such an approach would initially lead to overcrowded schools and the need either to expand capacity or to find informal ways of discouraging large numbers of students from attending particular schools. Expanding capacity to meet market demand would be expensive, wasteful, and impractical. The capital costs of expansion are not trivial and are hard to justify when there is excess capacity at other schools. The use by schools of informal methods of limiting demand would most likely be even less acceptable than the enrollment scheme approach that New Zealand chose. At least in that approach, a school's enrollment scheme had to be made public, which in principle gives parents some right to appeal a negative enrollment decision. No such safeguards would be available in an informal system.

USE RANDOM BALLOTING TO ALLOCATE SCARCE SPACES. The original design of Tomorrow's Schools maintained enrollment zones but provided for some limited parental choice of schools. As the *Tomorrow's Schools* policy paper put it, the goal was to "ensure that students can attend a state school reasonably convenient to their home, to give parents maximum choice, and to make the best use of existing school plant." This approach gave control of the enrollment process to the Ministry of Education, which was authorized not only to define the capacity of schools but to negotiate the definition of the home zone whose residents would have an automatic right to attend. In the event that there were more out-of-zone applicants than places, seats would be filled by ballot.[5] This system lasted only one year because in 1991 the design of Tomorrow's Schools was fundamentally altered by abolishing enrollment zones and introducing full-scale parental choice.

Using a random balloting process to decide who will be able to attend oversubscribed schools has obvious appeal. Such a method is transparent and seems fair in that it appears to give equal opportunity to all parents. Random selection, however, is not free from problems, particularly when applied to a system in which all students are choosing schools. It is one thing for there to be a basic system of public schools in which every child has an assigned school but in which children can, if they wish, apply to another school. In that case, a child who loses the lottery for the school of choice has another viable alternative, namely the public school to which he or she is assigned.

However, when all schools are essentially choice schools, as became true in New Zealand after 1991, such a balloting scheme is much less feasible or desirable. Consider, for example, the Auckland area in which some of the fast-growing suburbs have an abundance of students, many of whom might be interested in competing for several of the best schools. It is hard to imagine how a random selection process would work in such a situation.

5. *Tomorrow's Schools* (1988: sec. 5.3.2).

If the process of matching students and schools were decentralized to the school level, the process could end up being incredibly time-consuming and wasteful. Would students have to apply to many schools to ensure acceptance by at least one school? As the random selection process is implemented, how would a school determine how many students to accept, given that it could not predict how many of the students it accepted would enroll? Although random selection could perhaps be done on a centralized basis rather than at the school level, some of the alleged benefits of school choice would be lost if all schools knew they would end up with a full allotment of randomly selected students no matter how they performed. The main criticism of a truly random process that takes into account the preferences of individual families alone, however, is that there would be no balancing of community interests against individual interests in the student assignment process.

Based on these concerns, we are not convinced that random balloting is the ideal way of rationing scarce places in a whole system of education, in which every student ultimately needs to have a school.

IMPLEMENT MANAGED OR CONTROLLED CHOICE. Managed or controlled choice is a logical extension of the centralized random balloting approach but differs in that it would require some conscious balancing of competing interests. Under this approach, students would be assigned to schools based on their preferences in a way that balanced their interests against the interests of other students and the community as a whole. These community interests might well vary from place to place. Some communities, for example, might deem it crucial to maintain ethnic, racial or socioeconomic balance among schools. That was the community interest, for example, in the development of one of the best-known programs of controlled choice, that of Cambridge, Massachusetts.[6] Alternatively, or in addition, a community might place weight on maximizing the use of the existing facilities or resources. For example, it might want to ensure that the schools that offer Japanese language and culture programs are allocated enough students with those interests to make the programs viable.

Controlled choice brings its own set of trade-offs and requirements. For example, it could undermine some of the alleged benefits of competition, because unpopular schools would not lose as many students as they

6. For a description of the Cambridge program, see Fiske (1991: chap. 7).

would under an unmanaged system.[7] Nevertheless, a well-designed system of controlled choice would maintain many of the benefits that choice offers to students and parents as educational consumers. The requirements for a fair system of controlled choice have been laid out elsewhere.[8]

The bottom line is that it is impossible to sustain a system in which all parents are completely free to select the school their child will attend. Some mechanism must be devised for rationing places in popular schools, and this inevitably involves constraints on choice. The challenge is to keep the constraints from falling disproportionately on students from disadvantaged families, as is likely to occur when schools can select their students, and to implement the system in a way that appropriately weighs the interests of competing groups.

Low-Performing Schools

The problems of schools serving concentrations of disadvantaged students will not be solved by school autonomy and parental choice. To the contrary, reforms of this type exacerbate the problem of such schools.

Much has been written about the problems of urban school systems and the fact that in many schools in large U.S. cities student performance is unacceptably low, given the demands of today's economy. While many explanations for this low performance are offered, including the challenges of educating concentrations of disadvantaged students, some critics of urban education in the United States attribute the problem to excess bureaucracy and to inappropriate incentives for schools to improve. To such

7. The city of Boston, Massachusetts, tried to address this issue in the controlled-choice plan introduced in 1989, the goals of which were to provide student choice, guarantee school desegregation, and promote school improvement. To encourage improvement, the rank orderings of student preferences were published with the hope that administrators of the least-chosen schools would recognize the need to improve. In addition, the intent was for the school board to give special attention to upgrading the least-chosen schools, a component of the plan that has been difficult to implement. See Willie, Alves, and Hagerty (1996).

8. Fiske (1991: 195–97) lists the following requirements: parents must have a range of high-quality alternative schools from which to choose, every child must have a crack at every school, all parents must be educated about their options, transportation must be made available to those who cannot afford it, all parties must acknowledge that choice will cost more, and districts must be ready with training.

critics, school autonomy and parental choice provide hope for improvement. Autonomy would give schools the flexibility—and parental choice would give them the incentive—to improve. Failure to improve their educational offerings would lead to a loss of students and funding.

The New Zealand experience indicates that these expectations are misplaced for the schools at the bottom. There is little doubt that parental choice made it possible for many students to escape from low-performing schools and thereby to improve their educational experiences. However, there is also little doubt that parental choice significantly exacerbated the problems faced by many schools serving concentrations of disadvantaged students. Over the period since the beginning of Tomorrow's Schools, schools in South Auckland and other low-income urban areas have become repositories for increasing concentrations of difficult-to-teach students. These schools enjoy the same operational flexibility as other self-governing schools, and they share the same incentives as other schools to improve the quality of their programs in order to attract more students and more funding. In some cases they appear to be well managed. Nevertheless, they find themselves unable to compete successfully in the academic marketplace.

Although these schools faced difficult challenges long before the Tomorrow's Schools reforms, the reforms complicated their problems. Such schools had the least-educated pools of parents from which to select trustees, and negative publicity from the Education Review Office in some cases had devastating effects on their public image. The introduction of parental choice meant that they lost large numbers of students, including a disproportionate number whose families valued education enough to exercise choice. The emergence of enrollment schemes as a marketing technique also made it possible for popular schools to avoid the hassle of dealing with difficult-to-teach students and to ship them down the decile scale to schools with empty seats, which were obliged to accept them.

One potential benefit of the new governance arrangement is that the failures of such schools are more visible and less easily ignored than under the old system. Despite the logic of the market model, which would be to let failing schools go out of business, the New Zealand government has been reluctant for political reasons to close such schools. Another conspicuous limitation of the market model is that the market has failed to create sufficient incentives for new schools to move into these areas and offer alternative educational programs for difficult-to-teach students. Had such schools materialized, the ministry would presumably have been more willing to close down failing schools.

The problem with applying the market solution to failing schools is that every child must have access to some school. If there is no room in nearby schools for children who are in failing schools, or if the nearby schools are also failing, political pressures coalesce to keep even a failing school operating. In light of this political reality, a preferred approach would be to figure out how to turn failing schools around.

NEW ZEALAND'S APPROACH TO FAILING SCHOOLS. Initially, New Zealand's approach was to do little or nothing for failing schools. In cases of severe governance breakdown, the Ministry of Education stepped in and used the power granted to it under Tomorrow's Schools to replace the board of trustees with a commissioner. Other than that, it did very little until political pressures from a variety of sources, including publicity in the media and a major report by the Education Review Office, forced it to recognize that the hands-off approach was not working and that the problems of such schools were sufficiently serious to warrant attention.

Once the Ministry of Education decided to intervene, it focused primarily on bolstering the management capacity of such schools. It chose that approach because it was the only form of intervention consistent with the principle of self-governing schools. Any direct substantive policy interventions from the center would undermine the principle. Presumably, some of the ministry's efforts to improve management have achieved their objective. Nevertheless, even with good management, which many of these schools now appear to have, they still find themselves unable to compete effectively in the educational marketplace. The improvement of managerial capacity, while perhaps necessary, turned out to be insufficient in and of itself to solve the competitive problems of schools with disproportionate numbers of difficult-to-educate students.

In mid-1999 some of these troubled schools received favorable reports from the Education Review Office, and it appears that they may be working their way back to viability. Administrators at the schools attribute the turnaround to a variety of factors, including infusions of significant new funds that have made it possible for them to address issues such as teachers' training and the students' need for supervised homework centers.[9]

9. *New Zealand Education Review,* June 11, 1999: 9.

OTHER APPROACHES.   The ministry's preoccupation with bolstering managers runs counter to the advice of the independent Education Review Office in its public report on South Auckland schools.[10] Although the ERO couched many of its policy recommendations to the ministry in managerial terms, it also acknowledged that such schools face serious problems that are outside their control and recommended, among other things, policies to address the challenges they face in attracting and retaining high-quality teachers. Such problems cannot be addressed by the schools themselves because the government controls salary schedules and the supply of teachers through its funding for teachers' educational programs. Given that the problems are not exclusively managerial, other strategies need to be considered. At this point, the New Zealand experience provides little guidance. Hence we simply mention a few possibilities.

—*Financial assistance.* Scholars vigorously debate whether additional funds would lead to higher academic performance in troubled schools.[11] In New Zealand, low-decile secondary schools receive about 30 percent more per pupil funding from the state than their more privileged counterparts, so despite their lesser success in raising funds from parents and foundations, they end up with more funds. Even with this funding advantage, however, these schools are at a major competitive disadvantage. We have little basis from the New Zealand experience to argue that providing more money to such schools would solve their problems. To the extent that the problems are broader than the schools themselves, some more systematic form of intervention could well be required.

—*A return to residential zoning.* Some critics of the Tomorrow's Schools reforms have proposed returning to the previous system of basing school enrollment on residential attendance zones, with the proviso that such zones be defined with attention to the ethnic and economic mix of families. This proposal is founded on the belief that the socioeconomic mix of students is the most important determinant of educational quality and, therefore, that schools with a mix of students are preferred to the more segregated schools that emerge from a system of parental choice.[12]

10. Education Review Office (1996).

11. See, for example, the overview chapter and articles in Burtless (1996).

12. A return to zoning was the preferred solution of the Smithfield project (1995: 55). Interestingly, the authors changed their view later (Lauder and Hughes [1999: 136]), arguing instead for some form of managed choice.

Returning to a system of school attendance zones, however, would eliminate parents' right to choose their child's school, a right that most New Zealanders, having had a taste of it, would probably be loath to surrender. Moreover, given the segregation of residential areas, most educational gains from such a policy change in low-income areas would come at the expense of those families who would otherwise have exercised their choice and moved their children to other schools. Finally, any attempt to balance the socioeconomic mix of school attendance zones could be thwarted in part by the residential location decisions of wealthy households. New Zealand's recent partial move back to the concept of residential attendance zones was motivated not by a concern for failing schools but rather by a concern for the rights of parents to have access to a conveniently located school.

—*Major extended interventions, with support for teaching and learning.* Another strategic possibility would begin with the recognition that governance changes alone are not going to solve the problems of schools serving concentrations of disadvantaged students. Instead, the problems need to be confronted head-on with major interventions focused on teaching and learning. The New Zealand experience provides little insight about what might work in this regard, since the government is only now beginning to address the issue. However, policies to address the problems such schools face in recruiting and retaining teachers, as called for by the Education Review Office, provide one example of the types of intervention that may be required.

Thus the main lesson from New Zealand is a negative one: governance and management changes alone are not going to solve the problems of overburdened schools. This negative lesson has a clear implication for policymakers. If a country cares about the students in such schools, it must be prepared to experiment with large-scale interventions specifically directed at the educational challenges faced by such schools.

Self-Governance Combined with Competition

The fact that no one in New Zealand wants to return to the old system of a centralized Department of Education working through regional boards of education is to some extent a commentary on how bureaucratically encrusted the previous regime had become. Nevertheless, the country's experience with Tomorrow's Schools provides considerable vindication for the notion of self-governance in and of itself. In saying so, we must add the significant qualification that both its positive and negative effects are magnified when self-governance is embedded in a system of parental choice and market competition.

Self-governance worked for most schools in the sense that they managed to recruit and elect a sufficient number of parents to fill their boards of trustees. Moreover, in contrast to Chicago's experience with local school councils, the number of people running for school boards has not declined substantially over time.[13] In addition, although teachers and school administrators have experienced additional workloads, on the whole they appear to be generally pleased with their new operational latitude. Self-governance has worked much less well for a significant number of schools, many of which serve disadvantaged students. For some schools, the main problems occurred during the start-up period, but for others the managerial problems have persisted. A study by the Education Review Office found that 34 percent of decile 1 schools had inadequate means of assessing student achievement, versus only 10 percent of decile 10 schools. Other areas in which lower-decile schools showed significantly more problems include compliance with legal requirements, methods of judging the performance of their staff, financial and property management, and overall governance.[14]

Gladstone Primary School, Ponsonby Intermediate School, and Aranui High School have enthusiastically embraced their new autonomy and have transformed themselves into quite different, and successful, institutions. Such dramatic transformations of whole schools would not have been possible under the system that Tomorrow's Schools replaced. Nevertheless, however, we also note that changes of this magnitude require unusually energetic and visionary principals; while more such people could perhaps be recruited into positions of educational leadership, they are not likely to be the norm in any field, including education. The last few years have seen the emergence of a number of able young principals in South Auckland and other low-income areas who approach the running of urban schools with quite different attitudes than their predecessors,

13. In Chicago, the number of parents running for local school councils reached a peak of 17,096 in 1989, declined to 7,539 in 1993, and to 7,289 in 1998. See comments by Jeffery Mirel in Bryk (1999: 112).

14. Education Review Office (1998: app. 2).

and this is a hopeful sign. Nevertheless, while the governance changes of Tomorrow's Schools gave schools new opportunities and relieved them of many onerous restrictions, they did not guarantee an enhanced supply of bold innovators. For that reason, self-governance should be viewed as permissive rather than determinative as far as dramatic transformations of schools are concerned.

The fact that New Zealand's self-governing schools are embedded in a system in which parents have choice and schools compete for students has clear implications for the way self-governance operates in practice. When high-income parents choose a school, they can enhance its reputation and ultimately its ability to manage its own affairs; and when these more advantaged parents leave a school, they can hurt the school's reputation and damage its ability to manage. Ponsonby Intermediate provides an example of the first situation. While significant credit undoubtedly goes to the principal, Iain Taylor, for changing the school's image, his success was facilitated by the fact that the school, located in an area undergoing regentrification, was able to draw students with more advantaged backgrounds away from other schools. The higher socioeconomic status of the incoming students further enhanced the image of the school. Indeed, Taylor acknowledges that the fact that the school was well located to attract such students was an important factor in his decision to accept leadership of a school that others had written off.

Several secondary schools in South Auckland also exemplify these issues. The schools in that area of low-income immigrant families started out with the problem of having to draw for their boards of trustees on parents with low levels of education and skill. Parental choice of school only served to exacerbate the challenge. The parents who were most committed to education and might have been the best candidates to serve on the boards took their children out of such schools and moved them elsewhere, leaving an even smaller pool of talent and interest from which to draw. In addition, the publication of reports from the Education Review Office that were intended to induce better management made the situation worse. Poor reports further diminished the reputation of the schools, which in turn made it more difficult for the schools to retain students and attract good teachers.

NEW ZEALAND'S APPROACH TO SCHOOLS WITH GOVERNANCE PROBLEMS. The Tomorrow's Schools legislation gives the minister of education the power to dissolve a board of trustees and to appoint a commissioner with full governance and managerial authority in cases of mismanagement, incompetence, dishonesty, or unlawful behavior.[15] Thus in cases of extreme governance failure, the minister can step in.

This remedy of replacing the board with a commissioner is far too extreme for the typical situation of a poorly managed school. New Zealand's approach to such schools is to hold them publicly accountable through critiques by the Education Review Office. Publication of these reviews is designed to put public pressure on the schools to improve; and although the reviews provide information to the schools in the form of the actions required to meet legal obligations, they are not designed to provide policy guidance and advice. Indeed, policymakers believe that it would be inappropriate to combine monitoring and advice in the same agency. While the separation of those functions can be defended conceptually, the downside in the New Zealand context is that some of the policy advice and guidance functions that were available in the old system have largely fallen between the cracks of the new system. Moreover, publication of the reports can exacerbate the problems of struggling schools. Although the information in the reports can be useful to schools and to parents, these reports can be counterproductive when, as happened in some cases, negative reports fail to take into account actions the school is taking to address the identified problems.

In addition to its reports on individual schools, the Education Review Office distills what it has learned from its many school reviews about what makes for effective and ineffective schools.[16] Through this mechanism, the ERO shares information among schools, sending signals to schools and their boards about what makes an effective school. To date these reports have not been based on a sophisticated evaluation of what works or does not work but rather on what ERO reviewers have identified, given their particular perspective on school effectiveness.

STRATEGIES FOR MAXIMIZING THE BENEFITS OF SELF-GOVERNING SCHOOLS. Despite these activities, many schools serving concentrations of disadvantaged students in New Zealand remain woefully ineffective, as measured either by the Education Review Office's criteria for effectiveness or by the market's criteria of parents and students voting with their feet. As a result, the government has been forced to intervene. We have

---

15. Education Act of 1989, sec. 107.
16. Education Review Office (1998).

discussed the need for significant intervention in support of teaching and learning at unsuccessful schools. Here we list strategies that address governance issues more generally.

—*Retention of some operational functions at the center.* A good example of a function that needs central attention is combating truancy. In the spirit of decentralization, the Tomorrow's Schools reforms gave individual schools the responsibility for dealing with truants. In a competitive situation, however, schools with full rolls have little incentive to deal with difficult students whose place is readily taken by other students. In this situation, the interests of the system as a whole should not be entrusted to individual schools acting in their own interests. Recognizing this problem, the Ministry of Education has reinstituted a central office to combat truancy.

—*Recognition that all schools need some operational support.* The level of such support will vary from school to school, but it should be regarded as a normal part of the functioning of a decentralized school system. Schools will make much better use of their autonomy if they are not required to reinvent wheels in areas such as finance, property management, and professional development. Economies of scale can also be obtained by making such services available to schools, at least on an optional basis, from central authorities. The Education Review Office urged such services, declaring that "the Government may need to design different interventions and consider whether a greater degree of central direction is necessary to ensure that the learning opportunities of students are not placed at risk."[17] In principle such support could also come from the private sector.

—*Development of new governance arrangements for some schools.* Some schools are likely to require major support in order to remain viable institutions. Such support may mean the establishment of an entirely different governance system. It may call for the formation of natural clusters of schools: it may make sense for schools to pool their human and other resources through the formation of joint boards of trustees, feeder patterns, and other departures from a strict model of autonomous schools.

The lesson from New Zealand with regard to self-governance is similar to that in the previous section on failing schools: the combination of self-governance and a competitive environment will not have salutary effects

17. Education Review Office (1988: 33).

for the entire range of schools. Policymakers need to be prepared from the outset to intervene on behalf of schools that are not successfully managing themselves.

Lessons for Charter Schools

One approach to school reform to which New Zealand's experience with Tomorrow's Schools is directly relevant is the charter school movement in the United States. This movement has attracted considerable support in the last few years, and the number of charter schools has grown from none in 1990 to more than 1,200 in 1999. The Clinton administration has made expansion of the notion part of its educational policy.

U.S. charter schools are public schools in the sense that they receive government funding and are ultimately accountable to the same public authority—typically a school district or a state department of education—as other public schools. What differentiates charter schools is that they are not operated directly by the government. Rather, they are usually established and managed by voluntary associations of parents, educators, citizens, and others who come together around a common vision of education. Some charter schools are sponsored by preexisting organizations such as community groups, teachers' unions, churches, and even private businesses. Although in some cases regular public schools have converted to charter status, the majority of charter schools are started from scratch.

The sponsoring organization draws up a charter explaining the educational program it plans to offer and the goals it seeks to accomplish. Public school officials then evaluate the applicant's educational and business plans as well as the capability of the individuals involved to implement it and, if satisfied, issue the charter. The government provides funding to charter schools on a per pupil basis and exempts them from the need to follow many of the usual rules and procedures imposed on other public schools, including the need to conform to central collective bargaining agreements in hiring teachers. In return, charter schools agree to be held accountable to the state for meeting the goals laid out in its charter. If the school fails to do so, the government can revoke the charter.

The educational system established by the Tomorrow's Schools reforms in New Zealand bears some striking similarities to the charter school phenomenon. However, there are also some significant differences. Most important, charter schools constitute a minority of schools in the United

States and operate on the fringes of the state educational systems, whereas in New Zealand all schools must assume a high level of operational autonomy. The Tomorrow's Schools reforms forced all schools to become self-governing whether or not they wanted to and whether or not they had the demonstrated capacity to do so. Significantly, elected members of school boards in New Zealand do not usually come together around the sort of common educational vision that characterizes the boards of most charter schools in the United States.

Another difference is that in New Zealand the boards of individual schools have not had to face the capital funding challenge faced by many charter schools in the United States. Because New Zealand's autonomous schools converted from existing public schools, the facilities were already there and the government retained ownership of them. In contrast, any charter school in the United States that starts from scratch faces serious challenges in coming up with the funds needed to start a new school.

Because of these differences it would not be accurate to characterize the Tomorrow's Schools reforms as having established a whole country of charter schools. Nevertheless, there are sufficient parallels to ask what insights Tomorrow's Schools might offer proponents and critics of charter schools in the United States and elsewhere. We suggest that there are two main lessons.

Charter Schools on the Fringe versus a Whole System

There is a big difference between a few charter schools operating on the fringe of a public school system and a whole system of self-governing schools functioning in a competitive environment. When there are just a few charter schools, the government can be assured that if a school does not meet the needs of a particular child, that child will have a guaranteed place in a traditional public school, over which the government has direct operational control. Such a guarantee would seem to be important in a system of compulsory education. Thus when charter schools are limited in number, they can be given the flexibility to be innovative and to take educational risks. For some children they may be very effective; for others they may not be.

The New Zealand experience suggests, however, that a government's willingness to accept the diversity represented by charter schools might change if charter schools became the majority of schools or even a significant minority. Recall that the original architects of the New Zealand reforms envisioned that each school would have its own unique educational vision and objectives. However, as the reforms proceeded it became clear that, although the government encouraged local schools to come up with their own educational goals, such local goals were secondary to those imposed from the center in the form of the National Education Guidelines. The government has an interest in ensuring that its own national purposes will be served, and the New Zealand experience suggests that it will use its powers of funding and accountability to vigorously assert this interest. The relevance of this point is already clear in the United States in the related context of school vouchers. Some proponents of the use of vouchers for religious schools in the United States have warned about the possibility that this could lead to greater government regulation of such schools, and the evolution of the Tomorrow's Schools reforms suggests that such fears are justified.[18] We are, however, inclined to emphasize the other side of the coin: that the state has an obligation to ensure that schools are spending the public's tax dollars in a responsible way.

A related issue draws on the policy lesson emphasized earlier—that when a large number of schools are choice schools, the issue will inevitably arise about how to allocate spaces in oversubscribed schools. The implications for charter schools should be clear. As long as they are few in number, it is reasonable to require that they allocate their scarce places through random balloting. If charter schools were to become the norm, however, all the same issues raised earlier would reappear. Because balloting may not work well for a whole system of schools, a form of controlled or managed choice would most likely be required.

Thus we conclude that U.S. charter schools may better serve the goal of diversity and innovation if they remain limited in number and do not become the norm.

Accountability for Charter Schools

New Zealand's approach to accountability is worth considering for charter schools and possibly for public schools more generally. Although there is general agreement in the United States about the importance of holding charter schools accountable for results, the jury is still out on the ques-

18. Loconte (1999).

tion of how well states will succeed in doing so. Scholars on both sides of the charter school debate have looked at accountability and found it wanting.[19] The power to revoke school charters is available and has been used in a few cases on grounds of educational inadequacy, but it is likely to be too crude a tool for true accountability. Charter documents are often too vague to serve as the basis for charter revocation, and states frequently have no good means of holding their public schools, much less their charter schools, accountable for performance. Even in states with sophisticated test-based accountability systems for all their schools, authorities cannot use the system to make decisions about charter renewals or about major interventions unless they are willing to specify up-front standards for such renewal, something that no state has yet done.

The New Zealand approach to accountability provides a potential model. Under this system, charter schools would be periodically inspected by an independent agency that would review the school's operations and evaluate the school relative to the accountability standards spelled out in the school's charter. The reviews from such an agency should be made available, at a minimum, to the school and the state chartering agency. The review would provide the school and its board with helpful information from an outside objective source on the areas in which the school was falling short and in which it needed to improve. It would be useful to the chartering agency in making decisions about whether to intervene during the charter period and about whether to renew a school's charter. The New Zealand model also calls for public distribution of such reviews. A charter accountability model along these lines has already been established by Massachusetts and deserves consideration by other states as well.

This approach to accountability works quite well in New Zealand, although care would need to be taken to avoid some of its pitfalls. New Zealand's Education Review Office is effective in part because of its independence from the Ministry of Education. In addition, it has credibility because of the high quality of the professionals on its staff and because of its strong leadership. The ERO initially focused more on processes than on educational outcomes, and such an approach was probably justified for schools that were newly self-governing, with many elected board members who had little idea of what was involved in running a school and in

19. See *UCLA Charter School Study* (1998); Finn and others (1997). For guidance on charter school accountability, see Manno (1999).

complying with the legal requirements. Its subsequent introduction of effectiveness reviews, which were designed to determine the extent to which the school was effectively monitoring the progress of students toward the goals laid out in the school's charter, seems particularly relevant for the U.S. situation. While the absence of national test results in New Zealand has hampered the review agency's ability to say much about student outcomes, the ERO approach provides a model for the other outcomes and processes that a review agency might usefully examine.

Lessons for Voucher Schemes

Another approach to school improvement that has attracted considerable attention in recent years is educational vouchers. Under this approach, the state assigns a specific amount of funding for each student and then gives parents a voucher, or chit, for this amount, which they can trade for a year of education at the school of their choice. Schools then compete to enroll students and obtain the per pupil funding that comes with them. Proponents of voucher systems argue that they would enhance the quality of education by giving parents a greater voice in determining where their children attend school and by forcing schools to improve their offerings as a means of attracting students.

Voucher schemes come in various forms. Full voucher systems allow parents to take their state funding to any school, public or private, while partial voucher systems either limit parental choice to public schools or provide lesser amounts of funding for students who opt for a private school. The term *voucher* is also used to describe plans under which the government or foundations offer scholarships to students, usually from low-income families, to attend private schools. Two American cities, Cleveland and Milwaukee, are currently operating small and highly controversial publicly funded programs of the latter type, and a number of private organizations and individual citizens have established scholarship programs to subsidize attendance of low-income students at private schools. Some school reformers in the United States have been pushing for full-scale voucher experiments that would give students the choice of attending either public or private schools at public expense.

New Zealand's system of education has been described by one educational expert as a quasi-voucher system.[20] Even before Tomorrow's Schools,

---

20. Wylie (1998).

the country subsidized the tuition of the 3.5 percent of students who attend private schools, albeit at a level below the amount of per pupil spending for those in state schools. The reforms of 1991 embraced many of the central features of vouchers, notably parental choice, competition for students among schools, and the linking of school funding to the number of students the school is able to attract.

New Zealand, however, stops short of having a full voucher system in the sense that some school funding, including the targeted funding for educational achievement programs, is still given directly to schools on the basis of factors other than simply the number of students they attract. Some individuals and organizations in New Zealand, most conspicuously the Business Roundtable, have urged the government to move to a full-fledged voucher approach.

Targeted Individual Entitlement Program

Actually, New Zealand does in fact have one small true voucher program: the targeted individual entitlement (TIE) program. This program, which provides funds for low-income students to attend private schools, illustrates how such a program might work in practice. Of the country's 127 private schools, 62 were interested in participating, and 43 were declared eligible by the ministry. Some schools were apparently rejected on the grounds of being "small and religion based."[21] The program, which is aimed at low-income families, has attracted parents who are better educated and work in higher-skilled occupations than their peers in other eligible families. They are also disproportionately Pakeha (that is, European) relative to the low-income population as a whole, and minority students are underrepresented in the program relative to their prevalence within the low-income population.[22]

One of the big issues surrounding the introduction of the TIE program was the basis on which schools would select the students. Despite a Treasury Department recommendation that students be chosen randomly, participating private schools insisted on the right to select students based on interviews with families and students. Participating schools make no bones about looking for low-income students who are talented in academics, the arts, and, in the case of boys schools, rugby. Thus there is little doubt that cream skimming occurs in the TIE program.

21. Wylie (1998: 107).
22. Wylie (1998: 107).

Vouchers and Concentrations of Disadvantaged Students

The role of private schools aside, a key feature of vouchers is that funding is linked to students, not to schools. If a voucher program provides the same amount of money for all students, such a program would put schools with a disproportionate number of difficult-to-educate students at a disadvantage relative to other schools. Because these students are more costly to educate, such schools would find it difficult if not impossible to provide education of comparable quality.

In recognition of this fact, some voucher advocates recommend that disadvantaged students be given larger vouchers than other students. The larger vouchers, the theory goes, would compensate schools for the higher costs that these students impose. That in fact is the funding strategy of the TIE program. As of 1995, students received a scholarship that exceeded by 10 percent the average per pupil cost of educating a student in the public school system.[23]

Although this differential funding arrangement sounds appealing, it has a basic flaw. In effect, it assumes that the extra costs associated with disadvantaged students are related to the student alone and have little to do with the mix of students in a school. If in fact there is a concentration effect, so that the educational challenges facing a school are disproportionately greater as the proportion of disadvantaged students increases, a better way to compensate schools for the educational challenges they face is to direct additional funds to schools based on the mix of students in the school. That is what New Zealand currently does through its program of targeted funding for educational achievement (TFEA). Through that program, schools get additional funding, which varies with the mix of students they serve as estimated by the average characteristics of the census blocks in which the students live. The advantage of this approach is that it targets the funds to the schools facing the greatest educational challenges.

Attaching differential dollar amounts to individual students raises additional practical, ethical, and political problems. From a practical point of view, it is difficult to determine a measure of educational disadvantage that can be applied fairly to individual students. Presumably, the appropriate measure of disadvantage is some complicated combination of parental income, parental educational level (especially of the mother), living

23. Wylie (1998: 104).

conditions, and ethnicity. Gathering such information for each student would be a formidable, if not impossible, task. Any census block approach of the type used by New Zealand that is suitable for making an estimate of a school's overall mix of students would be too imprecise for a specific student. In the absence of good information, the more likely scenario is that students would be classified by some simpler—and less appropriate—measure, such as family income or ethnicity. In addition to this nontrivial practical problem, that vouchers of differential magnitudes could stigmatize students by labeling them as being poor or otherwise educationally disadvantaged. Finally, a political problem arises having to do with the willingness of the voting public to support programs that would provide larger educational vouchers to disadvantaged children.

This political problem is not unique to voucher programs. It also applies to differential funding for schools. One difference is that additional funding for schools can be more readily connected to objective and measurable school differences that data have shown correlate with educational success. However, even equity-based programs targeted to schools face political challenges. Although the original ministry proposal for TFEA funding called for directing the funds only to schools in the bottom three deciles, political considerations soon forced the funds to be distributed more broadly up the decile rankings, eventually to include decile 9 schools. This evidence from New Zealand does not bode well for a voucher funding formula that would differentiate in a significant way among students.

Vouchers and the Supply of Schools

One of the clearest lessons to emerge from the New Zealand experience with parental choice is that, when the supply of schools is limited, as it has been in New Zealand, students from the most advantaged families are the major beneficiaries. This finding highlights the importance of school supply to the outcomes of a choice system.

A major reason that school supply has been limited in New Zealand is that the government owns the schools and has been understandably reluctant to build new schools or to expand existing schools when there are existing schools with excess capacity. Some seem to believe that a voucher program would solve the supply-side problem. Because students would be able to use their vouchers in private schools, existing private schools with excess capacity would have new customers for their schools, existing private schools would have incentives to expand, and new private schools would be established. The hope would be that the larger number of schools would result in a broader array of educational programs for all students, including low-income students, and, through competition for students, in a higher overall quality of education.[24]

The New Zealand experience with a quasi-voucher system sheds little light on this key question of how the supply of schools would respond to a large-scale voucher program. However, it does suggest that there is no free lunch, because new or expanded schools impose capital costs that must ultimately be borne by someone, whether taxpayers or private individuals. Based on our review of New Zealand's quasi-voucher system, we predict that many of the concerns raised in the following section would be exacerbated in a true voucher program.

Broad Concerns

In the absence of national test data that would allow us to determine whether overall student achievement has increased, we can say little about the overall benefits of New Zealand's reforms. Despite the lack of such information, however, we have little doubt that the system has been beneficial for many students and schools. Indeed, as of 1997, three of four students were in schools that might be classified as successful based on the market criterion that they were at capacity or that their enrollments grew by more than 5 percent between 1991 and 1997. Of course, because market conditions vary across metropolitan areas, a fast-growing area such as Auckland is likely to generate a higher proportion of successful schools than other areas. But even in Auckland, the picture is not all rosy: 5 percent of primary and intermediate school students and 10 percent of secondary school students were in schools that were failures according to the market test.

An examination of the benefits and problems associated with the Tomorrow's Schools reforms leads us to suggest three broad areas of concern to policymakers in other countries who are interested in how self-governing schools function in a competitive environment.

24. Hill (1999).

Polarization of Student Enrollment

Enrollment and census data document the extent to which the Tomorrow's Schools reforms caused a significant movement of students from low-decile to high-decile schools. Although both Pakeha and minority families participated in this movement, the former were more aggressive in taking advantage of the choice option than Maoris or Pacific Islanders. As a result, ethnic minorities have become increasingly concentrated in low-decile schools at both the primary and secondary levels, and enrollment in state schools is more polarized than it was on the eve of Tomorrow's Schools. Piecemeal evidence from a ministry-financed study also suggests that enrollment patterns have become more segregated socioeconomically. In addition, the distribution of students among winner and loser schools indicates a clear pattern: losing schools have disproportionate numbers of minority students and rank low in terms of the socioeconomic status of their clientele.

One can reasonably ask whether such ethnic and socioeconomic polarization is a problem. We believe it is. The Hippocratic oath taken by new physicians begins with the declaration, "First do no harm," and a similar admonition seems relevant to educational policymakers. To be sure, polarization by race, ethnic group, and socioeconomic status is increasingly common in most industrialized countries, even in traditionally egalitarian New Zealand, and some additional polarization in the schools might have occurred even if parental choice had not become an option. Moreover, in countries such as the United States that are more culturally diverse than New Zealand, one would presumably find less agreement among parents as to which schools are the most desirable. There might thus be less pressure to get children into a narrow list of schools.

Nevertheless, however, we believe that the basic forces unleashed by parental choice—including the tendency to judge school quality by the mix of a school's student body—are likely to push systems toward greater ethnic and socioeconomic polarization under almost any circumstance. While state school systems cannot be expected to solve all social problems, they should at a minimum not exacerbate existing inequities. Ideally, they should serve to offset them. Thus organizing a state system of compulsory education in such a way that it reinforces existing tendencies toward polarization should be a matter of concern.

Winners and Losers

The preceding chapters show that the Tomorrow's Schools reforms had significant differential impact on the fortunes of many schools. Schools that were successful in adapting to the new conditions saw their enrollments increase, and those with enrollment schemes gained control of the mix of students they admitted. Unsuccessful schools, on the other hand, watched their rolls decline, sometimes in spiraling fashion, and many became repositories for a disproportionate number of dysfunctional students.

The fact that the Tomorrow's Schools reforms produced both winner and loser schools comes as no surprise. Indeed, it shows that the system worked. Any competitive situation presumes that some participants will succeed and others will fail. The creation of such losers becomes problematic, however, when competition is introduced into the operation of an educational system that the public deems so important that it makes school attendance compulsory. Is it defensible on moral, practical, or other grounds to organize a state educational system so that you know from the outset that, if the system functions the way it is supposed to function, you will seriously exacerbate the problems of some schools? Two conditions might justify such a policy.

The first condition would be realized if competition led to an overall improvement of the system as a whole. In such a situation some schools might appear to be unsuccessful by virtue of declining enrollment but still be prodded by the competitive environment to offer a better academic program than before. Such schools would be failures in relative terms but successes in absolute terms, and all students, including those in supposedly unsuccessful schools, would be winners.

We do not have the systematic test score data needed to determine which schools have improved the quality of their academic offerings under Tomorrow's Schools and which have not. Given the fact that the most desirable schools are now in an enhanced position to attract the brightest students and to tailor high-powered academic programs to them, we must presume that the academic levels of some schools have risen under Tomorrow's Schools. However, we can confidently say that schools that have lost enrollment and that have taken on greater concentrations of dysfunctional students as a result of Tomorrow's Schools are worse off than they were before. Thus whatever the benefits to some institutions and some students, the Tomorrow's Schools reforms have *not* produced a rising tide that raises all boats and increases the overall quality of the entire system.

The second condition that might justify a system set up to create unsuccessful schools and loser students would be realized if the Ministry of Education, cognizant of the fact that competition inevitably leads to unsuccessful schools, stood ready with a safety net to intervene once schools began to fail. As with the first condition, this second condition has not been met in New Zealand. The Ministry of Education was slow to recognize the need to provide support for schools in such low-income areas as South Auckland. Moreover, when political pressure compelled it to intervene, it did so in a minimalist way, placing unwarranted faith in the capacity of good management to solve problems that were at least partially beyond the control of the schools. The Ministry of Education's reluctance was understandable given that the Tomorrow's Schools model offered no conceptual justification for such intervention. Any such intervention would violate the principle of self-governance as well as call into question the assumption that competition leads to better education. Eventually, however, the ministry was forced to act.

That some schools will inevitably be unsuccessful in an educational system designed around the principles of self-governance and competition need not require the rejection of those organizing principles. However, it does pose a serious policy challenge to the designers of an educational system. The challenge is how to ensure that the educational needs of students in unsuccessful schools are met while at the same time preserving the benefits of self-governance and choice for others. At a minimum, policymakers should be aware from the outset that there will be losers as well as winners, and they should be prepared to intervene earlier rather than later in order to prevent damage.

Balancing the Interests of Competing Stakeholders

Any state educational system has a multitude of stakeholders with differing interests. The central government has broad goals such as educating citizens and training workers, while students, teachers, administrators, local communities, future employers, and other stakeholders all have their own claims on the system. Each of these stakeholders has legitimate interests, but there will be times when these interests clash. In such situations those who manage the system need to find ways of balancing them.

The major thrust of the Tomorrow's Schools reforms was to free parents, educators, and even entire schools from the stifling constraints of the previous centralized and highly bureaucratic system in order to release energies that would lead to an improved state educational system. To a large extent this objective was accomplished—but at a price. The old system, cumbersome and inefficient though it may have been, nevertheless had mechanisms for ensuring that the interests of particular stakeholders did not take undue precedence over those of other stakeholders or of those of the system as a whole.

The new system addresses such issues in one of two ways. First, it gives primacy to the rights of current parents in a particular school. The ink was hardly dry on the reform legislation when a dispute arose over the decision by the board of a primary school in Wellington to add two more grades so that parents would not have to send their children to a nearby intermediate school. This decision pitted the interests of a particular set of parents against those of other stakeholders, including other primary schools in the area and parents who feared the loss of an intermediate school option for their children. In keeping with the principles of self-governance, the Minister of Education declined to intervene, on the ground that the wishes of current parents in a school must prevail. Subsequent ministers have backtracked from this position.

Second, the new system puts its faith in the capacity of a competitive marketplace to balance competing interests. Thus until very recently over-subscribed schools have had the right to accept and reject students with little reference to how their decisions would affect either other schools or the system as a whole. Such a policy has contributed to ethnic and socio-economic polarization of student enrollment and has interfered with the interests of parents who would like their child to attend a nearby school but for whom there was no such school available. The initial faith of New Zealand policymakers in the capacity of the market alone to deal with such issues turned out to be naïve, and the new enrollment policies represent acknowledgment of this lesson.

Our purpose in raising the issue is not to suggest that the decision of the minister in the Wellington dispute was wrong or that the enrollment scheme of any particular school is unjust. Rather, we suggest that more attention be paid to the question of how to strike the best balance between the interests of competing stakeholders and the system as a whole. This question is, of course, a complex one. Indeed, stated broadly, it is *the* central issue for any democracy and any democratic institution.

The reform plan proposed by the Picot task force and subsequently incorporated into the Tomorrow's Schools policy document did anticipate the need for such structures. The initial reforms included a provision for community forums on education to discuss issues that transcended individual schools, and such a forum was convened for the Wellington controversy. When its work was dismissed by the minister as irrelevant, though, the forum concept was abandoned. Likewise, parent advocacy councils, which were designed to address the power imbalance between parents and educational professionals by supporting individual parents in dealings with the Ministry of Education, never got off the ground. Other countries might consider ways to ensure permanent status for such institutions.

Observations about Comprehensive Reform

Among the most striking characteristics of the Tomorrow's Schools reforms are that they were comprehensive and that they have been sustained over a long period of time. The reforms entailed the creation of entirely new structures for financing, governing, and managing state schools and introduced new approaches to enrollment policy and accountability. In the process, they redefined many of the presuppositions, values, and relationships on which the state educational system operates, including the nature of the relationship of local schools to central authorities and the rights of individual students and families vis-à-vis the system as a whole. Rarely has any country engaged in such a sustained and far-reaching overhaul of its educational system. It is worth reflecting for a moment on some of the lessons that emerge from the comprehensive nature of the Tomorrow's Schools reforms.

Evolutionary Nature of the Reform Process

The state system of compulsory education as it now exists in New Zealand did not emerge full-blown and Phoenixlike from the ashes of the old one. The original design of Tomorrow's Schools brought about changes, mainly having to do with governance and management, that were intended to correct certain perceived problems of the old system. Within two years, however, the reform process took on a life of its own and began to evolve in ways neither intended nor foreseen by its architects.

Part of the evolution can be seen as healthy reality checking. As time passed, political and educational leaders gained a clearer understanding of which parts of the reform were working well and which were creating problems and needed to be modified. For example, the Ministry of Education realized that the truancy function had fallen through the cracks and set up a small office to deal with it. On a more substantial level, officials were obliged to concede that a significant number of unsuccessful schools lacked the capacity for self-governance and that different arrangements had to be made for them.

Other changes resulted because public school reform is ultimately a political process and as such is susceptible to change as proponents of particular approaches gain and lose power. The notion of self-governance of schools, for example, was embraced by a Labour government for reasons having to do with community voice and good management, but it was maintained and molded by the National government that assumed power in 1991 for reasons more closely related to distrust of centralized government and faith in the value of market competition. Likewise, the concept of parental choice was originally introduced in quite limited fashion as a populist gesture aimed at giving parents a greater voice in primary and secondary education. The National government expanded the notion because it saw choice as an accountability and efficiency-enhancing mechanism and as a way of reducing the influence of government.

The political nature of school reform also means that some reforms will be either blocked or implemented in piecemeal fashion. Bulk funding of teachers' salaries, for example, was endorsed by the Labour government in its policy document, *Tomorrow's Schools,* but it has yet to be completely implemented, largely because of opposition from teachers.

New Zealand's experience with Tomorrow's Schools thus suggests that school reformers in the United States and other nations should think about school reform as a dynamic and evolutionary process, not as a fixed program. They should also be prepared for the possibility that their ideas may be taken in unintended and unexpected directions.

Tensions and Trade-Offs among Policy Objectives

The Tomorrow's Schools reforms pursued a number of major policy objectives. Among them were improving educational quality, enhancing parental and community involvement in local schools, achieving greater managerial efficiency, controlling costs, minimizing the role of the state, and achieving equity. Different participants in the reform effort gave different weight to these values, and the relative importance of the various goals fluctuated. Conflicts inevitably arose between some of these goals, and the architects of the reforms were forced to make trade-offs.

The most serious conflicts among the competing policy objectives of Tomorrow's Schools involved equity. Some important steps were taken to ensure the continuation of New Zealand's egalitarian traditions in education. Among the most notable was the 1995 targeted funding for educational achievement program, which allocated additional state funding for low-decile schools to offset some of the burden of educating disproportionate numbers of difficult-to-educate students. In many other ways, however, when equity concerns came into conflict with other policy objectives, it was equity that suffered.

Equity, defined as high-quality education for all students, would require a significant amount of government expenditure to offset the overwhelming disadvantages faced by schools serving at-risk students. Likewise, a truly equitable system of parental choice would require that the government subsidize transportation costs for low-income families and provide information centers and services in multiple languages so that all parents would be fully informed about the various options. The government, however, was consistently more concerned with containing costs to the state than with neutralizing transportation burdens and information as factors that inhibit parental choice. By placing heavy emphasis on parental choice but declining to make the financial investment needed to ensure that all families could exercise this choice, the Tomorrow's Schools reforms further polarized the system.

The New Zealand experience with school reform illustrates that the collective voice option works much more effectively for middle- and upper-income families than it does for poor, uneducated families. That does not mean that vehicles for collective decisionmaking, such as school boards of trustees, are undesirable for schools serving the children of poor families. Rather it means that such schools are at a significant disadvantage relative to those with a more educated pool of parents as prospective board members.

Similarly, conflicts arise between equity concerns and an accountability system that does not take into account the socioeconomic status of students. Schools that serve disadvantaged students and that add much to the learning of their students receive no recognition of that accomplishment. Such lack of recognition in turn makes it difficult for them to recruit high-quality teachers. One way to reduce this conflict between equity and quality is to develop measures of school quality that take into account the background of students.

The New Zealand experience with Tomorrow's Schools supports the view that a country cannot have its cake and eat it too. New Zealand was not able to achieve higher educational quality for all students with lower costs and no loss of equity while giving significantly more power to parents. Instead, the New Zealand experience illustrates the significant trade-offs among these policy objectives.

No Panaceas

The New Zealand experience also suggests the limits of particular ideas and theories. Some, though by no means all, of the architects of Tomorrow's Schools seemed to believe that governance reforms based on ideas such as community voice, market competition, and choice had the capacity in and of themselves to bring about major improvements in the quality of New Zealand's state educational system. In many cases these ideas were borrowed from other fields, such as management theory or economics, with the expectation that they could be readily adapted to the delivery of public education.

If nothing else, New Zealand's experience with school reform, starting in 1989, illustrates that there are no panaceas in school reform. The core ideas of Tomorrow's Schools that persisted over time—self-governance, parental choice, market competition—proved to have both benefits and complications. Proponents of particular reforms may argue with some justification that their pet idea never really got tried. Some say the only true test of the validity of parental choice would be a full-scale voucher system. Likewise, it can be argued that the self-governance of schools has not been fully tested because the Ministry of Education was never able to overcome political opposition from teachers' unions and school trustees to fully implement the bulk funding of teachers' salaries. Along the same line, it is tempting to wonder how self-governance of schools would have played out had a new government not added parental choice to the mix—a move that substantially complicated the task of schools serving concentrations of disadvantaged students.

The story of the Tomorrow's Schools reforms suggests that many of the concepts now being exchanged in the global marketplace of ideas about school reform are unlikely ever to be implemented in pure form. Indeed, this is probably a good thing, for such ideas have no meaning apart from particular contexts. Teachers' unions may or may not have been driven primarily by concerns about job security in resisting bulk funding, but they also raised some legitimate educational reasons for going slowly. Likewise, self-governance proved to have real value, but experience shows that it has severe limitations, which its advocates in the Ministry of Education are now belatedly acknowledging.

New Zealand's experience with Tomorrow's Schools demonstrates that reformers in other countries who are tempted to put their faith in simple governance solutions to complex questions of educational quality are likely to find them wanting. It also demonstrates that overreliance on simplistic solutions can cause considerable harm to both individuals and schools unless policymakers are willing to anticipate from the outset the limitations of such solutions and to build in appropriate safeguards.

A | *Persons Interviewed and Schools Visited*

Persons Interviewed

Primary and Secondary Schools (principals, teachers, students, trustees)

Annan, Brian
Baragwanath, Susan
Bates, Terry
Blair, Ashley
Brader, Robyn
Brockenshire, Ann
Burt, Caroline
Campbell, Bruce
Campbell, Janice
Cassily, Jackie
Chou, Joyce
Clarke, Eric
Clarke, Marie
Crossman, Kerry
Dale, Colin
Davis, Jackie
Derbyshire, Ellen

DuChatinear, Alistair
Evans, Carol
Feehan, Sister Frances
Fisher, Rona
Forbes, Diane
Gavin, Bill
Grant, John
Hart, Janet
Hodge, David
Huntington, Beth
Jones, Tim
Jurgensen, Susanne
Lancaster, Neil
Lawson, Don
Lee, Peter
Lee, Sungjin
Lewis, Brent M.
Lilley, Teresa
Ling, Ming
Lockie, Warren
Luke, Sharmaine

Lynch, Jenny
Mareko, Caroline
Marshall, Graeme
Matthews, Wendy
McLeod, Margaret
Moir, John
Morrison, Doreen
Moses, Roger
Mossop, Lois
Murray, Bruce
Naden, Joe
Nesbitt, Peggy
Ngatai, Margaret
Osterika, Eliza
Paitai, Mary
Parbhu, Ramon
Park, Laures
Peke, Lynley
Peters, Jim
Phillips, Stan
Plummer, Graeme
Prestidge, Lyall
Ranfurly, Bonny
Rees, Alwyn
Ridley, Jenny
Robb, Brian J.
Russell, John
Schumacher, Richard
Scott, Marge
Siohane, Phoederly
Stanley, David V.
Stanley, Jill
Staples, Robin
Stone, Angela
Sutton, Bill
Tapp, John
Taylor, Iain C.
Tekere, Trina

Thompson, Dennis
Trembath, Murray
Vink, Buino
Vivien, Rosemary
Waiora, Puna
Ward, Bronwyn
Ward, Caroline
White, Kevin
Williams, Murray
Woods, Rob

*Government (Ministry of Education,
Education Review Office, Treasury
Department, Parliament, and others)*
Aitken, Judith E.
Bakker, Carl
Bowden, Robin
Bushnell, Peter G.
Carpenter, David
Connolly, Martin
Crawford, Ron
Donnelly, Brian
Fancy, Howard
Gordon, Liz
Heslop, Jane
Hodgson, Pete
Lange, David
LaRocque, Norman
Little, Struan
McMahon, Tim
Mersi, Peter
Milbank, Gorham
Mitchell, Brian
Moore, Robyn
Norris, Marion
Patterson, Desiree
Pedersen, Eric
Philips, David

Pole, Nicholas
Rae, Ken
Robertson, Pam
Sinclair, Mary
Turner, Gay
Vella, Mark
Wendt, Jennifer
Whitney, Lynn
Wilson, Graeme
Wilson, Jessica

Educational Organizations
(teachers' unions, trustee
associations, research
institutes, and others)
Aikin, Sandra
Allen, Guy
Ashworth, Yvonne
Bowkett, Te Makou
Cross, Bronwyn
Hamilton, Bill Te Huia
Hicks, Carol
Irwin, Michael
Kelly, Janet
Keon, Andrew
Kerr, Jan
Mitchell, Linda
Newport, Ray
Penitito, Cathy
Shone, Sue
Willetts, Rob
Wylie, Cathy

Universities
Ballantyne, Ann
Barrington, John
Barton, Bill
Boston, Jonathan

Clark, Megan
Colquhoun, Philip M.
Crooks, Terry
Gaffney, Michael
Gibson, Kendall
Grimes, Arthur
Hawk, Kay
Hawke, Gary
Hughes, David
Martin, John
Penitito, Wally
Robinson, Viviane
Scott, Claudia
Scott, David
Stephens, Bob
Watson, Sue
Wilson, Tony

Miscellaneous
Alan Duff
Butterworth, Graham
Butterworth, Susan
Capper, Philip
Cassie, Fiona
Elley, Warwick
Farland, Karen
Fernyhough, Christine
Gilling, Donald
Hart, Bob
McAree, Fiona
McQueen, Harvey
Pattillo, Ann
Picot, Brian
Plested, Bruce
Rivers, Jan
Scott, Lynn
Smelt, Simon J.
Wilson, Ken

Schools Visited

Auckland Area
Bairds Mainfreight Primary School
Edendale School
Ferguson Intermediate School
Gladstone School
Hillary College
Kaipara College
Mount Albert School
Otahuhu College
Ponsonby Intermediate School
Southern Cross Campus
Tamaki College
Tangaroa College
Te Kura Kaupapa Maori o Hoani
Waititi

Christchurch
Aranui High School
Aranui School
Hillmorton High School
Mairehau High School
Papanui High School
Rowley School

Dunedin
Kaikorai Valley College

Napier
Flaxmere College
Napier Community Activity Center
Wycliffe Intermediate School

Wellington Area
Aotea College
Cannon's Creek School
Heretaunga College
Hutt International Boys School
Hutt Valley High School
Lyall Bay School
Mana College
Newtown School
Petone Central School
Porirua College
Porirua School
Russell School
School for Teenage Parents
Seatoun School
Saint Frances de Sales School
Taita College
Tawa College
Thorndon School
Upper Hutt College
Waitangirua Intermediate School
Wellington College
Wellington East Girls College
Wellington Girls College

B | *Other Research*

THIS APPENDIX BRIEFLY describes the study designs of the two empirical studies by other researchers to which we refer several times in the text.

New Zealand Council for Educational Research (NZCER) Surveys

The NZCER surveys were undertaken in 1989, 1990, 1991, 1993, and 1996 by Cathy Wylie. Principals, teachers, and trustees of a national sample of 239 primary and intermediate schools were surveyed. For a subsample of 26 schools, a cross section of parents was surveyed. The aim of the series was to describe the experiences of people involved with primary schools, to find out what difference the reforms have made to New Zealand schools, and to see whether the reforms were improving education for low-income and Maori children. The 1997 report by Cathy Wylie, *Self-Managing Schools Seven Years On: What Have We Learnt?*, summarizes the 1996 survey results and for many responses compares the results to findings for previous years.

The 239 schools represented 10.5 percent of all nonprivate primary and intermediate New Zealand schools in 1989. The sample was stratified to be proportionately representative of the 1989 distribution by type of school, location of school, roll size, proportion of Maori enrollment, and whether the school was state or integrated. For each survey round, questionnaires were sent to the principals of the sample schools, to two randomly chosen trustees at each school, and to one to three teachers at each school, depending on school size. The sample sizes in 1996 (and response rates) were as follows: 181 (76 percent) principals, 270 (57 percent) trustees, and 361 (66 percent) teachers. The resulting samples were largely representative of national school and population characteristics. The findings for principals were most representative of the schools, and the trustee and teacher findings are quite representative, with some imbalances relating to the proportion of Maori enrollment and location.

Fifty-two percent (676) of the 1,297 parents who were sent questionnaires responded. In the 1996 sample, parents with higher educational qualifications and with professional or skilled work were overrepresented relative to their distribution in the nation.

Smithfield Project

Financed by the Ministry of Education, this longitudinal study of the impact of the marketization of education on primary and secondary schools had three phases. In phase 1 (1992–93), the authors examined the creation of an educational marketplace and assessed its impact on parental and school choice. During that phase, the researchers collected baseline data on a cohort of 3,297 students in two cities and one rural area. In phase 2 (1994–96) and phase 3 (1997–98), the researchers focused on impacts on school effectiveness and student outcomes. The project, undertaken by a distinguished team of educational sociologists headed by Hugh Lauder and David Hughes, produced eight reports for the ministry between 1994 and 1998. In 1999, Lauder and Hughes published many of the findings in *Trading in Futures: Why Markets in Education Don't Work*. See the appendix to that book for a more detailed description of their methodology.

The Smithfield sample included twenty-three secondary schools, one in a rural area and eleven each in two cities that the researchers called Green City and Central City. The researchers identified the primary and intermediate schools that fed into the secondary schools and approached the parents of all students in year seven (comparable to sixth grade in the United States) in those schools. Seventy-six percent of the urban parents who were approached participated in the study. The initial questionnaire elicited ethnic and socioeconomic information.

To measure socioeconomic status, the researchers relied on a modified form of the occupation-based Elley-Irving index, which is frequently used in New Zealand research. The original index classified occupations based on the income and educational levels associated with them, with 1 being high status and 6 being low status. The Smithfield researchers modified the index to apply to families rather than to individuals and to include prior occupations for currently unemployed family members.

In 1993 the researchers gathered test score data from the feeder schools for their sample of students, supplementing these data with testing of their own. The additional tests included tests of student aptitude and measures that allowed the researchers to develop an index of self-concept. In May 1997, they gathered information on student performance on school certificate examinations. Because not all students had taken the school certificate examination, scores for some students had to be approximated by sixth-form certificate results.

In 1994 the researchers collected additional context data for the feeder schools, and in 1995 they systematically visited classrooms in each of the sample schools.

In addition to the initial survey, a subsample of urban parents were surveyed in 1994 to solicit answers to four questions relating to the secondary schools they were interested in and to which they had applied for their children. Because of a low initial response to a mail survey, follow-up telephone calls were made, raising the response rate to 72 percent. However, response rates remained low for minority parents. A third questionnaire was distributed in 1996 eliciting information on parental involvement in the schools.

The Smithfield project, a major and impressive undertaking, permitted an in-depth analysis of parental choice and school performance in parts of two cities over time. It should be noted, however, that not all the analyses are based on the full sample of schools or parents; much of the analysis is based on subsets of four or six schools in Green City or on subsamples of urban parents.

References

Auckland Uniservices Limited. 1997. *A Review of ERO: Final Report to the PPTA*. Auckland.

Austin Report. 1997. *Achieving Excellence: A Review of the Education External Evaluation Services*. Wellington: State Services Commission.

Ballantyne, Ann Lorraine. 1997. *Power or Partnership? An Analysis of the Role and Political Positioning of the New Zealand School Trustees Association in the Implementation of the Tomorrow's Schools Reforms, 1989–1994*. Delta Research Monograph 13. Massey University, Educational Research and Development Centre.

Barrington, John. 1981. "School Government in New Zealand: Balancing the Interests." In *The Politics of School Government*, edited by George Baron, 157–80. Pergamon Press.

Barro, Steven. 1996. "How Countries Pay for Schools: An International Comparison of Systems for Financing Primary and Secondary Education." Paper prepared for the Consortium for Policy Research in Education, University of Wisconsin, Madison.

Boston, Jonathan, John Martin, June Pallot, and Pat Walsh. 1996. *Public Management: The New Zealand Model*. Oxford University Press.

Belich, James. 1996. *Making Peoples: A History of the New Zealanders from Polynesian Settlement to the End of the Nineteenth Century*. Allen Lane/Penguin.

Bell, Cathie, and Debbie Dawson. 1991. "Bulk Funding Plan Delayed: Smith's Move Soothes Trustees, Colleagues." *Dominion Sunday Times*, April 14, 1991.

Birch, Bill. 1995. *Budget and Fiscal Strategy Report, 1995*. Wellington: Treasury Department.

Brandl, John E. 1998. "Governance and Educational Quality." In *Learning from School Choice*, edited by Paul E. Peterson and Bryan C. Hassel, 55–82. Brookings.

Brown, Sue. 1996. "Special Education 2000: Developing a Policy for Inclusive Education in New Zealand." *New Zealand Annual Review of Education* 6:141–56.

Bryk, Anthony S. 1999. "Policy Lessons from Chicago's Experience with Decentralization." *Brookings Papers on Education Policy, 1999*, 67–128.

Burtless, Gary, ed. 1996. *Does Money Matter? The Effect of School Resources on Student Achievement and Adult Success*. Brookings.

Butterworth, Graham, and Susan Butterworth. 1998. *Reforming Education: The New Zealand Experience, 1984–96*. Palmerston North, N.Z.: Dunmore Press.

Butterworth, Susan. 1993. *The Department of Education, 1877–1989: A Guide to Its Development*. Wellington: Ministry of Education.

Chubb, John, and Terry Moe. 1990. *Politics, Markets, and America's Schools*. Brookings.

Codd, John, and Liz Gordon. 1991. "School Charters: The Contractualist State and Education Policy." *New Zealand Journal of Educational Studies* 26(1): 21–34.

Codd, John, Richard Harker, and Roy Nash. 1990. "Introduction: Education, Politics and the Economic Crisis." In *Political Issues in New Zealand Education*, 2d ed., edited by John Codd, Richard Harker, and Roy Nash, 7–21. Palmerston North, N.Z.: Dunmore Press.

Education Review Office. 1994. *Annual Report, July 1993 to 30 June 1994*. Wellington.

———. 1996. *Improving Schooling in Mangere and Otara*. Wellington.

———. 1997. *Improving Schooling on the East Coast*. Wellington.

———. 1998. *Good Schools, Poor Schools*. Wellington.

Elley, Warwick B. 1991. "How Well Do New Zealand Students Achieve by International Standards?" Canterbury Region, Post Primary Teachers' Association.

ESRA (Economic and Social Research Associates Ltd.). 1997. *A Critique of the Technical Feasibility Study Prepared by the University of Otago Consulting Group*. Report to New Zealand School Trustees Association.

Ferguson, Ronald, and Helen F. Ladd. 1996. "How and Why Money Matters: An Analysis of Alabama Schools." In *Holding Schools Accountable: Performance-Based Reform in Education*, edited by Helen F. Ladd, 265–98. Brookings.

Finn, Chester E., Jr., and others. 1997. *The Birth-Pains and Life-Cyles of Charter Schools*. Charter Schools in Action, Final Report, pt. 2. Washington, D.C.: Hudson Institute.

Fiske, Edward B. 1991. *Smart Schools, Smart Kids: Why Do Some Schools Work?* Simon and Schuster.

Funding Working Group. N.d. *Tomorrow's Schools: Report of the Funding Working Group to the Implementation Unit*. Wellington.

Gerritson, John. 1998. "Assessment May Result in League Tables." *New Zealand Education Review*, October 14, 1998.

Gilles, Stephen G. 1998. "Why Parents Should Choose." In *Learning from School Choice*, edited by Paul E. Peterson and Bryan C. Hassel, 395–408. Brookings.

Gordon, Liz. 1992. "The State, Devolution, and Educational Reform in New Zealand." *Journal of Education Policy* 7(2): 187–203.

Hanushek, Eric. 1994. *Making Schools Work*. Brookings.

———. 1997. "Assessing the Effects of Schools' Resources on Student Performance: An Update." *Educational Evaluation and Policy Analysis* 19(2): 141–64.

Harker, Richard, and Roy Nash. 1996. "Academic Outcomes and School Effectiveness: Type 'A' and Type 'B' Effects." *New Zealand Journal of Educational Studies* 32(2): 143–70.

Hawk, Kay, and Jan Hill (1996). *Towards Making Achievement Cool: Achievement in Multi-Cultural High Schools (AIMHI)*. Massey University, Educational Research and Development Centre

Henig, J. R. 1995. *Rethinking School Choice*. Princeton University Press.

Hill, Paul T. 1999. "The Supply Side of School Choice." In *School Choice and Social Controversy: Politics, Policy, and Law*, edited by Stephen D. Sugarman and Frank R. Kemmerer, 140–73. Brookings.

Hotere, Andrea. "Standards May Go." *New Zealand Education Review*, May 6, 1998.

Jencks, Christopher, and Susan Mayer. 1990. "The Social Consequences of Growing Up in a Poor Neighborhood." In *Inner-City Poverty in the United States*, edited by Laurence E. Lynn Jr. and Michael G. H. McGreary, 111–86. Washington, D.C.: National Academy Press.

Kelsey, Jane. 1997. *The New Zealand Experiment: A World Model for Structural Adjustment?* Updated ed. Auckland University Press.

Krueger, Alan. 1997. *Experimental Estimates of Education Production Functions*. Cambridge, Mass.: National Bureau of Economic Research.

Ladd, Helen F., and Edward B. Fiske. 1999. "The Uneven Playing Field of School Choice: Evidence from New Zealand." Paper prepared for the annual conference of the Association of Public Policy Analysis and Management, Washington, D.C.

Lauder, Hugh. 1993. *Democracy, the Economy, and the Marketisation of Education*. Inaugural address, delivered September 27, 1991, Victoria University of Wellington. Victoria University Press.

Lauder, Hugh, and David Hughes. 1999. *Trading in Futures: Why Markets in Education Don't Work*. Buckingham, N.Z.: Open University Press.

Laxon, Andrew. 1994. "Inequality Seen in Bulk Funding." *New Zealand Herald*, October 14.

———. 1996. "Paper Shows 'Real' Agenda for Education." *New Zealand Herald*, February 10.

Livingston, Ian D. 1994. "The Workloads of Primary School Teachers." Wellington: Chartwell Consultants.

Loconte, Joe. 1999. "Schools Learn That Vouchers Can Have a Hidden Cost." *Wall Street Journal,* January 26.

Manno, Bruno V. 1999. *Accountability: The Key to Charter Renewal.* Washington, D.C.: Center for Education Reform.

Mansell, Ruth Lillian. 1993. "Community Forum on Education in Wellington's Eastern Suburbs: A Case Study on Choice and Democratic Community Participation in New Zealand Education Policy." Master's thesis, Victoria University of Wellington.

McCulloch, Gary. 1991. "School Zoning, Equity, and Freedom: The Case of New Zealand." *Journal of Education Policy* 6(2): 155–68.

Ministry of Education. 1993. *National Education Guidelines.* Wellington.

———. 1995. *Resource Entitlement for School Staffing: Report of the Ministerial Reference Group.* Wellington.

———. 1996. *Research Bulletin,* No. 7 (November 1996). Wellington: Research and International Section.

———. 1997a. *New Zealand Schools: A Report on the Compulsory Schools Sector in New Zealand, 1996.* Wellington.

———. 1997b. *Government Expenditure on Education: 1994.* Wellington: Data Management and Analysis Section.

———. 1998a. *Assessment for Success in Primary Schools.* Green Paper. Wellington.

———. 1998b. *New Zealand Schools: A Report on the Compulsory Schools Sector in New Zealand, 1997.* Wellington.

———. 1998c. *Operational Funding for New Zealand Schools, 1998.* Wellington.

Mitchell, David, and others. 1993. *Hear Our Voices: Final Report of Monitoring Today's Schools Research Project.* University of Waikato, Monitoring Today's Schools Research Project.

Moe, Terry. 1984. "The New Economics of Organization." *American Journal of Political Science* 28 (November): 739–77.

Nechyba, Thomas J. 1999. "School Finance Induced Migration, and Stratification Patterns: The Impact of Private School Vouchers." *Journal of Public Economic Theory* 1(91): 5–50.

OECD (Organization for Economic Cooperation and Development). 1994. *School: A Matter of Choice.* Paris.

———. 1995. *Schools under Scrutiny.* Paris.

———. 1998. *Education at a Glance: OECD Indicators, 1998.* Paris.

Peterson, Paul E. 1999. "Top Ten Questions Asked about School Choice." *Brookings Papers on Education Policy, 1999,* 371–405.

Peterson, Paul E., and Bryan C. Hassel, eds. 1998. *Learning from School Choice.* Brookings.

Pole, Nicholas. 1997. "Needs-Based Resource Allocation in Education via Formula Funding of Schools." Case Study 5: New Zealand. Paris: UNESCO.

———. 1999. "Formula Funding of Schools in New Zealand." In *Needs-Based*

Resource Allocation in Education via Formula Funding of Schools, edited by Kenneth N. Ross and Rosalind Levačič, 228–49. Paris: UNESCO.

Post Primary Teachers' Association. 1997. *Meeting the Challenge of Growth: The Emerging Crisis in Our Secondary Schools.* Wellington.

Rae, Ken. 1991. "Secondary School Enrollment Schemes: A Case Study in Policy Change and Its Implementation." In *Education Policy and the Changing Role of the State,* edited by Liz Gordon and John Codd, 107–15. Massey University, Department of Education.

Scott, Graham, Ian Ball, and Tony Dale. 1997. "New Zealand's Public Sector Management Reform: Implications for the United States." *Journal of Policy Analysis and Management* 16(3): 357–81.

Smithfield Project. 1994. *The Creation of Market Competition for Education in New Zealand.* Phase 1, first report. Wellington: Ministry of Education.

———. 1995. *Trading in Futures: The Nature of Choice in Educational Markets in New Zealand.* Phase 1, third report. Wellington: Ministry of Education.

Snook, Ivan. 1997. "The Issue of Bulk Funding." Paper for a seminar in Auckland (September).

Statistics New Zealand. 1997. *New Zealand Official Yearbook, 1997.* Wellington.

Task Force to Review Education Administration. 1988. *Administering for Excellence: Effective Administration in Education.* Wellington.

Taylor, Iain. 1997. "Marketing in Schools: Does It Have All the Answers?" *New Zealand Journal of Educational Administration* 12:5–9.

Thrupp, Martin. 1997a. "Shaping a Crisis: The Education Review Office and South Auckland Schools." In *Education Policy in New Zealand: The 1990s and Beyond,* edited by Mark Olssen and Kay Morris Matthews, 145–61. Palmerston North, N.Z.: Dunmore Press.

———. 1997b. "School Mix and the Outcomes of Educational Quasi-Markets." In *Education Policy in New Zealand: The 1990s and Beyond,* edited by Mark Olssen and Kay Morris Matthews, 372–90. Palmerston North, N.Z.: Dunmore Press.

Tomorrow's Schools: The Reforming of Education Administration in New Zealand. 1988. Wellington.

Treasury Department. 1987. *Government Management: Brief to the Incoming Government, 1987.* Vol. 2. *Education Issues.* Wellington.

UCLA (Amy Stuart Wells and others). 1998. *UCLA Charter School Study.* Los Angeles.

University of Otago Consulting Group. 1997. *Developing a School Resourcing Model: Technical Feasibility Study.*

Wagemaker, Hans, ed. 1993. *Achievement in Reading Literacy.* Wellington: Ministry of Education.

Whitty, Geoff. 1997. "Creating Quasi-Markets in Education: A Review of Recent Research on Parental Choice and School Autonomy in Three Countries." In

Review of Research in Education 22, edited by Michael W. Apple, 3–47. Washington, D.C.: American Educational Research Association.

Williamson, O. E. 1985. *The Economic Institutions of Capitalism.* Free Press.

Willie, Charles V., Michael Alves, and George Hagerty. 1996. "Multiracial, Attractive City Schools: Controlled Choice in Boston." *Equity and Excellence in Education* 29(2): 5–19.

Willis, Deborah. 1992. "Educational Assessment and Accountability: A New Zealand Case Study." *Journal of Education Policy* 7(2): 205–21.

Witte, John. 1996. "School Choice and Student Performance." In *Holding Schools Accountable: Performance-Based Reform in Education*, edited by Helen F. Ladd, 149–76. Brookings.

Wylie, Cathy. 1994. *Mixed Messages from New Zealand.* Wellington: New Zealand Council for Educational Research.

———. 1997. *Self-Managing Schools Seven Years On: What Have We Learnt?* Wellington: New Zealand Council for Educational Research.

———. 1998. *Can Vouchers Deliver Better Education? A Review of the Literature, with Special Reference to New Zealand.* Wellington: New Zealand Council for Educational Research.

———. N.d. *Primary Principals' Experiences of ERO Reviews, 1995–96.* Wellington: New Zealand Council for Educational Research.

Wylie, Cathy, Jean Thompson, and Cathy Lythe. 1999. *Competent Children at 8: Families, Early Education, and Schools.* Wellington: New Zealand Council for Educational Research.

Zimmer, Ron W., and Eugenia F. Toma. 1999. "Peer Effects in Private and Public Schools across Countries." *Journal of Policy Analysis and Management* 19(1): 75–92.

Index